The Older Worker and the Changing Labor Market

As the country's workforce ages, the changing labor market must address unique challenges as well as surprising opportunities. This book presents leading scholars and researchers providing valuable insights into the challenges facing older workers in the contemporary workplace as well as offering perspectives on the demands presently being placed on employers to adapt to and accommodate the needs of these workers. This book focuses on the analysis of current trends in older workers, work, family, and personal life issues, and ways to transform today's workplace to value older workers.

This book offers practitioners the opportunity to fully grasp the current situation for older workers by presenting the latest research. This helpful resource provides professionals with best practices and innovative approaches to support aging employees. This book is extensively referenced and contains several tables to clearly present data. It is a valuable text for employers, human resources professionals, employee assistance programs, work/family professionals, gerontologists and aging studies professionals, educators, and students.

This book was published as a special issue of the *Journal of Workplace Behavioral Health*.

Judith G. Gonyea is Professor and Chair of the Research Department at the Boston University School of Social Work. The author of more than 90 publications, much of her research focuses on the economic and health status of older Americans, particularly the cumulative effects of social and economic inequalities on the life experiences of older adults. Her recent scholarship explores the changing nature of intergenerational family relations, family caregiving, and the interface of work and family in contemporary American society. Dr. Gonyea currently serves on the editorial boards of *Public Policy and Aging Report, Research on Aging,* and *Journal of Gerontological Social Work.* She is a Fellow in the Gerontological Society of America and an elected member of the National Academy of Social Insurance.

The Older Worker and the Changing Labor Market

New Challenges for the Workplace

Edited by Judith G. Gonyea

Routledge
Taylor & Francis Group

LONDON AND NEW YORK

First published 2009 by Routledge
2 Park Square, Milton Park, Abingdon, Oxon, OX14 4RN

Simultaneously published in the USA and Canada
by Routledge
711 Third Avenue, New York, NY 10017

Routledge is an imprint of the Taylor & Francis Group, an informa business

Typeset in Times by Value Chain, India

British Library Cataloguing in Publication Data
A catalogue record for this book is available from the British Library

ISBN10: 0-7890-3771-8 (hbk)
ISBN10: 0-7890-3772-6 (pbk)
ISBN13: 978-0-7890-3771-8 (hbk)
ISBN13: 978-0-7890-3772-5 (pbk)

CONTENTS

About the Contributors

Ronald H. Aday, PhD, is Professor and Chair of the Sociology and Anthropology Department at Middle Tennessee State University in Murfreesboro, TN. A social gerontologist, he has published 3 books and over 40 book chapters and articles focused on policy issues related to intergenerational issues, health and wellness, senior centers and aging inmates.

Geri Adler, PhD, is Assistant Professor in the Graduate College of Social Work at the University of Houston. Dr. Adler has a PhD and MSW degrees in Social Work from the University of Minnesota, St. Paul as well as a BA in Rural Sociology from the University of Wisconsin, Madison. Her research interests and scholarship is in transportation and driving, and older adults, dementia, gerontological social work and health care social work.

Nicole Batsch, BS, is the Director of Early Stage Programs for the Greater Illinois Chapter of the Alzheimer's Association. Prior to that, she developed senior wellness programs in Tucson, AZ and was involved in the development of the "Powerful Tools for Caregivers" Program at the Mather LifeWays Institute on Aging. The web-based version of this program was awarded an Association for Work Life Progress Award for Innovation in 2006. Ms. Batsch has a BS in Psychology and a graduate certificate in Gerontology from Florida State University in Tallahassee, FL.

Robert W. Boyce, PhD, FACSM, is Assistant Professor of Exercise Science in the Health and Human Sciences Department at the University of North Carolina at Wilmington NC. His research focuses on the application of the principles of ergonomics and exercise to increase performance in clinical and occupational settings. Awarded the title of Fellow by the American College of Sports Medicine, Boyce holds their highest preventive and rehabilitative certificate, Clinical Exercise Physiologist.

Jan Civian, EdD, is a Senior Consultant at WFD Consulting in Newton, MA. A survey research specialist, she conducts broad needs assessments to understand domestic and global workforce issues concerning dependent care, flexibility, women's advancement, work/life support, and employee engagement and retention. She has a BA from Wellesley College, MA from Stanford University and EdD from Harvard University.

Angela L. Curl, PhD, is Assistant Professor in the School of Social Work at the University of Missouri. She is a Fellow of the University of Missouri's Interdisciplinary Center on Aging and a Faculty Affiliate of the Women's and Gender Studies Department. Dr. Curl has a PhD in Social Welfare from Case Western Reserve University, a MSW from The University of Alabama, and a BS in Social Work from Taylor University. Her aging research interests include retirement and health of married couples. Currently a Hartford Foundation Geriatric Social Work Faculty Scholar, she is engaged in the study, "The impact of retirement on heart problems: A multilevel dyadic analysis of longitudinal secondary data."

Eric Dahlin, MS, is a doctoral candidate in the Sociology Department at the University of Minnesota. His dissertation focuses on the effects of firm innovation on financial performance. In addition, he has done research on the U.S. women suffrage movement, citizenship, social networks in the workplace and cross-national inequality.

Jerry W. Hedge, PhD, is a senior research psychologist at RTI International who has been involved in personnel research in both the public and private sectors for more than 25 years. His expertise encompasses work and aging, career development, performance measurement, personnel selection, and training program design and evaluation. He holds a doctorate in Industrial/Organizational Psychology from Old Dominion University, and is a Fellow of the Society for Industrial and Organizational Psychology and the American Psychological Association. In 2006 he co-authored *The aging workforce: Realities, myths and implications for organizations.*

Don Hilber, MS, is Manager of Performance Analysis for the Houston Independent School District. He holds a MS in Economics from the University of Wisconsin- Madison. He previously managed accountability measures for career and technology education, labor market information, employment forecasting and regional economic analysis for federal and state.

Linda Hollinger-Smith, RN, PhD, FAAN, is Vice President of Mather LifeWays Institute on Aging in Evanston, IL. She has a PhD in Gerontology, a MS in Medical-Surgical Nursing with dual majors in gerontological nursing and nursing services administration, and BS in Nursing from the University of Illinois at Chicago. A Fellow of the American Academy of Nursing, Hollinger-Smith has worked in the field of aging for over 25 years and published more than 50 journal articles, book chapters and research abstracts on various aging topics. In addition to leading the Institute, she holds faculty appointments at both Rush University Medical Center and the University of Illinois at Chicago.

Gayle Kehoe, MA, is currently an adjunct faculty member at Middle Tennessee State University in Murfreesboro, TN. Her research and scholarship interests focus on senior centers and older women's lives.

Erin L. Kelly, PhD, is Associate Professor of Sociology at the University of Minnesota. Dr. Kelly studies the adoption, implementation, and consequences of anti-discrimination and "family-friendly" policies in U.S. workplaces. She has recently examined non-compliance with the Family and Medical Leave Act, how U.S. companies manage flexible work arrangements, and the development and diffusion of sexual harassment policies. Currently, Dr. Kelly is co-principal investigator, with Dr. Phyllis Moen, of the Flexible Work and Well-Being Center, part of the National Institutes of Health Network on Work, Family, Health & Well-Being. This research examines how increased schedule control affects employees' health and well-being, as well as the work process and the organizational culture.

Daniel Kuhn, MSW, is the Director of the Professional Training Institute for the Greater Illinois Chapter of the Alzheimer's Association, based in Chicago, IL. He completed a master's degree in social work at the Jane Addams College of Social Work at the University of Illinois-Chicago and he is a licensed clinical social worker. He has been active as a social worker, educator, and researcher in the fields of health care and aging with several organizations in his native Chicago for the past 35 years. He has authored or co-authored more than 50 books, book chapters, journal articles, training manuals, and videos. His most recent book, co-authored with Jane Verity, is *The Art of Dementia Care*.

Tracy L. Madvig, MS, an organizational psychologist, works as a consultant to industry primarily through involvement in the conduct of large-scale individual and organizational assessments, mainly employee surveys, assessment centers, and selection and development systems. Madvig has a MS in Industrial/Organizational Psychology from California State University, San Bernardino. Her research and publication interests include the aging workforce and retirement issues, as well as generational trends in the workplace.

Phyllis Moen, PhD, holds the McKnight President Chair in Sociology at the University of Minnesota. She studies and has published numerous books and articles on occupational careers, retirement, families, health, gender and social policy, as they intersect and as they play out over the life course. Her two most recent books are *It's About Time: Couples and Careers* (2003) and *The Career Mystique: Cracks in the American Dream* (2005, with Pat Roehling). The *Career Mystique* earned the 2005 Award for Excellence in Sociology and Social Work from the Association of American Publishers Professional and Scholarly Publishing Division. She is the principal investigator of the Flexible Work and Well-Being Study, part of the National Institutes of Health Network on Work, Family, Health & Well-Being. This research investigates how shifts in the organization of work impacts family, health and productivity so as to offer employees greater scheduling latitude.

Judith Presser, MS, is a Senior Consultant at WFD Consulting in Newton MA. An expert in employer-sponsored dependent care programs, she has worked with numerous clients in the development and implementation of a variety of strategies to meet their employees' work-life, child, and elder care needs. More recently, she has begun to focus on the issues of working caregivers and the aging workforce, and has developed a number of innovative approaches to supporting them. She earned her BA from Vassar College and her MS from Yeshiva University.

Kenneth S. Shultz, PhD, is a Professor in the Psychology Department at California State University, San Bernardino. Dr. Shultz earned his PhD and MA degrees in Industrial and Organizational (I/O) Psychology from Wayne State University, as well as a BA in Honors Psychology from the State University of New York (SUNY), College at Potsdam. His primary areas of research include aging work force and retirement related issues, as well as applied psychological measurement. He has published over 35 refereed articles, numerous book chapters, and two books on these topics, including the recent co-edited volume, *Aging and Work in the 21st Century* (2007, Psychology Press, with G.A. Adams).

Donna L. Spencer, MA, is a doctoral candidate in the Sociology Department at the University of Minnesota. As a Senior Research Fellow in the State Health Access Data Assistance Center at the University of Minnesota, she brings more than 15 years of experience in public health and social science research designed to inform federal and state policy. Spencer's general areas of concentration are the life course, demography, work and labor markets, and law and social policy. Her primary research interests are in the areas of work and family and work and retirement. Her dissertation uses Current Population Survey data to examine longitudinal trend in access to employer-based health insurance among part-time workers in the U.S.

Diana Stork, PhD, is Associate Professor and Chair of the Management and Economics Department at Emmanuel College in Boston, MA. She holds a PhD from Columbia University, a MBA from Boston University and a BA in Psychology from Oberlin College. Her areas of interest include organizational behavior, human resources management, business ethics, leadership, and diversity as well as survey design and statistics. She has authored and co-authored numerous journal articles and a book, *Leading Biotechnology Alliances* (2001, with A. Sapienza). Stork recently completed terms as a member of the Board of Directors of the Eastern Academy of Management and Ethics Advisory Council of the Society of Human Resource Management.

Aloen L. Townsend, PhD, is Associate Professor of Social Work in the Mandel School of Applied Social Sciences at Case Western Reserve University. She holds a joint appointment in Sociology, is a Faculty Affiliate of the University Center on Aging and Health, and is an Associate Member of the Cancer Prevention, Control, and Population Research Program of the Case Comprehensive Care Center. She received her PhD in Social Psychology from the University of Michigan, Ann Arbor. Her primary research interests are in adult development and aging, family relationships, mental and physical health, and the interface between families and formal care systems. The author of numerous articles and book chapters, her current research investigates the impact of cancer and comorbidities on psychosocial quality of life of middle-aged and older married couples.

Donald L. Venneberg, PhD, is Assistant Professor in the School of Education at Colorado State University, Fort Collins. In this role he teaches graduate courses in the field of organizational performance and change. His research agenda focuses on workforce development trends and policy with particular regard to the intergenerational workforce, the aging workforce and the retention, recruitment and effective utilization of older workers. He was formerly a senior executive in U.S. General Services Administration, where he led large organizations delivering supplies and technology services to federal agencies. His last position was the Deputy Chief Information Officer for the agency.

Vida Wilkinson, PhD, is Director of Development for the Gillette College Foundation in Gillette, WY. Dr. Wilkinson has a PhD in Education and Human Resource Studies from Colorado State University and a BS in Mathematics Education from Minot State University. The focus of her dissertation was on the Workforce Investment Act of 1998 and the creation of partnerships among employment, community college, and economic development agencies for workforce development efforts. Her career background includes teaching, research, training coordinator, and fundraising. She has a particular interest in the role of government policy and the need for partnerships in workforce development, economic development, and community development.

Foreword:
America's Aging Workforce:
A Critical Business Issue

The coming tidal wave of 76 million baby boomers reaching age 65, the traditional age of retirement in the U.S., in the next 15 years has not escaped public attention. As they increasingly enter the ranks of America's older population, these "aging boomers" are predicted to have significant impacts on all aspects of our society, including our health, housing, educational, and business institutions. Indeed, the challenge of an aging population has raised concerns not only in the U.S., but in a number of developed countries, about having sufficient numbers of skilled workers to maintain economic productivity as well as the sustainability of national pension systems (Hardy, 2006). Thus, developed countries, including the U.S., are responding to these aging demographics by restructuring their old-age insurance programs to either encourage or require later exits from the workforce and developing programs to retrain older workers in skills for today's marketplace (AARP, 2006).

In this volume we explore whether the business sector is "thinking strategically" about the aging of the U.S. workforce. Two key questions addressed by the authors are: Whether American businesses are actively engaged in identifying and implementing strategies by which they might better utilize older workers' energies, talents, and expertise?; and What are the internal and external facilitators and barriers influencing organizations' efforts (or lack of efforts) to redesign jobs, benefits and/ or work environments to be more responsive to older workers?

The volume also explores the implications of the changing patterns of labor force participation among older Americans as well as shifting work and retirement preferences among current and future older workers for American businesses. As many of the authors note, increasing the supply of older workers not only requires that attention be directed toward removing the barriers which impact older adults' continued employment, but also necessitates creating new work opportunities and incentives which appeal to a "mature workforce." Also emphasized is a viewpoint that the phenomenon of the "aging of the workplace" cannot be explored in isolation; rather, it must be examined within the broader context of a changing U.S. business environment. Over the past several decades, the U.S. economy has undergone a major transformation from blue-collar manufacturing and agricultural economies toward white-collar technology, service, and knowledge-based economies. Globalization, or global competition, has often led to corporate mergers, acquisitions, and shifts in market shares. The current employment strategy is toward the creation of lean or smaller core workforces; thus, employers have downsized and outsourced, and increasingly focused on the use of temporary assignment-based or project-type work.

To date, much of the discourse about the implications of the aging of the U.S. labor force for American businesses has been cast somewhat negatively; that is, older workers are typically viewed as presenting yet another set of challenges for corporate America. However, as these authors suggest, the aging of the labor force might also be viewed as offering opportunities for companies to adopt new business strategies. The adoption of a "life cycle approach" to labor force activity, for example, may offer Americans of all ages greater flexibility in how they engage in employment as well as provide American businesses more opportunity to create the requisite skilled multigenerational workforce to meet the demands of our technology-driven and knowledge-based national economy.

THE AGING OF THE U.S. WORKFORCE

It is often noted that the aging of the U.S. workforce reflects three demographic trends: the increasing numbers of older adults, rising life expectancies, and lower birth rates. Not only is there a dramatic increase in numbers of older adults than ever before; but individuals are living longer. The percentage of the U.S. population aged 65 and older was only 4% in 1900; however, today, older adults comprise slight more than

12% and are expected to reach almost 20% of our nation's total population by 2030. While in 1900 life expectancy at birth in the U.S. was only 47 years of age and 5 million Americans were age 65 or older; today, life expectancy at birth has increased to 77 years of age and 35 million Americans are 65 and older (Federal Interagency Forum on Aging Related Statistics, 2006).

Correspondingly, the U.S. Bureau of Labor Statistics' projections suggest that, in the upcoming decades, adults age 55 and older will comprise an increasingly larger percentage of the American workforce. Currently, workers age 55 and older represent 13% of the workforce, but they will reach 17% by 2010 and be at 19% by 2050. At the same time, younger workers between the ages of 25 and 54 are projected to decline from 71% in 2000 to 67% in 2010 and to 65% in 2050. By 2012, the median age of the U.S. labor force will be 41.4 years of age (Toosi, 2002).

Two different scenarios are often offered about the implications of the aging of the U.S. workforce for American businesses. The first scenario predicts a pending "workforce shortage" and a "brain drain" as a result of older adults choosing to exit the labor market. This viewpoint holds that in the upcoming decades labor demands will simply outstrip supply; and the shortage of skilled workers, coupled with the loss of institutional memory, will lead to declining productivity. The second scenario proposes the opposite trend; that is, rather than a shortage of workers, businesses will be faced with an abundance (even an over-abundance) of older workers who want to remain on the job (Cappelli, 2004).

A growing number of experts, however, suggest there is a need for more complex or targeted analyses which examine the labor supply-labor demand match by industry sector or type to gain a more accurate picture (Penner, Perun, & Steuerle, 2003). Adopting this strategy, Geri Adler and Don Hilber (in this volume) address the question of whether the types of jobs being created will, in fact, enable older workers to remain in the workplace. Using a multi-stage approach, they: (1) calculate the proportion of older workers to all workers in 20 major U.S. industries, (2) compare the obtained proportions to the expected rate of job growth in the 20 industries, and (3) compute the overall degree of relative shortages or surpluses generated by any mismatches taking into account the industry size. Their analysis revealed that four industries–health care and social assistance, professional and technical services, administrative, and educational services-will account for over one-third of jobs in 2014. Moreover, faced with job growth and replacement needs, Adler and Hilber suggest these four sectors will present the majority of employment opportunities for future cohorts of older workers.

OLDER WORKER TRENDS

Determining the current and future number of older workers in the labor force depends, of course, on one's definition of "older worker." The Age Discrimination in Employment Act (ADEA) protects American workers aged 40 and older. Eligibility for membership in AARP (formerly the American Association of Retired Persons) starts at age 50; yet, nearly half of current AARP members are actively engaged in the paid labor force. Further, a sizeable proportion of older adults do not identify as being among the ranks of the elderly; a 2000 National Council on Aging survey found that one-third of Americans in their 70s perceived themselves to be middle-aged.

Focusing on those individuals who have remained in the workforce beyond the traditional retirement age of 65, the Bureau of Labor Statistics reveals an upward trend since 1985 in labor force participation rates for both men and women. For men aged 65 to 69, their participation rate rose from 25% in 1985 to 34% in 2005, and for women aged 65 to 69, their rates increased from 14% in 1985 to 24% in 2005. The presence of workers age 70 and older has also continued to climb in recent decades; in 2005 almost 14% of men and 7% of women aged 70-plus were in the paid labor force (Federal Interagency Forum on Aging Related Statistics, 2006).

Rajnes (2001) notes that two competing hypotheses are offered to explain this upward trend. The first proposes that the economic cycle–a strong economy and low unemployment–has created a favorable labor market that offers all workers, including older workers, more options. The second hypothesis proposes that a series of more permanent labor market changes, such as changes in public and private pensions, has led to individuals remaining in the labor market longer.

In fact, one of the primary reasons individuals identify for remaining in the workforce longer is financial or the need for money. For many older workers, stagnating wages as well as growing gaps in their pension and health care benefits are pressuring them to remain in the workforce (Hudson & Gonyea, 2007). The common metaphor for retirement income security in America is a stool resting on three financial legs: Social Security, employee-pension plans, and savings. Yet each of these legs is becoming shakier (Gonyea, 2005). Social Security will not replace as much pre-retirement income for future retirees due to recent legislative changes, including: (1) the progressive increase in the normal retirement age (for the receipt of full benefits) from 65 to 67 years of age, (2) the introduction of Medicare Part D (drug) benefits, as well as the rising costs of Medicare Part B (health care) benefits, claiming a larger percentage of a beneficiary's check; and (3) the increased taxation of Social Security benefits under the personal income tax, as the exemptions are not indexed to inflation (Munnell, 2006). Based on these three factors, Munnell (2006) projects that Social Security's pre- retirement income replacement rate will decline from 38.5% today to only 29.4% by 2030.

Although the proportion of U.S. workers who participate in an employment-based retirement plan has remained at about half of the workforce between the ages of 21 and 64 years of age since the 1970s, in the past two decades, there has been a major shift in the types of employer-sponsored pension plans, from traditional defined-benefit (DB) plans to defined-contribution (DC) plans, such as 401(k) and 403(b) plans. The percentage of workers with a DB plan decreased dramatically from 80% in 1985 to only 33% in 2003 (Federal Interagency Forum on Aging Related Statistics, 2006). While the full impact of this shift in pension income for future cohorts of retirees is not yet fully known, the DC plans are generally viewed as bringing lower and more volatile returns than DB plans. The DC plans currently average only about 42,000 dollars, considerably less than what workers would be guaranteed under a traditional DB plan (Munnell, 2006). And, the personal saving rates among Americans in 2005 was a −0.5 saving rate, the first negative rate since 1933 (U.S. Department of Commerce, 2006).

Retirement Transitions

Although the above identified macroeconomic trends suggest that older adults will need to remain in the workforce longer in order to ensure a financially secure retirement; historically, the popular image of retirement in the U.S. has been that of working until one reaches the age of 65 then exiting completely from the paid workforce and living off the income generated from retirement sources. Yet, as Hardy (2003) notes, only about half of today's older workers experience retirement this way. For a growing number of older Americans, retirement is no longer a single event or a one-time transition from full-time work to a complete withdrawal from the labor force soon after a 65th birthday. Older workers are increasingly retiring gradually by transitioning from full-time employment to part-time employment or partial retirement. Some older workers are ending their career jobs, retiring, and then entering "bridge" jobs or choosing self-employment; and, still others interrupt their retirement with episodic employment, often on specific time-limited projects.

While retirement is often viewed as a voluntary transition, it is important to recognize that for a number of Americans their exit from the paid labor force is involuntary or forced. Disability, labor market obstacles, and/or family obligations may force individuals to exit from the labor force at earlier ages. Using data from Waves 1 to 4 of the Health and Retirement Survey (HRS), Szinovacz and Davey (2005) found that almost one out of every three retired workers perceived their retirement as forced. In fact, more than half (55%) of retirees ages 51 to 59 in the HRS survey reported that a health condition or impairment limits the amount or type of paid work they can do and they were three times more likely to be in fair or poor health compared to the working counterparts (National Academy on An Aging Society, 2000).

Flippen and Tienda's (2000) analysis of the HRS data revealed that Blacks and Hispanics were more vulnerable than Whites to involuntary job loss in the pre-retirement years and were more likely to exit the labor force through pathways other than retirement. Higher rates of chronic illness and functional limitations experienced by both these groups suggest that they were "pushed" from the labor force at earlier ages than Whites. The HRS data also revealed that that African Americans, Hispanics, and women experienced more involuntary job separation in the years immediately prior to retirement, and that these periods of joblessness often resulted in permanent labor force withdrawal (Flippen & Tienda, 2000).

Recognizing the plight of lower-income older adults who are unemployed or underemployed, the federal government created the Senior Community Service Employment Program (SCSEP). First authorized under the Economic Opportunity Act in 1965 and today standing as Title V of the Older Americans Act, the SCSEP currently assists some 47,000 lower-income adults aged 55 and older transition into the labor force through subsidized employment with locally-based community service organizations. The benefits of the SCSEP to participants are, however, farther reaching than just economic gains. As Ronald Aday and Gayle Kehoe's analysis (in this volume) of older workers in three SCSEP sites found, the participants reported better physical and psychological health, including a greater sense of personal empowerment emerging from their work experience.

In fact, a growing body of empirical literature suggests that there are multiple pathways to retirement reflecting many different life course trajectories. Indeed, work-family lives–or the intersection of the worlds of work and family–have changed dramatically in the past several decades as increasing numbers of women spend the majority of their adult years in the paid labor force. In this volume, also using the HRS dataset, Angela Curl and Aloen Townsend focus on the retirement patterns of 1,118 White and Black dual-earner married couples during the eight-year period of 1992 to 2000. As Curl and Townsend note, "for married individuals, retirement is a couple-level event where the retirement of one spouse often affects the life circumstances of both" impacting areas such as household income, health insurance coverage, household routines and schedules, and marital quality. In fact, not only did their results underscore the growing complexity of retirement, but they also revealed the degree to which couples' lives are linked (Kim & Moen, 2002). While there were distinct gender differences (i.e., husbands were more likely to transition directly from work to complete retirement), both the number and types of transitions were related within couples.

WORK AS A PART OF RETIREMENT

The pending retirements of the members of the baby boomer generation has revealed shifting expectations of retirement. National surveys consistently show that many baby boomers are planning to continue to engage in paid employment during their retirement years. The AARP (2003) survey of workers over the age of 45 found that almost 70% of respondents plan to continue working in retirement. Slightly more than one-third (34%) said they would work part-time out of enjoyment or interest, about one-fifth (19%) for needed income, 10% to go into business for themselves, and 6% would work full-time doing something else.

Baby boomers often identify a desire for social connection as well as the opportunity to engage in meaningful work and make a contribution to the community as important factors that would influence their future decisions about engaging in work during their retirement years. The MetLife Foundation/Civic Ventures 2005 *New Face of Work Survey* revealed that half of the surveyed American adults age 50 to 70 expressed interest in work in retirement that helps communities and those in need.

In fact, many reported that they did not want to wait until age 65 to shift into a second career nor did they view this next chapter of their worklife as less significant than their prior work. Among the surveyed individuals who were considering work in their retirement years, the four most important aspects of this future employment were: staying involved with other people (59%), a job with a sense of purpose (57%), having an additional income source (52%), and a job that benefits or helps the community (48%).

Many of these above reasons were articulated by the twelve individuals who were participants in Donald Veeneberg and Vida Wilkinson's qualitative study of retirees' motivations and experiences in re-entry to the workplace. Venneberg and Wilkinson (in this volume) document both the human capital (i.e., skills and knowledge) and social capital (i.e., social network, contacts and resources) that these retirees offered their organizations. Yet, they also identify the types of barriers the retirees faced, including the need to gain new knowledge and skills to meet current work challenges, to adjust to a new role or status, and to transition from a leader to a follower in the organization. Finally, the authors note that although these retirees felt they still had much to contribute to an organization or field, they typically sought to do so under "less stressful and more flexible work arrangements."

This strong desire by many retirees for more flexible employment options, often expressed as an interest in part-time or episodic employment, may match well with America's new work economy. Tracy Madvig and Kenneth Shultz (in this volume) suggest that retirees' interest in flexible work arrangements may align well with corporate America's shift toward the greater utilization of temporary, contract and consultant-type workers. The re-hiring of retirees, who possess knowledge of organizational operations, policies, and culture, for temporary work assignments may be more cost effective for companies than the hiring new external workers. Drawing upon survey data from approximately 1,000 retirees from a southern California utility company, Madvig and Schultz therefore begin to explore what factors might predict a retirees' interest in returning to their previous employer in a voluntary or paid work capacity. Central to their analysis is the concept of employer-employee reciprocity; that is, if an organization treats an employee fairly and creates a supportive work environment then that individual is more likely to engage with the organization, either on a volunteer or work basis, as a retiree.

Supportive Work Environments

In fact, as Diana Stork (in this volume) emphasizes, young and older workers share strikingly similar views on what constitutes a "good job" and a "positive or supportive work environment." Her comparison of 663 younger workers (age 30 and younger) and older workers (age 45 and older) revealed that for both age groups the ideal job entailed doing work that engendered pride and feelings of being trusted as well as having a good relationship with one's supervisor. Also critical were rewards, benefits, and time for health, wellness and family. Although important to both age groups, older workers expressed greater interest than did younger workers in having challenging work, task variety, and control over their work (e.g., how, when and where work was performed).

Flexibility in work, allowing individuals greater balance between their work and personal or family life is highly desired by workers of all ages. While work-family conflicts are often perceived to be an issue primarily for younger families, it is estimated that about 15% of America's adult population cares for a chronically ill or disabled adult family member aged 50 or older, and nearly six out of ten of these adult caregivers are employed (International Longevity Center-USA, 2006). Moreover, as the National Alliance for Caregiving and AARP 2004 survey revealed the costs of this caregiving is often borne by both the employees and employers. Work-related adjustments include arriving late or leaving work early, using personal or sick days or taking a temporary leave of absence, reducing work hours, refusing work-related travel, overtime work, or relocations, turning down new assignments or promotions, leaving the work force, and early retirement. The stresses of attempting to balance the dual demands of caregiving and paid work may also place these individuals at risk for poorer physical health (i.e., lower immune system) and emotional health (i.e., depression, anxiety). On average, family caregivers provide this care for more than four years. A 1997 analysis by the Metropolitan Life Insurance Company estimated that the annual national productivity costs of these work-related caregiving adjustments for corporate America is between 11.4 billion dollars to 29.billion dollars.

Nationwide, there are a growing number of collaborations or partnerships between corporations and nonprofit health and social services organizations to develop resources to better support employees with caregiving responsibilities. Yet, as Daniel Kuhn and his colleagues (in this volume) note, although the internet is now the leading source of information for caregivers, the utility of internet-based caregiver information and education has rarely been evaluated. Working with the American Business Collaboration for Quality Dependent Care (ABC), the nonprofit organization Mather LifeWays adapted their community-based six-week caregiver education program, *Powerful Tools for Caregivers* (PTC) into an on-line course that corporations might offer their employees. The PTC on-line course–available 24/7–was viewed as offering the greatest flexibility to busy individuals; and, while the on-line PTC offered social interaction through web chats and discussion boards, (unlike workplace-based groups) individuals did not have to self-identify. As Kuhn reports in this volume, their preliminary evaluation of PTC-online suggests that web-based resources hold considerable promise as both attractive and effective strategies for supporting busy caregivers juggling multiple life demands.

Robert Boyce (also in this volume) argues that to create supportive work environments for older employees, companies must ultimately adopt a more integrative approach-linking ergonomics, health promotion, and employee assistance. Although older Americans are much healthier than in the past and jobs have become less physically demanding, age-related physiological changes (i.e. changes in cardiovascular, musculoskeletal, nervous, and sensory systems) still affect job performance and many contemporary jobs involve stress and/or strain (i.e., repetitive motion, stationary positions).

The Americans with Disabilities Act (ADA), enacted in 1990, prohibits discrimination of individuals with disabilities and mandates reasonable accommodations (i.e., job restructuring, modified work schedules, and making existing facilities accessible). As the baby boomer generation ages, and experiences more age-related disabilities, they will undoubtedly change the impact that the ADA has on the workplace. Yet, the ADA focuses on accommodation on an individual basis; and Boyce argues that American corporations need to do more to prepare for an aging workforce. Boyce, a proponent of transgenerational or universal design of the workplace, suggests such an approach can improve performance and safety for workers of all ages. (In fact, Boyce's case study at a call center revealed that about 4 out of every 10 workers, regardless of age, reported high levels of discomfort in their lower backs.) Ultimately, the principles of universal design with respect to the workplace offer economic benefits to employers through decreases in the number of injuries and disabilities sustained by employees on the job, reductions in the number of individual workplace accommodations, increases in employees' job performance, morale and productivity, and declines in the rate of employee absenteeism and job turnover.

TRANSFORMING AMERICA'S WORKPLACES

Transforming or changing America's workplaces to better utilize the human and social capital of older workers, as well as creating work environments that present job opportunities that are attractive to a mature workforce, will not be an easy task. Although the Age Discrimination in Employment Act (ADEA) protects against age discrimination for persons aged 40 and older and prohibits mandatory retirement at any age (except in jobs for which age is considered a bona fide criterion of ability), many employers continue to have negative stereotypes of older workers. Surveys consistently find that both employers and older employees believe that age bias remains a problem in the workplace; employers are seen as harboring negative perceptions of older workers' flexibility, adaptability, technological competence and willingness to learn new skills (AARP 2003; McCann, 2004).

As Jerry Hedge and Gayle Kehoe (in this volume) emphasize, employers need to examine how their corporate culture affects its policies and practices towards investment in older workers. They stress that "there are probably more policies and decisions that are implicitly age-based than those which are explicitly so . . . It is the implicit ones that are the most difficult to detect and change." Moreover, Hedge and Kehoe argue that a strong commitment or buy-in from top management is essential to development and implementation of effective human resource management practices which are attractive to older adults.

There is ample evidence that both current and future older Americans want to remain active in the labor force in their later years; however, they wish to "work differently." Considerable recent attention has been focused on the option of phased retirement, in which older workers gradually depart the workforce through shorter work weeks, flexible hours, or some other arrangement. In fact, surveys consistently demonstrate older persons' interest in pursuing this option. For example, a 2004 national cross-sectional survey found that one out of three older workers would phase out of work if the option was available rather than retire completely. Almost two-thirds of workers over the age of 50 reported hoping to phase into their retirement; many hoping to work part-time (63%) or work part-time (48%) before withdrawing completely from the labor force (Watson Wyatt, 2004). However, few employers currently make the option of phased retirement available to their employees, either formally or informally.

Barriers to employers implementing phased retirement policies extend beyond the organization's culture; as Erin Kelly and her colleagues (in this volume) emphasize organizations' policies and practices are constrained by multiple federal laws and regulations. The widespread confusion that exists about how phrased retirement programs should be structured to comply with the intersecting laws of the Employee Retirement Income Security Act (ERISA), the Age Discrimination in Employment Act (ADEA) and IRS tax code has prevented many companies from moving forward to implement such programs. In fact, Kelly and her co-authors note that the title for their piece, "Making Sense of a Mess" was derived from both the confusion and frustration they heard expressed repeatedly from key stakeholders in the workplace, including human resource managers, benefit specialists, and work-life professionals.

Underlying much of employers' and employees' frustration is a growing recognition that these regulatory statues (i.e., ERISA, ADEA, tax codes) are based on an increasingly outdated assumption of a clear bifurcation between the life stages of work and retirement, a policy version of "structural lag" (Riley & Riley, 1994). As Phyllis Moen astutely comments in the 2005 MetLife Foundation/Civic Ventures, *New Face of Work Survey*:

> [T]here is a fundamental problem with this education-employment-retirement lock step. Its outdated, forged by 20th century polices and practices that don't match up with 21st century realities. As a result, this tidy life package puts limits on education, work, service, and leisure possibilities for all Americans and is age-graded, building age segregation and discrimination–of all types–into all our institutions. (p.13)

Indeed, a strong argument could be made that the redesigning of America's work model, from a linear to cyclical one, would benefit workers of all ages–young adult, midlife, and older workers. Equally important, establishing flexibility as an organizational value may be a "sound business practice" as America's workplaces become increasingly multigenerational.

CONCLUSION

Once considered an oxymoron, "working in retirement" is now being viewed as the new reality. Surveys consistently find that a large percentage of the baby boomer generation reports that they plan to keep working during their retirement years, at least on a part-time or episodic basis. Healthier and better educated than previous older generations, baby boomers feel they still have much to contribute to their organization, field, and/or community during the second half of their lives. Unfortunately, most anticipate they will face considerable difficulties in finding these flexible and/or alternative work arrangements. In publishing this volume focused on *The Older Worker and the Changing Labor Market* we hope to contribute to the growing national dialogue on strategies to foster public and private sector policies that support, retain, and engage older workers as well as promote workplaces that are responsive to the increasingly diverse multigenerational workforce of the 21st century.

Judith G. Gonyea, PhD
Boston University
School of Social Work

REFERENCES

AARP. (2003). Staying ahead of the curve 2003: The AARP working in retirement study. Retrieved from http://assets.aarp.org/rgcenter/econ/multiwork_2003.pdf.

AARP (2006). Rethinking the role of older workers: Promoting older worker employment in Europe and Japan. *Issue Brief 77*, Washington, DC: Author.

Cappelli, W. (2004). Will there really be a labor shortage? *Public Policy & Aging Report, 14, 3,* 1-6.

Federal Interagency Forum on Aging Related Statistics. (2006). Older Americans 2006: Key indicators of well-being chartbook. Retrieved from http://www.agingstats.gov.

Flippen, C., & Tienda, M. (2000). Pathways to retirement: Patterns of labor force participation and labor market exist among the pre-retirement populations by race, Hispanic origin, and sex. *Journal of Gerontology: Psychology and Social Sciences, 55,* S14-S27.

Gonyea, J. G. (2005). The economic well-being of older Americans and the persistent divide. *Public Policy & Aging Report, 15(2),* 1-11.

Hardy, M. (2006). Older workers. In R.H. Binstock and L.K. George (Eds), *Handbook of aging and social sciences* (6th ed., pp. 201-218). CA: Academic Press.

Hudson, R. B., & Gonyea, J. G. (2007, forthcoming). The evolving role of public policy in promoting work and retirement. *Generations.*

International Longevity Center-USA. (2006). *Caregiving in America.* USA: Author.

Kim, J. E., & Moen, P. (2002). Retirement transitions, gender and psychological well-being: A life course, ecological model. *Journal of Gerontology Psychological Sciences, 57*(B), 212-222.

McCann, L. (2004). Age discrimination in employment: Why its predicted demise is off the mark. *Public Policy & Aging Report, 14, 3,* 7-10.

MetLife Foundation and Civic Ventures. (2005). New Face of Work Survey. Retrieved from http://www.civicventures.org/publications/surveys/new_face_of_work/new_face_of_work.pdf.

Metropolitan Life Insurance Company. (1997). The MetLife study of employer costs for working caregivers. CT: Author.

Munnell, A. H. (2006) Policies to promote labor force participation of older people. CRR WP-2006-2. MA: Center on Retirement Research at Boston College. Retrieved from http://www.bc.edu/crr.

National Academy on An Aging Society. (2000). Who are young retirees and older workers? DC: Author.

National Alliance for Caregiving and AARP. (2004). Caregiving in the United States. Retrieved from http://www.aarp.org/rgcenter/il/us_caregiving.pdf.

National Council on Aging. (2000). Myths and realities: 2000 survey results. Washington, DC: Author.

Penner, R. G., Perun, P. & Steuerle, E. 2003. Letting older workers go. *Brief Series, 16,* DC: Urban Institute.

Rajnes, D. (2001). Phased retirement: Leaving the labor force. *EBRI Notes, 22,9.* Washington DC: Employee Benefits Research Institute.

Riley, M. W., & Riley, J. W. (1994). Structural lag: Past and future. In M.W. Riley, R. L. Kahn & A. Foner (Eds.), *Age and Structural Lag.* New York: Wiley.

Szinovacz, M. E., & Davey, A. (2005). Predictors of perceptions of involuntary retirement. *Gerontologist, 45,* 36-45.

Toosi, M. (2002). A century of change: The U.S. Labor Force, 1950-2050. *Monthly Labor Review, 125,* 15-28.

U.S. Department of Commerce. (2006). Personal savings rate. *National Economic Accounts.* Washington, D.C.: Bureau of Economic Analysis. Retrieved from http://www.bea.gov/briefrm/saving.htm.

Watson Wyatt. (2004). Phased retirement: Aligning employer programs with worker preferences. MD: Author. Retrieved from http://www.watsonwyatt.com/research/resender.asp?id = w-731&page = 1.

Retirees Who Returned to Work: Human and Social Capital Implications for Organizations

Donald L. Venneberg
Vida D. Wilkinson

INTRODUCTION

Everyone is the age of their heart.

–Guatemalan Proverb

THE AGING WORKFORCE AND FUTURE WORKER AND SKILL SHORTAGES

The population and the workforce of the United States and several other developed countries are continuing to age. In the United States the large cohort of *Baby Boomers* makes up the bulk of the current workforce. The Boomers are followed by a much smaller generational cohort, *Generation X*, born in the years 1965 to 1979. Also, in the United States the birth rate is just at/or below the replacement rate. This low birth rate will generate fewer younger workers to replace those who are older and may soon begin to exit the workforce (Herman et al., 2003). Between 2000 and 2050 the aging population will result in a projected increase from 22% to 38% in the number of people over age 65 who will be supported by decreasing numbers of active workers aged 15 to 64 (Gordon, 2005). Concerns are also being raised about the potential impact of the significant loss of skills and experience as the aging workforce begins to retire (Delong, 2004; Gordon, 2005; Dychtwald et al., 2006).

These potential shortages of skilled and experienced workers will necessitate a reconsideration of government and organization policies and practices in order to retain older workers and rehire those who have retired from the workforce. Most organizations in the United States, however, have not yet begun to take action to capture and/or retain the knowledge base represented of older workers.

HUMAN AND SOCIAL CAPITAL CAPACITY OF OLDER WORKERS

Part of the problem with understanding the knowledge and skills held by older workers comes from the way human capital investment has traditionally been evaluated. Geroy and Venneberg (2003) described a human capital construct where (1) human capital *capacity* is composed of skills, knowledge and the influence of attitude and other intrinsic variables, and (2) human capital capacity is both *passive* and *active*. Passive capacity is that knowledge that the individual gains and is available for potential/future use. Active capacity is knowledge that the individual gains and is available for immediate use. In economic terms, passive capacity represents the stock of knowledge available and not currently utilized, while active capacity is the explicit information that is currently flowing through the organizational system.

We further posit that social capital capacity is also passive and active. Lin (2001) offers an operational definition of social capital that includes both resources and outcomes: "investment in social relations by individuals through which they gain access to embedded resources to enhance expected returns of instrumental or expressive actions." Instrumental action is the obtaining of resources not currently possessed by the worker for active use. Expressive action is the maintenance of resources currently possessed by the worker which can be used at any time (active) or are kept in reserve (passive). Passive social capital capacity is also similar to that espoused by Burt (2000) in his *structural hole* argument. Burt defines social capital in terms of the information and control advantages of being a broker in relations between people otherwise disconnected in social structure. In other words, these relationships are non-redundant sources of information, are available to the individual for future use, and are more additive than overlapping. Coleman (2000) maintains that active social capital capacity is necessary in order for organizational information to be accessible for all individuals. Depending on the desired outcome, having access to appropriable active and passive social capital capacity is an asset to individuals and/or organizations.

Older workers typically have a large store of human capital capacity from their years of training, skill and knowledge development and work experience. A great deal of this human capital capacity is active and used on a day-to-day basis to accomplish tasks and reach organizational objectives. Much of the capacity is also passive and available for use on other tasks and jobs. Older workers also generally have a large store of social capital, represented by their broad networks of social relationships with both those outside the organization and those within the organization. These human capital capacities and social capital relationships could be leveraged by organizations for the furtherance of organization ends. However both the human capital and the social capital held by older workers are often under-valued or overlooked by organizations, resulting in a loss of the capacity of these capitals to their operations and their ability to meet goals and objectives (Dess & Shaw, 2001).

PROBLEM STATEMENT

In order to effectively capture and utilize the social and human capital assets represented by older workers, organizations will need to develop an understanding of the workplace needs of older workers and retirees who may wish to return to the workforce. A missing element in developing this understanding is the meaning that retirees who have returned to work ascribe to their experience.

METHODOLOGY

Research Purpose

A recent study (Venneberg, 2005) was conducted to discover and describe the meaning retirees ascribe to the experience of retiring and then returning to paid work, and developing implications for organizations from the experiences as voiced by the study participants.

Research Question

The question to be answered by the study was what is the perspective of the retiree who seeks to find the essential nature of the experience of retiring and returning to paid work from retirement?

SELECTION OF METHODOLOGY FOR THE STUDY

Most of the recent research on older workers and retirees has been done using telephone or written surveys for data collection. This method yielded quantifiable data that was analyzed for purposes of describing the current situation and behavior of older workers and retirees, to project their possible future behavior. Where the participants surveyed were a randomly selected sample representative of the population of older workers or retirees, some generalizations were made about the population being studied.

The survey research method is limited, however, for the exploration of the *meaning* retired persons ascribe to the return to paid work, which may shed light on why they chose to return to work after retirement. Also, since much of the current survey research is prospective, it suffers from the limitation that actual behavior may differ from what is reported. What was needed, therefore, was an interpretive phenomenological analysis (Willig, 2001) of the meaning retirees ascribe to the phenomena of returning to work after retirement.

Criterion Sampling

A criterion sampling approach was used to select twelve retirees (seven men and five women) to participate in the study. The criteria for participant selection were that:

1. The participant had retired from an organization or his or her own business and was receiving income from a pension or annuity, social security or other government provided benefit, from personal assets or from a previously owned and actively managed business; and
2. the participant had returned to working for pay on a full or part-time basis, either in their pre-retirement type of work and/or organization or another organization or type of work, or was operating their own business.

The criteria of being retired and subsequently returning to work was chosen based on the limited or lack of research on the decision to return to work after retirement (Rocco et al., 2003).

Data Collection and Analysis

The primary form of data collection was through in-depth interviews of participants, using the open-ended question "What has been your experience with retiring and then returning to paid work or to operating your own business?", with appropriate follow up questions, to elicit non-directed responses (Seidman; 1998; Willig, 2001). All interviews were conducted between October 2004 and January 2005.

The outcomes of the study were emergent *themes* and the *essence* of how the participants experienced the phenomenon of retiring and returning to work (Creswell, 1998; Moustakas, 1994; Willig, 2001).

FINDINGS

Themes

From this study, two sets of themes emerged through the voices of the participants, some of which supported and some of which differed from the dimensions of prior research on how older workers used their human and social capital capacity in organizations. Four primary themes emerged; and three to seven specific *sub-themes* emerged within these primary themes.

The participant's primary and sub-themes are shown in Tables 1a and 1b, with the themes (primary in bold) cited by the male participants in the first seven columns (unshaded) and the themes cited by the female participants in the last five columns (shaded).

Some of the themes which emerged were consistent with the findings of prior research. For example, the impetus to retire due to job stress or the desire to return to work because of a feeling of the loss of social interaction or the need for mental stimulation is consistent with earlier research (Montenegro et al., 2002).

However, the results of this study revealed some themes which differed from or added additional meaning to the findings of earlier research. This was particularly true of some of the themes that emerged from women participants. These new themes are felt to be important to inform future organizational decisions on the effective use of the human and social capital of older workers, and are discussed briefly in the following sections.

TABLE 1a. Primary and Sub-Themes of Participants' Experiences with Retiring and Returning to Work, by Gender (Shaded = Female)

Participant / Theme	3 M	4 M	5 M	6 M	7 M	8 M	9 M	1 F	2 F	10 F	11 F	12 F
Reasons for Retiring												
Planned - Financially or Mentally Prepared	X	X				X	X	X	X		X	X
Did Not Plan - Event or Opportunity			X		X				X		X	
Spouse Retired, Family, other things					X				X		X	X
Job Stress or Conflict			X	X	X	X	X	X			X	X
Reasons to Return to Work												
More to Contribute	X	X		X	X		X		X	X		
Spouse Working						X		X	X			X
Social Interaction	X		X	X			X			X	X	X
Identity tied to Work			X	X		X				X	X	
Stay Engaged/In Touch with Field	X	X			X	X	X			X	X	
Extra Income	X		X	X	X				X	X	X	X
Transition to Retirement		X	X		X	X			X			X
Barriers or Challenges to Returning to Work												
Orgs. do Not Understand Needs of Retiree Employees	X		X		X	X						
New Role, Status, Salary	X		X	X		X		X	X			
Need to Build New Reputation	X	X										
Younger Colleagues or Supervisors	X	X	X									
Need for New Knowledge or Skills								X	X		X	X
New Network and Interview Skills		X							X		X	
Work-Life Balance			X					X	X	X		

TABLE 1b. Primary and Sub-Themes of Participants' Experiences with Retiring and Returning to Work, by Gender (Shaded = Female)

Participant / Theme	3 M	4 M	5 M	6 M	7 M	8 M	9 M	1 F	2 F	10 F	11 F	12 F
Why This Org. or Work												
Knew Org., People and they Solicited Me	X	X	X	X	X		X	X		X		X
Org. Uses Experience, Knowledge, Contacts	X	X	X	X	X	X		X		X		X
Enjoy Work, People, Teamwork	X		X	X	X	X	X	X	X	X		X
Mentor/Help Others			X				X	X		X	X	X
No Supv. Duties, Promotion Pressure	X	X	X	X	X	X	X					
Part time, Flexible Schedule/Assignment	X		X	X	X	X	X	X	X		X	X
Pay and Benefits	X						X	X		X		X

Decision to Retire, Barriers or Challenges to Returning to Work and Gender Differences Among Participants

Four of the men and four of the women who participated in the study had financially planned or were mentally prepared for retirement. For example one of the women stated:

> We started probably in our early 50s planning for our retirement, which is late. It cost quite a bit for us to do it but we figured . . . we were looking at getting 75% of my salary . . . and then we looked at, well maybe it would be nice to have 80% and we started looking back at ways we could do it.

All five of the women in this study, including the four who had *planned for their retirement*, had worked in jobs which provided them with a defined benefit annuity. This group may thus differ from the norm for women retirees found by others. Schulz (2001) for example noted that women have often had more irregular work patterns and therefore are dependent for retirement on benefits from a spouse or a limited amount of Social Security payments. Other studies have also found that a gap in the level of pensions between men and women, while closing somewhat, still remains (Even & Macpherson, 1994) and that there is continued segregation of women into gendered lower paying professions with lower access to training (Schulz, 2001; Simpson & Stroh, 2002; Tomaskovic-Devy & Skaggs, 2002).

On the other hand, the women in this study may presage the results of the 2004 Retirement Confidence Survey by the Employee Benefits Research Institute (EBRI) that currently employed women and men are about equal in their level of confidence that they will have adequate income and assets in retirement to support a comfortable lifestyle.

Three of the women and one of the men were influenced in their decision to retire by the fact that their spouse had or soon would retire from their job or career. For example, one of the male participants stated; "We kind of made an agreement when I did retire and my wife retired at the same time, actually a few months earlier."

This finding is consistent with some of the recent studies on the marital status impact on the retirement decision (Szinovacz & DeViney, 2000), spousal influence on retirement decisions (Smith & Moen, 1998), and the retirement decision in dual career families (Gustman & Steinmeier, 2000), all of which suggested the linkage of spouses' decisions.

In the area of *barriers or challenges to returning to work* four of the women, but none of the men, cited a need to gain *new knowledge and skills* as a challenge to returning to work. For example, one woman participant who trained her subordinate to take her job upon retirement was then rehired to fill the lesser position stated that: "And so for that four years between when I hired [my replacement] and I retired I wasn't doing it [the lesser position] and . . . I didn't stay on top of it so I had to learn the process all over again.'"

Notably, these four women shifted to a different, if related, type of job where new technology or processes were in use compared their pre-retirement jobs. In contrast, all of the men in the study returned to doing work that was similar to their pre-retirement jobs so they may have had or at least acknowledged less need for skill and knowledge development.

Three of the women, but only one of the men felt that the maintaining their *work-life balance* was a barrier or challenge to returning to work. As one of the women said:

> *I'm trying to discern where that [work] fits in with my role as a wife, and my husband's doctorate program and being supportive to him which is pretty time consuming right now for him. Do I want to do it [work] everyday where I have to go someplace else to do that, and then that would also add stress around our house?*

No Feeling of Age Bias in the Decision to Retire or Return to Working

Notably absent as a reason cited by both the men and the women for deciding to retire was a feeling that they were encouraged to leave their organizations because of their age. Also, none of the participants felt that age was a barrier to returning to work or to the organization or type of work they chose after retiring. This may be considered unusual given the studies that reflect that a youth culture in the United States weighs against organizations valuing older workers (Auerbach & Welsh, 1994; Goldberg, 2000) and that outright age discrimination exists in the workplace (Johnson & Neumark, 1997; Montenegro et al., 2002; Seagrave, 2001).

Challenges of the Intergenerational Workplace

One of the men cited the lack of respect by younger colleagues of his experience; whereas, another of the men felt that working younger colleagues kept him challenged. None of the women participants cited issues relating to working with younger fellow workers.

Adjustment to a New Role or Status and the Need to Build a New Reputation in a Post-Retirement Job or Organization

Four men in the study cited a need to make a *role or status adjustment* in their post-retirement job and organization as a challenge in returning to work. Two men further found that they had to build a new reputation in their new organization since their prior reputation did not carry over. For all of these men, this role and status and reputation adjustment was one of moving from being a manager or leader to being more actively involved as the provider of a service. For example, one of the men stated:

> *As a consultant you have zero power, it seems, so you're lucky to get people sometimes to even answer the phone, to be willing to talk to you. So yes, that was a major change. I just want to be a part of a team.*

Two of the women also cited a status adjustment, but they differed from the men. One woman, who was a manager prior to retirement, did not find the shift to a non-managerial position difficult but was concerned about *adjusting to a lower salary* level:

I also had a certain level of salary that I wanted which [I thought] could have been gained by working part-time. I didn't necessarily have to take a full-time position based on my retirement money and based on other factors; I had decided X amount of dollars would probably suffice. I was kind of amazed at how little they were paying [here] for some of the jobs that I interviewed for.

Another woman had to adjust to a change in role from being the person in the office who provided advice and knowledge on the processes and program of the office, to being in a subordinate position in the same office.

The Move from Leader to Follower

All of the men in the study had led organizations and supervised people in their careers were no longer interested in being supervisors, managers and leaders after they retired. For example, one of the participants said:

I didn't want to be a manager; I didn't want the headaches, the work hours and all. I just wanted to have a regular job . . . I just wanted to come in and do my work during the day and leave. Someone who's retired like me . . . just wanted to do the work and get paid for it, I had no aspirations of being manager or moving up.

In addition, these men did not wish to treat their post-retirement jobs as a second career but as a means to continued satisfaction with work.

Acceptance That They Have More to Contribute

Two of the women in the study and five of the men said they were not ready to fully retire from work because they felt that they had more to contribute in the way of experience, knowledge, and skill to an organization or their field of work. As one of the men said:

As I grow older I want to think–'Oh, I can still play with these guys.' And if you do it every day and it's working, you're continuing to give yourself some positive feedback. I hope I'm making a contribution that they like.

One of the women stated a similar reason to return to work: ". . . I guess I'm not ready yet to just be retired." Also, all but one of the men and three or the women felt that their post-retirement organization accepted them as being able to fully contribute to organizational goals and objectives. As one of the men said ". . . .they know the value of the expertise. They're doing their best to bring that back."

Opportunity to Mentor or Help Others

Four of the women and two of the men cited the opportunity for mentoring or helping others as one of the things they found to be satisfying about their post-retirement work. One of the men stated this feeling well:

> . . . there is an opportunity to try and help some younger people out. They aren't always that interested but once in a while you find one that you feel is worthy of some attention and you try and channel them, as best you can, to do the right things.

Extra Income and Pay and Benefits

In prior research (Montenegro et al., 2002), the need for income was a strong motivator for prospective retirees to continue working. In this study, five of the eight participants who cited extra income as a factor in their return to work decision saw the income as "nice to have" for vacations and other pursuits. Only three cited extra income as a key factor in their decision to return to work. In two of these three cases, the participants had income needs caused by circumstances that did not affect the others (one had a young child and one was divorced).

Three of the women and two of the men said that the pay and benefits they received were a factor in their decision to work for their post-retirement organizations. Of those five, three cited extra income as a *need* in retirement. One of the men needed extra income to pay off some debts, and one to cover his loss of assets in a divorce prior to retiring while one woman who returned to work with a state agency cited the need to lower her health benefit costs:

> When you work for the state you could work like one hour a month and you get all the benefits . . . and the big mover is health insurance . . . our insurance is a little more than $700 a month . . . and through the state it's going to be I think $200, so [it's] a major difference and [for] the same coverage.

The Importance of Social Interaction in the Workplace

Three of the men and three of the women said that they missed the social interaction aspect of work when they retired and that this factor was important in their decision to return to work. One woman stated this need very well:

> *One of the reasons I wanted to do it [work] was social. . . You need playmates and all your playmates are working. So for me a big part of it is social.*

Essence of the Retiree's Experience

The primary and sub-themes themes that emerged from the analysis of the voices of the participants provided the essence of their experience with retiring and then returning to work: *I am not ready to fully retire because I have more to contribute, and I want to continue to work but under less stressful and more flexible work arrangements.*

CONCLUSION

Some of the findings of this study fit the dimensions of the application of human and social capital capacity of older workers (see Table 2).

As can be seen in Table 2, some of the key findings supported the literature on human and social capital. For example, the difference between gaining active or passive human capital can be seen in the first two items under *human capital* in Table 2. Four of the women stated a desire to gain *active* human capital through increased knowledge and skills to perform the current job. On the other hand, none of the men in the study wished to gain additional *passive* human capital capacity to move ahead in the organization.

The last item in Table 2 under the *social capital* heading reflects the importance of social networks that the organizations used in the hiring process. Six of the men and three of the women were hired based on social networks. Also, the need to redevelop personal social networks for finding a job played a key role in the job seeking process for three of the participants (one man and two women).

A dimension that included both human and social capital for nine of the participants was that the organization used their existing experience, knowledge, and contacts.

TABLE 2. Human and Social Capital Dimensions of Retirees Experiences with Returning to Work

Human Capital	Social Capital
♦ No desire to gain new knowledge and skills to move ahead in the organization (all men) ♦ Desire to gain new knowledge and skills to improve performance on the job (four women) ♦ One size does not fit all for training and development (generational difference) ♦ More to contribute from experience, knowledge and skills (five men and two women) ♦ No desire for supervisory duties (all men)	♦ Need to re-build or re-define or build new network to find a new job (one man and two women) ♦ Adjustment to change in status (four men and two women) ♦ Desire to move from leader to follower (all men) ♦ Opportunity to mentor and/or help others (two men and four women) ♦ Knew organization and solicited/hired by the organization (six men and three women)
Organization values and uses my experience, knowledge and contacts (six men and three women)	

Limitations

As with most qualitative studies that focus on a small number of participants who are not representative of a population, the findings and conclusions of the study can only be applied to the participants themselves and not to the population as a whole (all those who have retired and then returned to work).

Implications for Organizations and the Need for Further Research

The study of retirees who returned to the workforce provides an initial exploration of the dimensions of the issues through their lens. It is hoped that their experiences will provide insight to organizations for planning and implementing programs for the retention and recruiting of older workers. Further research needs to be conducted on the use of the human and social capital capacity of older workers by organizations to meet their workforce needs and accomplish their organizational objectives.

REFERENCES

Auerbach, J. A. & Welsh, J. C. (1994). *Aging and competition: Rebuilding the U. S. workforce*. Washington, DC: National Planning Association.

Burt, R. S. (2000). The contingent value of social capital. In E. L. Lesser (Ed.), *Knowledge and social capital: Foundations and applications* (pp. 255-286). Boston: Butterworth-Heinemann.

Coleman, J. S. (2000). Social capital in the creation of human capital. In E. L. Lesser (Ed.), *Knowledge and social capital: Foundations and applications* (pp. 17-41). Boston: Butterworth-Heinemann.

Creswell, J. W. (1998). *Qualitative inquiry and research design: Choosing among the five traditions.* Thousand Oaks, CA: Sage.

DeLong, D. W. (2004). *Lost knowledge: Confronting the threat of an aging workforce.* New York: Oxford University Press.

Dess, G. G. & Shaw, J. D. (2001). Voluntary turnover, social capital, and organizational performance. *Academy of Management Review, 26,* 446-456.

Dychtwald, K., Erickson, T. J. & Morison R. (2006). *Workforce crisis: How to beat the coming shortage of skills and talent.* Ambridge, MA: Harvard Business School Press.

Employee Benefit Research Institute (2004), *Retirement confidence survey, 2004: Retirement confidence fact sheet.* Washington, DC: Employee Benefit Research Institute, American Savings Education Council & Mathew Greenwald & Associates.

Even, W. E. & Macpherson, D. A. (1994). Gender differences in pensions. *The Journal of Human Resources, Special Issue: Women's Work, Wages and Well-Being, 29*(2), 555-587.

Geroy, G. D. & Venneberg, D. L. (2003). A view to human capital metrics. In A. M. Gilley, J. L. Callahan, & L. L. Bierema, (Eds.), *Critical issues in HRD: An agenda for the twenty-first century* (pp. 87-103). Cambridge, MA: Perseus Books.

Goldberg, B. (2000). *Age works: What corporate America must do to survive the graying of the workforce.* New York: The Free Press.

Gordon, E. E. (2005). *The 2010 meltdown: Solving the impending job crisis.* Westport, CT: Praeger.

Gustman, A. L. & Steinmeier, T. L. (2000). Retirement in dual-career families: A structural model. *Journal of Labor Economics,* 18-3; 503-545.

Herman, R. E., Olivo, T. G., & Gioia, J. L. (2003). *Impending crisis: Too many jobs too few people.* Wincester, VA: Oakhill Press.

Johnson, R. W. & Newmark, D. (1997). Age discrimination, job separations and employment status of older workers: Evidence from self-reports. *Journal of Human Resources, 32*(4), 113-129.

Lin, N. (2001). *Social capital: A theory of social structure and action.* New York: Cambridge University Press.

Montenegro, X., Fisher, L. & Remez, S. (2002), *Staying ahead of the curve: The AARP work and career study conducted for AARP by Roper ASW.* Washington, DC: AARP.

Moustakas, C. (1994). *Phenomenological research methods.* Thousand Oaks, CA: Sage.

Rocco, T. S., Stein, D. & Lee, C. (2003), An exploratory examination of the literature on age and HRD policy development, *Human Resource Development Review,* 2-2: 155-180.

Schulz, J. H. (2001). *The economics of aging,* (7th ed.). Westport, CT: Auburn House.

Seagrave, K. (2001). *Age discrimination by employers.* Jefferson, NC: McFarland & Co.

Seidman, I. (1998). *Interviewing as qualitative research: A guide for researchers in education and the social sciences* (2nd ed.). New York: Teachers College Press, Teachers College, Columbia University.

Simpson, P.A. & Stroh, L.K. (2002). Revisiting gender variation in training. *Feminist Economics, 8*(3), 21-53.

Smith, D. B. & Moen, P. (1998). Spousal influence on retirement: His, her, and their perceptions. *Journal of Marriage and the Family, 60*(3), 734-744.

Szinovacz, M. E. & DeViney, S. (2000). Marital characteristics and retirement decisions. *Research on Aging, 22*(5), 470-498.

Tomaskovic-Devy, D. & Skaggs, S. (2002). Sex segregation, labor process organization, and gender earnings inequality. *American Journal of Sociology, 108*(1), 102-128.

Toossi, M. (2004). Labor force projections to 2012: The graying of the U.S. workforce. *Monthly Labor Review, February, 127-2*: 37-57.

Venneberg, D.L. (2005). *The experiences of retirees and their decision to return to the workforce: Implications for organizations.* Unpublished doctoral dissertation. Colorado State University, Fort Collins, CO.

Willig, C. (2001). *Introducing qualitative research in psychology: Adventures in theory and method.* Buckingham, England: Open University Press.

Zempke, R., Raines, C. & Filipczek, P. (2000). *Generations at work: Managing the clash of veterans, boomers, xers and nexters in your workplace.* New York: AMACOM.

Modeling Individuals' Post-Retirement Behaviors Toward Their Former Organization

Tracy L. Madvig
Kenneth S. Shultz

INTRODUCTION

Over 2.5 million people retire each year in the United States (Adams & Beehr, 2003; Feldman, 1994), and the numbers are increasing with the Baby Boomer cohort nearing retirement age. Demographics show that even though individuals are living longer, they are retiring from their careers at younger ages, although often later re-entering the workforce once retired (Hayward et al., 1994). For example, 84% of 60 year olds were part of the labor force in 1970. By 1986, the percentage dropped dramatically to 70%, and more recently in 1993 has remained relatively stable at 69% (Census Bureau, 1995). As a result of this trend, more and more organizations in both the United States (Hedge et al., 2006; Rosen & Jerdee, 1985; 1988) and the European Community (Snel & Cremer, 1994) are beginning to examine their retirement and staffing policies with regard to the aging workforce (Taylor et al., 2005).

In addition, in the past century we have seen a shift from mostly blue collar-type industries, such as agriculture and manufacturing, to today's white collar technological and knowledge based economy (Drucker, 2001). With these changes we are seeing a shift from taking part in mostly core staff or line work, towards participating in more variable temporary, assignment-based, and project-type work. This has lead to the utilization of more temporary, contract, and consultant-type workers within organizations (Shultz, 2001). While these practices appear to be part of the new, cutting edge employment philosophy of the 21st century, organizations are still experimenting with successes and failures in terms of who (what type of people or employees) are best to hire for variable work. Should they staff these positions internally, or seek external hires? Might an organization's own retirees serve as a valuable source of flexible workers (Hirshorn & Hoyer, 1994)? The changing concept of retirement will be explored next using traditional, modern, and future frameworks.

The Changing Nature of Retirement

Feldman (1994) defines retirement as, "the exit from an organizational position or career path of considerable duration, taken by individuals after middle age, and taken with the intention of reduced psychological commitment to work thereafter." This definition takes a more psychological perspective on retirement as opposed to the traditional view regarding the receipt of Social Security benefits and private pensions

(Adams & Beehr, 2003). Thus, how we define retirement has changed to that of another transitional developmental stage, not just the end of employment for an individual (Sterns & Kaplan, 2003).

Atchley (1971; cited in Atchley, 2000) stated that the retirement process begins when individuals recognize that some day they will retire. He also found that most adults expect to retire (less than 10% do not) and most of them expect to retire before age 65. Since almost everyone expects to retire and retirement has such a tremendous impact on individuals' lives, the planning and decision-making processes preceding retirement, and how they affect overall retirement satisfaction, have been the most studied aspect of retirement (Atchley, 2000; Taylor & Doverspike, 2003).

Another important, though less studied, factor in this retirement equation involves post-retirement behaviors toward the organization individuals retired from. How do people feel about the organization they retired from? Would they be willing to return to that organizational on a part-time or voluntary basis? Could such post-retirement behaviors be operating in a similar fashion to employee reciprocity (Settoon et al., 1996), in which an employee behaves in certain organizationally-beneficial ways because of past fair and supportive treatment of the employee by the organization?

Correlates and Predictors of Post-Retirement Behaviors

The primary intention of this study was to examine variables that may influence a retired individual's decision to engage in post-retirement behaviors that would be beneficial to the organization. Such "behaviors" might include attitudinal support and loyalty, volunteering (e.g., mentoring, community spokesperson), or re-employment capacities (e.g., independent contractor, consulting, part-time or seasonal work). Another aim of this study was to identify key factors, such as perceptions relating to the organization, perceptions relating to retirement, and variables relating to the individual's meaning of work, and to demonstrate how they may be related to post-retirement behaviors. Finally, it is hoped that in understanding these influential variables, we can better examine how organizations can influence them, as well as discuss the individual and organizational benefits of post-retirement behaviors directed toward one's former organization.

POST-RETIREMENT BEHAVIORS

The premise for predicting post-retirement behaviors stems from the concept of employee reciprocity, which is derived from the combination of Blau's concept of social exchange and Gouldner's norm of reciprocity (Eisenberger et al., 1986). Blau (1964; see Eisenberger et al., 1986) theorized that "the basis for any exchange relationship can be described in terms of either social or economic principles." For the purposes of this study, the present authors concentrate on the social exchange principle, which is based on the trust that gestures of goodwill will be reciprocated at some future time. Generally, research findings suggest that an organization can establish high-quality exchange relationships with its employees by engaging in positive actions towards its employees. These positive actions on the part of the organization can create obligations for employees to reciprocate to the organization in positive, beneficial ways (Eisenberger et al., 1986; Konovsky & Pugh, 1994; Shore & Wayne, 1993). This obligatory exchange can be explained using the norm of reciprocity. This means that as an organization displays certain supportive functions, such as socialization procedures, career planning, socio-emotional networks, rewards systems, and fairness, individuals may feel obligated to reciprocate those actions. This would involve displaying behaviors or attitudes, such as organizational citizenship, in-role, or extra-role behaviors (e.g., person-organization value congruence, loyalty, and/or behavioral support), which are beneficial to the organization.

In the present study, a logical leap is made from employee reciprocity to proposing a similar form of post-retirement reciprocity as a possible mechanism in a retiree's decision to return to his or her retiring organization–in an employment or volunteering capacity. The assumption is that if an organization treated the employee in a fair, respectful manner and provided adequate support to the individual as an employee, that employee may be motivated to return the favor in some way as a retiree (e.g., become a community advocate, mentoring, working part-time as needed). Recognizing that reciprocity may only be one reason or motivation to volunteer or work at one's retiring organization, other common motivations behind volunteer behavior in general are also addressed.

Research has generally found volunteering behavior to be quite complex, yet common themes emerge from the exploration of volunteerism motivations. Mature individuals' motivations for volunteering, of interest here, tend to include altruistic, ideological, material/reward, status/

reward, social relationships, leisure-time, and personal growth as primary motivations (Fischer & Schaffer, 1993; Oken et al., 1998). Generativity, or the need to fulfill one's life goals and pass on their knowledge, could be added as another possible motivation for older workers to volunteer (Mor-Barak, 1995).

In today's changing workforce, not only are demographics shifting to an older labor force, but also organizations may be under-employed and may need to seek the assistance of retirees (Alley & Crimmins, in press). Additionally, with the work in organizations shifting from traditional core staff work to variable peaks and valleys in workloads, organizations may deem it necessary to adopt flexible staffing options, such as increased use of part-time workers, consultants, and even volunteers. Would it not be effective to rehire individuals–retirees–already familiar with the organization politics, culture, operations, and knowledge with a proven track record, instead of spending crucial time and money on high-risk, external hiring (Hirshorn & Hoyer, 1994)? Additionally, if organizations deem the practice of rehiring retirees necessary, practical, and ethical, how can they be sure retirees would want to be rehired? Because of these questions, it is necessary to examine factors such as an individual's perception of the organization, perception of retirement, and meaning of work and how these factors may predict a retiree's decision to return to the organization in a volunteer or work capacity. Therefore, we developed the model depicted in Figure 1, outlining our rationale below.

PERCEPTION OF THE ORGANIZATION

The proposed model (see Figure 1) hypothesizes that the retiree's perception of the organization factor consists of four measured variables–organizational identification, perceived organizational support, and retirement planning/preparedness (specifically, financial and employer provided planning/preparedness)–and that this factor predicts post-retirement behaviors.

Organizational Identification

"Identification with a psychological group" (IDPG) or organizational identification (OID) is defined as "the tendency of individuals to perceive themselves and their groups or organizations as intertwined, sharing common qualities and faults, successes and failures, and com-

Figure 1. Initial Conceptual Model Predicting Post-Retirement Behaviors

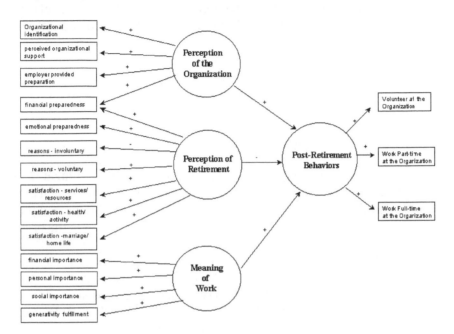

mon destinies" (Mael & Tetrick, 1992). Social Identity Theory is the basis for this type of cognitive formation, in that people define themselves in terms of their memberships in various social categories. Organizational identification has been associated with increased organizational citizenship and extra-role behaviors (Ashford & Mael, 1989; Mael & Ashforth, 1995). Examples of extra-role behaviors could be increased extra-curricular involvement (social activities, fundraising, volunteering), decreased absenteeism, increased creativity, increased performance, increased helping behaviors, and other behaviors of the sort. This relationship between OID and extra-role behaviors has been supported for employees; however, does this relationship hold true for former members of the organization such as alumni or retirees?

The implications of attachment and identification for retirees also finds support in work by Dorfman, Kohout, and Heckert (1985) among others, who show that retirees may be interested in returning to work, especially if they are dissatisfied with their retirement activities. Additionally, if a retiree has a relatively strong identification or at-

tachment to the retiring organization, that individual may prefer to return to the former employer, whereas those with low levels of
identification or attachment would probably not be interested in their
old firm. Therefore, this study will examine the relationship of organizational identity to a retiree's perception of the organization; more
specifically, organizational identification is hypothesized to be one of
the variables that comprise the perception of the organization factor in
the proposed model.

Perceived Organizational Support

Based on years of research in social psychology, the organizational
literature attests that a global exchange relationship exists between employees and the organization. Eisenberger et al. (1986) suggested that
employees form a global belief concerning the extent to which the organization values their contributions and is concerned over their well being. This belief has been labeled *perceived organizational support*
(POS). Empirical research has found POS to be positively related to performance of job duties, citizenship behavior, and organizational commitment (Eisenberger et al., 1986; Eisenberger et al., 1990; Shore & Wayne,
1993). These relationships can be explained in part by the reasoning that
high levels of POS are believed to create obligations within individuals
to repay the organization for that support (e.g., resources and/or
socio-emotional support provided) with positive attitude formation or
desired behaviors (e.g., citizenship behaviors) that support organizational goals.

For current employees, these attitudes can translate into desired behaviors that benefit both the individual and the organization. However,
what about retired employees? Do they retain a sense of obligation, in-
debtedness, or loyalty to the organization that would encourage attitude
formation (or attitude prolongation) and/or behavior modification that
reciprocates back to the organization? And if so, what can organizations
do to facilitate development of POS that would lead to desired post-retirement behaviors? Theory and common sense would tell us that development of formal and/or informal support mechanisms in organizations
would be the first step to development of an employee's perceived organizational support. Therefore, the proposed model hypothesizes that
perceived organizational support is a variable that partially comprises
perception of the organization.

Retirement Planning/Preparedness

Almost half a century ago, Thompson (1958) found that successful adjustment to retirement was associated with workers (pre-retirees) who had positive attitudes towards retirement, realistic views of retirement, and made realistic plans for their future prior to retirement. Thus, the importance of pre-retirement planning in regards to retirement satisfaction and adjustment is not a new revelation. Higher levels of adjustment, personal competence, and self-actualization have been found in retirees who participate in retirement planning programs offered through their organization (Dennis, 1988; Taylor & Doverspike, 2003).

Fretz, Kluge, Ossana, Jones, and Merikangas (1989) found that positive levels of retirement self-efficacy are associated with less pre-retirement anxiety. This finding suggests the importance of psychologically preparing for the retirement transition. However, most retirement planning programs do not include discussions that might facilitate psychological preparation for retirement (Forteza & Prieto, 1994). Taylor and Shore (1995) suggest that planning may have its strongest impact on individuals who are approaching, but not yet eligible for retirement, since many decisions central to choosing the retirement date are made by the time an individual is eligible for retirement. Still, many organizations do not have sponsored retirement planning. Modern retirement preparation programs are on the rise, but still mostly reflect financial planning and pension issues with few concentrating on psychological and life-style planning issues (Forteza & Prieto, 1994; Taylor & Doverspike, 2003).

The key aspect of any retirement planning initiative is to create a mindset of thinking and planning about the future which can help develop more realism and favorable attitudes, resulting in satisfaction with the decision to retire. The organization can play a critical role in this process by socializing employees early about the need for such long-term planning and providing concrete support through comprehensive employer sponsored retirement planning programs (Lindbo & Shultz, 1998; Spiegel & Shultz, 2003; Taylor & Doverspike, 2003). Our proposed model predicts that financial, emotional, and employer sponsored retirement planning/preparedness partially constitute a retiree's perception of the organization. Additionally, a similar relationship may exist between retirement planning/preparedness and the perception of retirement factor.

Perception of Retirement

The proposed model hypothesizes that the retiree's perception of retirement consists of the following measured variables–emotional retirement planning/ preparedness, financial retirement planning/preparedness, voluntary and involuntary reasons for retirement, and satisfaction with services/resources, health/activity, and marriage/home life in retirement. In turn, perception of retirement predicts post-retirement behaviors.

Researchers postulate many causes and correlates of retirement satisfaction, mostly encompassing individualistic variables such as health, income, activity level, shared leisure with spouse and offspring, occupational level, educational level and job satisfaction (Atchley, 2000). Even 40 years ago, Back and Guptill (1966) (cited in Atchley, 2000) found that an individual who was healthy, had a middle- or upper-class occupation (and therefore better retirement income), and had a high number of personal interests, felt minimal losses and therefore had greater retirement and life satisfaction. Therefore, satisfaction with retirement activities may be negatively related to an individual's willingness to go back to the old firm. Thus, the proposed model hypothesizes that retirement satisfaction in terms of service/resources, health/activity, and marriage/home life; partially comprise a retiree's perception of retirement.

Reasons for Retirement

In examining the decision to retire, the theory of planned behavior, which is an extension of the theory of reasoned action (Ajzen & Fishbein, 1980; Fishbein & Ajzen, 1975), was utilized. The central factor in the theory of planned behavior is an individual's intention to perform a given behavior. Intentions are assumed to encapsulate motivational factors that influence behaviors. Intentions can indicate how hard an individual will try to perform a behavior, and how much effort the individual plans to exert. Generally, the stronger the intention, the more likely performance of the behavior will occur (Ajzen, 1991). An important note however, is that the behavioral intention can only result in behavior if that behavior is under the control of the individual–if the person can decide at their own will that they will perform the behavior. Actual control also refers to non-motivational factors (e.g., time, money, skills, cooperation of others), such that it refers to the collective forces an individual has, required resources and opportunities *and* the intention to perform the behavior. Therefore, the theory of planned behavior differs from the original theory of reasoned action in the degree and inclusion of perceived behavioral control (Ajzen, 1991).

The theory of planned behavior appears to have a link to the retirement decision, in that (with the elimination of mandatory retirement) individuals examine their resources or actual control, such as financial independence, health status, and organization support paired with their intentions to retire, in making the decision to perform the behavior of officially retiring from an organization (Barnes-Farrell, 2003). These intentions and examination of resources can only occur at the point at which an individual realizes they will retire someday and begins both informally and formally planning for this transition. The employees' perception of their retirement choice as voluntary or involuntary is critical (Shultz et al., 1998). Traditionally, factors that have been shown to influence the decision to retire are: wanting to retire (engage in leisure activities instead of work), health limitations, loss of job, receipt of social security benefits, receipt of pension benefits, dislike of job, number of dependents still at home, housing, and retirement of spouse (Barnes-Farrell, 2003; Hansson et al., 1997).

Meaning of Work

Our proposed model (and the previous work of Mor-Barak, 1995) hypothesizes that an individual retiree's meaning of work consists of four measured importance variables–social, personal, financial, and generativity–and the meaning of work factor predicts retiree post-retirement behaviors.

Generally we examine the meaning of work for those people who are currently working; however, Mor-Barak (1995) identified the need to examine the meaning of work for mature individuals looking for work and/or retired individuals and how that meaning may affect their attitudes towards continued employment or a search for (part-time) employment. Studies have shown the positive effects of employment on mature workers, in that people tend to be more satisfied with their life, marriage, health, social networks, and mental states when employed (e.g., Bosse' et al., 1987; Mor-Barak et al., 1992; and Soumerai & Avon, 1983; cited in Mor-Barak, 1995).

Mor-Barak (1995) conducted a study, based on Alderfer's human needs theory and Florian's three factors of work (economic, social, and psychological), which expanded these two models to include one more very important factor, generativity. Generativity, originally named by

Erikson, is a developmental stage in which one wishes to share their knowledge, experiences, and ideas with others and make a difference in the lives of others (particularly the younger generation). Mor-Barak refers to this sharing by mature adults as training, supervising, teaching, and transferring knowledge and skills to younger workers. These ideas fit well into the authors' previous suggestions of retirees returning to the workplace to volunteer or work.

Mor-Barak's (1995) study utilizing a sample of 146 participants (age 50 and over) who were actively seeking employment, found the four factors accounted for 70% of the variance in the meaning of work scale (MWS). The implications of her study were that these four factors were particularly important for mature workers and retirees who wished to return to work, and that jobs that could provide for transfer of knowledge and experience would be most valued by mature workers. Mor-Barak called for organizations to utilize this segment of the population in its hiring practices for the company's benefit (e.g., via decreased hiring costs or knowledge transfer) as well as the individual's benefit (e.g., via financial independence, generativity, or social interaction). Therefore, the proposed model predicts social, personal, financial, and generativity importance to comprise the meaning of work factor.

PRESENT STUDY

Empirical research has been conducted on the previously stated variables to test various relationships in independent contexts utilizing college students, employees, and college alumni. However, currently there is no empirical research relating the three hypothesized factors–perception of the organization, perception of retirement, and meaning of work–utilizing a retiree population to predict post-retirement behaviors. The proposed model has the potential to serve individual and organizational needs by pointing out factors predictive of post-retirement work behaviors, serving to facilitate strategic staffing within organizations, as well as to promote individual fulfillment and satisfaction with life in retirement.

PHASE I–CONFIRMATORY FACTOR ANALYSIS (CFA)– THE MEASUREMENT MODEL

Figure 1 graphically depicts the hypothesized interrelationships lending to post-retirement behaviors. In regards to the relationship between the measured variables and the predictor and criterion constructs, the following hypotheses were proposed.

Hypothesis 1. Perception of the organization is a function of organizational identification (OID), perceived organizational support (POS), and retirement planning/preparedness (specifically, financial and employer provided planning/preparedness). More positive perceptions of the organization predicts a higher degree of organizational identification, perceived organizational support, and retirement planning/preparedness (specifically, financial and employer provided planning/preparedness).

Hypothesis 2. Perception of retirement is a function of emotional and financial retirement planning/preparedness, reasons for retirement (specifically, involuntary versus voluntary reasons for retirement), and satisfaction with life in retirement (specifically in regards to services/resources, health/activities, and marriage/home life). More positive perceptions of retirement predict more emotional and financial retirement planning/preparedness, more voluntary reasons for retirement, and more satisfaction with life in retirement (specifically in regards to services/resources, health/activities, and marriage/home life). A positive perception of retirement also negatively predicts involuntary reasons for retirement.

Hypothesis 3. Meaning of work is a function of financial, personal, social, and generativity importance. Greater meaning of work predicts more financial, personal, social, and generativity importance.

Hypothesis 4. Post-retirement behaviors are a function of interest in volunteering at or on behalf of the organization, working part-time or seasonal at one's retiring organization, and/or working full-time at one's retiring organization.

PHASE II–STRUCTURAL EQUATION MODELING (SEM)– THE STRUCTURAL MODEL

In regards to the relationship of the proposed predictor constructs to the criterion construct, the following hypothesis was proposed.

Hypothesis 5. Perception of the organization, perception of retirement, and meaning of work predict post-retirement behaviors. Specifically, more positive perceptions of the organization, negative perceptions of retirement, and greater meaning of work predict a greater likelihood of engaging in some form of organizational specific post-retirement behavior such as volunteering, working part-time, or working full-time.

METHODOLOGY

Participants

A survey was mailed out to 3,511 retirees of a southern California utility company. The 3,511 retirees were derived by randomly sampling half of the southern California population of the utility's retirees. The sample consisted of 2,881 men and 630 women. One thousand ten (1,010) retirees responded by returning their completed surveys, resulting in a 29% response rate. The sample was predominantly white males, with some college education, and relatively long tenure with the organization (>25 years); this was representative of the target population. Please see Table 1 for the detailed demographic breakdown.

Materials/Measures

Organizational identification was measured using Mael and Tetrick's (1992) scale for identification with a psychological group (IDPG), which consists of 10-items. For the current study, the scale had a total Cronbach's Alpha reliability of .86 (N = 935). Respondents were instructed to indicate the degree of agreement or disagreement with each statement using a 5-point Likert scale (1 = strongly disagree, 5 = strongly agree).

Perceived organizational support was measured using Eisenberger, Huntington, Hutchinson, and Sowa's (1986) Survey of Perceived Organizational Support (SPOS). The original scale consists of 36 items; however there is a 16 item short version—which was used in this study. The SPOS was developed to measure a "wide variety of ascribed organizational attitudes and possible actions relevant to employees' interests". Respondents were instructed to indicate the degree of agreement or disagreement with each statement using a 5-point Likert scale (1 = strongly disagree, 5 = strongly agree). The short version total SPOS had a Cronbach's Alpha reliability coefficient of .95 (N = 942).

Retirement planning/preparedness was measured by 14 questions, subdivided into three subscales, which were developed for this study. The directions for the scales asked the participants to rate their agreement with the statements using a 5-point Likert scale (1 = strongly disagree, 5 = strongly agree) to determine the extent of retirement planning (Financial–3 items, Emotional/Psychological–6 items, and Employer Sponsored–5 items) incurred. Internal consistency reliability estimates

TABLE 1. Participant Demographic Breakdown

Demographic	Frequency	%	Mean	Std. Dev.	Mode
Gender					
Men	818	84.6			
Women	149	15.4			
Ethnicity					
African American	17	1.7			
Asian	25	2.5			
Hispanic	40	4.0			
Native American	14	1.4			
White	808	80.0			
Other	7	.7			
Education Level					
Some High School	23	2.3			
High School Dipl.	134	13.3			
Some College	423	41.9			
Associate's Degree	170	16.8			
Bachelor's Degree	152	15.0			
Master's Degree	53	5.2			
Ph. D.	9	.9			
Other	33	3.3			
Retirement Status					
Completely Retired	798	80.4			
Retired/Working PT	107	10.8			
Retired/Working FT	87	8.8			

Demographic	Frequency	%	Mean	Std. Dev.	Mode
Age			66	9.81	58
Age when retired			58	4.63	55
(range 40 – 74)					
Tenure with organization			29	8.34	35
(range 3- 46)					
Year retired			1989	6.96	1996
(range 1960 – 1998)					

for the three subscales were: Emotional/psychological planning/preparedness .89 (N = 970), Financial planning/preparedness .75 (N = 978), Employer sponsored planning / preparedness .92 (N = 966).

Reasons for retirement were measured using a subscale of Floyd, Haynes, Doll, Winemiller, Lemsky, Burgy, Werle, and Heilman's (1992) Retirement Satisfaction Inventory of importance of reasons for retirement. Participants were presented 15 reasons for retirement in which they responded to Likert-type questions (from 1 = very unimportant to 6 = very important). We were not able to confirm the original authors' 4-factor structure (pursue own interests, circumstances, pressure from employer, and job stress). A CFA showed that a less than desirable fit was obtained, Bentler Bonnett = .627 and the Comparative Fit Index (CFI) = .645. Our sample data presented a more parsimonious factor structure (which also was more consistent with our theory around voluntary versus involuntary retirement) with two factors–named Involuntary Reasons for Retirement and Voluntary Reasons for Retirement. The two factors were comprised by combining the original authors' "job stress" and "pressure from employer" sub-scales to produce the Involuntary factor; and the original authors' "circumstances" and "pursue own interests" subscales to produce the Voluntary factor. The respective Cronbach alpha reliability estimates were .63 (N = 920) and .66 (N = 925).

Satisfaction with life in retirement was measured using a subscale of Floyd et al.'s (1992) Retirement Satisfaction Inventory of satisfaction with life in retirement. Participants were presented 11 aspects of their current life in which they responded to Likert-type questions (from 0 = not applicable [e.g., the health of my spouse] and 1 = very dissatisfied to

6 = very satisfied). Cronbach alpha reliability estimates for the three subscales which composed the scale structure were: satisfaction with health/activity .78 (N = 978), satisfaction with marriage/home life .70 (N = 949), satisfaction with services/resources .53 (N = 943).

Meaning of work was measured using Mor-Barak's (1995) Meaning of Work Scale (MWS), which consists of 16-items. The four subscales of the MWS had Cronbach alpha reliabilities of Social Contact .87 (N = 964), Personal .87 (N = 967), Financial .69 (N = 967), and Generativity .91 (N = 966)

Post-Retirement Behaviors. Retiree behaviors were measured by three, two part questions, developed for this study. A multiple choice scale was used to determine the level of interest the participant had in becoming involved with their retiring organization. The items measured four levels of interest: not interested, would consider, intend to, or actually engage in volunteer or work activities at or on behalf of their previous employer. Additionally, participants were asked to indicate their reasons for considering, intending, or behaving in those manners, by using a checklist technique following each question (36 possible reasons why/motivations were listed). For ease of analysis and interpretation, the latter three levels were collapsed to represent one overall interest scale for the respective activities (volunteering, working part-time or seasonal, and working full-time) and the questions were then dichotomized into 1 = interested and 0 = not interested.

PROCEDURE

The survey packet was mailed out to a sample of 3,511 retirees of a southern California utility company. Each participant was mailed a survey packet which included: a cover letter explaining the purpose of the study (to solicit retirement attitudes) and assurance of confidentiality, a contact name for questions, and a stamped return envelope to be returned to an outside vendor who entered the survey responses for data analysis. Participants were instructed to complete the questionnaire by following the directions on each scale, using the utility company as their reference organization. Participants had three weeks to complete and return the survey. Reminder cards were sent one week before the surveys were due.

The survey packet consisted of 92 items (see measures section above for scales used). Two additional items were added on behalf of the organization to measure the interest in full-time work as well as general interest in volunteering (at any organization other than itself). Additionally, several other demographic items were added as requested by the organization (i.e., shareholder status, last position held, and bargaining unit status), but were not relevant to the present study.

ANALYSES

Confirmatory factor analysis (CFA) was performed to confirm the hypothesized factor structure of the measurement model–the measured variables and the predictor constructs, thus testing hypotheses 1 through 4. Structural equation modeling (SEM) was performed to predict post-retirement behaviors, from the predictor constructs of perception of the organization, perception of retirement, and meaning of work, thus testing hypothesis 5.

RESULTS

Data Screening and Assumptions

Descriptive statistics were performed to screen the data. Table 2 displays the means, standard deviations, alpha reliabilities, and correlations among the 17 measured variables. Frequencies were performed to check for missing data and univariate outliers. Means and standard deviations were examined for each variable. Additionally, random scatter plots of residuals and histograms were performed and examined to check for normality. The assumptions of linearity and multivariate normality were evaluated through SPSS and EQS. The data showed slight multivariate kurtosis, according to the normalized estimate (>3), therefore robust statistics (e.g., Satorra-Bentler scaled chi-square, Satorra & Bentler, 1988) and maximum likelihood estimation were utilized.

The Hypothesized Model

Since this proposed theoretical model of post-retirement behaviors was new and previously untested, the retiree sample was randomly divided in half for model estimation; one half for model building (N = 507) and the other for cross-validation (N = 503). Missing data constituted roughly 2% of the total sample, therefore for ease of analysis in

TABLE 2. Descriptive Statistics–Means, Standard Deviation and Inter-correlations Among the 17 Measured Variables for Both the Developmental Sample and the Cross-Validation Sample

Variable Name	1	2	3	4	5	6	7	8	9	10	11	12	13	14	15	16	17
1. Organizational Identification	**.86**	.54	.35	.20	.15	-.17	.07	.00	-.01	.20	.12	.35	.40	.29	.12	-.02	.00
2. Perceived Organizational Support	.55	**.95**	.47	.28	.25	-.34	.12	.00	.08	.24	.19	.36	.33	.32	.03	-.17	-.13
3. Planning – Employer Sponsored	.35	.39	**.92**	.43	.41	-.21	.13	.05	.09	.15	.18	.22	.23	.20	.01	-.06	-.11
4. Planning – Financial	.30	.27	.36	**.75**	.68	-.25	.19	.18	.26	.08	.23	.18	.15	.19	-.02	-.14	-.22
5. Planning – Emotional	.23	.19	.42	.60	**.89**	-.28	.19	.14	.27	.13	.17	.11	.10	.17	-.07	-.18	-.21
6. Involuntary Reasons for Retirement	-.16	-.29	-.12	-.12	-.21	**.63**	.14	-.09	-.14	-.02	-.05	-.09	-.06	-.12	.14	.27	.22
7. Voluntary Reasons for Retirement	.10	.02	.10	.20	.15	.14	**.66**	.10	.15	.10	.05	.05	.03	.06	.04	-.05	-.05
8. Satisfaction with Health/Activities	.12	.08	.18	.21	.26	-.15	.09	**.78**	.37	.16	-.01	.03	.06	.06	.07	.13	.07

TABLE 2 (continued)

Variable Name	1	2	3	4	5	6	7	8	9	10	11	12	13	14	15	16	17
9. Satisfaction with Marriage/Homelife	.09	.08	.11	.23	.17	-.13	.16	.39	.70	.27	-.04	.05	.03	.06	-.10	-.04	-.05
10. Satisfaction with Services/Resources	.22	.25	.29	.21	.25	-.13	.04	.21	.18	.53	.00	.02	.22	.06	-.05	-.19	-.10
11. Meaning of Work – Financial	.13	.14	.22	.22	.25	.03	.07	.07	.05	.12	.69	.32	.18	.32	.00	-.05	-.09
12. Meaning of Work – Personal	.32	.40	.22	.17	.13	-.08	.04	.13	.02	.18	.31	.87	.45	.52	.18	.07	.01
13. Meaning of Work – Social	.39	.38	.29	.22	.17	-.05	.04	.06	.03	.24	.23	.46	.87	.33	-.01	-.11	-.03
14. Meaning of Work – Generativity	.25	.26	.23	.13	.10	-.01	.17	.11	.10	.16	.31	.51	.38	.91	.18	.11	-.00
15. Interest in Volunteering	.14	.07	.01	.01	-.05	.02	.05	.15	.00	-.02	.03	.16	.07	.14	-----	.50	.24
16. Interest in Working Part-time	-.04	-.07	-.09	-.11	-.17	.14	.01	.10	-.06	-.15	-.04	.07	-.07	.11	.49	-----	.42

34

Variable Name	1	2	3	4	5	6	7	8	9	10	11	12	13	14	15	16	17
17. Interest in Working Full-time	-.02	-.03	.02	-.17	-.19	.04	-.06	.12	-.12	-.14	-.06	.05	.02	.10	.28	.44	----
Development Sample Mean	36.	55.	16.	11.	22.	16.4	14.1	9.17	23.69	15.83	12.3	16.2	16.8	14.7	.29	.42	.12
Mean	02	19	48	42	79	5	4				1	7	2	8			
Development Sample	5.8	11.	4.4	2.1	4.2	6.85	5.50	2.23	4.93	4.82	1.94	2.39	3.72	2.88	.45	.49	.33
Standard Dev	0	40	0	1	1												
Cross-validation Sample	36.	55.	16.	11.	22.	16.2	13.9	9.05	23.55	15.66	12.4	16.2	17.0	15.1	.32	.45	.15
Mean	21	78	91	35	59	9	5				8	6	7	0			
Cross-Validation Sample	6.0	11.	4.2	2.0	4.2	6.28	5.36	2.32	5.02	4.87	1.86	2.39	3.58	2.78	.46	.50	.36
Standard Dev	2	07	0	4	0												

NOTE: Values in the diagonals are Alpha reliabilities based on the entire sample (N=920 to 966, depending on the scale). Values above the diagonal are for the development sample (N=507). Values below the diagonal are for the cross-validation sample (N=503).

35

EQS, linear interpolation was used as the imputation technique to replace missing data using the regression function of SPSS.

A confirmatory factor analysis was performed to test the measurement model (Hypotheses 1 to 4) using EQS for Windows on 17 scales of individual and organizational variables thought to be related to retirement attitudes. The complete hypothesized model (CFA & SEM) is presented in Figure 1.

In terms of the measurement model, the independence model that tests the hypothesis that all variables are uncorrelated was rejected, χ^2 (136, N = 507) = 1958.20, p < .01. Then, the measurement model itself was tested and a less than desirable fit was obtained, Satorra-Bentler scaled χ^2 (115, N = 507) = 561.64, p < .01, comparative fit index (CFI) = .76, indicating the model needed some modifications before it was a good fit.

Therefore, post hoc model modifications were performed in an attempt to develop a better fitting and more parsimonious model. On the basis of the Larange Multiplier statistics (see Ullman, 1996) and theoretical relevance, several modifications were made. Two cross-loadings were added to Factor 1 (Perception of the Organization) and Factor 2 (Perception of Retirement), emotional retirement planning/preparedness and involuntary reasons for retirement. One unreliable manifest variable–satisfaction with retirement services/resources–was removed due to its low reliability (r = .53) and low loading. The residuals were allowed to correlate for reasons for retirement–voluntary and involuntary (.25), as well as for satisfaction with retirement–health/activity and marriage/home life (.33). The measurement model was then tested again and support for it was found χ^2 (97, N = 507) = 284.77, p < .01, comparative fit index (CFI) = .900. In addition, every path from the measured variables to the predictor constructs was significant (p < .05). Now that we had estimated the fit of the measurement model, we could test the structural equation model.

MODEL ESTIMATION

Model building. Maximum likelihood estimation and Satorra-Bentler scaled χ^2 statistics were utilized when estimating the structural model (Hypothesis 5). The independence model that tests the hypothesis that all variables are uncorrelated was rejected, χ^2 (120, N = 507) = 1989.89, p < .01. Then, the hypothesized model was tested and it was less than desirable without a covariance estimation between F1, perception of the organization, and F3, meaning of work, Satorra-Bentler scaled χ^2 (95, N = 507) = 364.86, p < .01, comparative fit index (CFI) = .856. However, when the covariance between F1 and F3 was estimated, more support for the model was found, Satorra-Bentler scaled χ^2 (94, N = 507) = 250.45, p < .01, comparative fit index (CFI) = .916. A chi-square difference test indicated a significant improvement in fit between the independence model and the revised model, χ^2 diff (1, N = 507) = 114.41, p < .01. In addition, all three structural paths were significant at p < .05.

Cross-validation. Because of the model modifications, cross-validation on the holdout sample (N = 503) using maximum likelihood estimation and Satorra-Bentler scaled χ^2 statistics was performed. First, the measurement model (Hypotheses 1 to 4) was tested, indicating an acceptable factor structure, χ^2 (97, N = 503) = 284.76, p < .01, comparative fit index (CFI) = .892. The independence model that tests the hypothesis that all variables are uncorrelated was rejected, χ^2 (120, N = 503) = 1852.11, p < .01. Partial support was found for the revised model (Hypothesis 5), χ^2 (94, N = 503) = 262.68, p < .01, comparative fit index (CFI) = .903. While this CFI showed some shrinkage, slightly lower than the CFI for the model building sample, that was to be expected. The χ^2 /df ratio was less than three (χ^2 2/df = 2.79), indicating a reasonable fit. The significant χ^2 value is likely due to the large sample size (N = 503).

The percent of variance in the post-retirement construct accounted for by its predictors was 8.2%. Only Perception of Retirement, significantly predicted post-retirement behaviors at the p < .05 level. However, Perception of the Organization and Meaning of Work, were significant at p < .10. Although they were significant, the directions of some of the relationships were opposite to our hypothesized direction. The relationship of perception to organization (organizational identification; perceived organizational support; employer provided, financial, and emotional retirement planning/preparedness; and involuntary reasons for retirement) to post-retirement behaviors was −.20; the more positive the perception of the organization the less likely one would engage in the post-retirement behaviors studied.

However, as predicted, there was a negative relationship between perception of retirement (employer provided, financial, and emotional retirement planning/preparedness; voluntary and involuntary reasons for retirement, and satisfaction with health/activity and marriage/home life in retirement) and post-retirement behaviors, −.21; the greater perception of retirement, the less likely one would be interested in returning to the organization. Meaning of work positively predicted post-retirement behaviors, .25, therefore indicating that the factors comprising meaning of work–financial, personal, social, and generativity–predict post-retirement behaviors. The final structural model, with path coefficients, fitted on the cross-validation sample is presented in standardized form in Figure 2.

DISCUSSION

Proposed Model

The purpose of this study was to examine the proposed model in Figure 1, which included several factors thought to be predictive of the post-retirement behaviors of volunteering at or on behalf of the organization, working part-time at the organization, or working full-time at

Figure 2. Final Measurement and Structural Model Predicting Post-retirement Behaviors with Standardized Path Coefficients for the Cross-validation Sample (N = 503); * p < .05

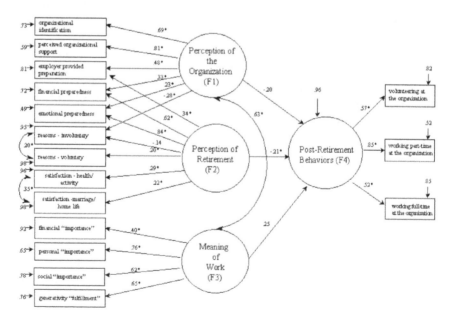

the organization. While some organizations have already begun to utilize flexible work arrangements with their retiree population for much needed work assignments and volunteer activities (Hishorn & Hoyer, 1994; Lublin, 1998; Rosen & Jerdee, 1988), we are unsure of why these arrangements do or do not work. Why would retirees want to return to work or volunteer at their former organization? In today's changing labor force it is crucial that we try to understand employees and retirees, as they are the mainstays of organizations, similar to a university/student/alumni relationship (Mael & Ashforth, 1992).

In addition, organizations are witnessing a steady exit of knowledge and experience due to an aging population that is sure to continue with the exit of the retiring Baby Boomers. If organizations were more knowledgeable of retiree attitudes, as well as motivations to continue or return to work, many more could benefit from the use of this valuable resource (Shultz & Adams, in press). Not only could organizations develop ways to attract and utilize their retirees, solving organizational labor dilemmas, but also retirees could discover ways to make their life in retirement more fulfilling and rewarding (Taylor et al., 2005). The proposed model presented five major hypotheses related to variables and factors that could be underlying this proposed dynamic. The following is a discussion of the results and implications of those hypotheses.

Hypothesis 1, dealing with the perception of the organization factor, was supported, as the aforementioned variables were positively predicted by perception of the organization. Perceived organizational support and organizational identification were the strongest path loadings (standardized coefficients .81 and .69, respectively). This made sense, as these two scales have been shown to be very strong indicators of organizational attitudes. This is consistent with previous research in organizational attitudes, identification, and support (Eisenberger et al., 1986; Mael & Tetrick, 1992). The positive affect that individuals receive from the organization is returned to the organization in the form of positive perceptions, just as negative affect, lack of support and possibly misidentification would lead to negative perceptions of the organization.

Additionally, two other measured variable paths were introduced as significant, emotional retirement planning/preparedness and involuntary reasons for retirement. The inclusion of emotional retirement planning/preparedness makes sense since the individual may seek and find this type of support from company peers, a manager, or other organizational resources. The significance of involuntary reasons for retirement was also reasonable, as this variable appears to have a direct link to the organization.

Hypothesis 2, which dealt with the perception of retirement factor, was partially supported, as significant paths emerged from all variables except involuntary reasons for retirement and satisfaction with services/resources in retirement. The strongest path loadings were from emotional retirement planning/preparedness and financial retirement planning/preparedness (standardized coefficients .84 and .62, respectively). This makes sense, as financial planning is typically at the forefront of people's minds when referring to retirement, as well as commonly on their minds when determining their comfort level in retirement. While emotional planning/preparedness levels may not have been high for a majority of retirees, this strong relationship to perception of retirement speaks to the importance of emotional readiness for retirement. Since it was the strongest path coefficient, this tells us emotional preparedness is most influential in a person's evaluation of their perception of their retirement.

Satisfaction with services/resources was deleted from the model because it had a non-significant loading on the factor, as well as low reliability ($r = .53$). We conclude the low loading and lack of reliability may be due to an unusually young and relatively affluent sample of retirees. The items that comprise the variable focus on services/resources in terms of governmental aid programs (e.g., social security, Medicare, subsidized housing, and nutrition programs), access to transportation, and services from community agencies and programs. While these are services and resources typically utilized by retirees, it does not seem appropriate for our sample. Very few are actually considered elderly and heavily dependent on governmental resources. For the most part they have generous retirement packages from the company. The responses in this variable were skewed and therefore deemed inappropriate. However, future frameworks may still wish to include this variable, as it is an important consideration for many older retirees.

An additional path emerged as significant in this factor, employer sponsored retirement planning/preparedness. While it also had significant cross-loadings on perception of the organization, a possible reason for the loading here could be the strong foundational link to retirement planning and the perception of retirement on the whole. Retirement planning and preparation (or lack of it) will more-than-likely have direct links to an individual's perception of their retirement. Therefore, perception of retirement was a function of all three types of retirement planning/preparedness variables, suggesting the importance of utilizing all three, not solely the most traditional financial planning aspect that most firms focus on. Not only do all three serve to comprise an individual's perception of retirement, but the fact that all three also significantly cross-loaded on the perception of the organization factor suggests the critical linkage between the organization and an individual's retirement planning.

Hypothesis 3, in regards to meaning of work, was fully supported in that all four variables were positively predicted to comprise the meaning of work for individuals. Interestingly, all four had strong path loadings: personal .76, generativity .65, social .62, and financial .40. However, it was even more interesting that financial importance had the lowest loading of the four, suggesting that personal, social, and generativity factors are much more important than just bringing home a paycheck. This lends support to the supposition of mature workers and retirees wanting to participate in meaningful, fulfilling activities (Mor-Barak, 1995).

These variables are bound to have profound implications for linking individual needs with organizational needs. If an organization is knowledgeable of the different forces underlying individual's work behavior, they can make attempts to better link people with jobs and/or activities (Mor-Barak et al., 1992). The same goes for retirees and their post-retirement work behaviors, especially since retirees can (and should) be particular about the types of activities they engage in during retirement.

Hypothesis 4, which dealt with post-retirement work behaviors, was fully supported. While all were significant, interest in working part-time or seasonal at the organization had the strongest path coefficient, suggesting that retirees are most interested in part-time or seasonal work opportunities (standardized coefficient .85). This appears to be related to the relatively young sample of retirees that responded to this survey. A large number of retirees took an early retirement offer from the company, therefore many of these retirees are young enough to continue to be interested in part-time work, or even full-time work, but may be stable enough, financially, to be most interested in part-time only. Working part-time would allow individuals to stay involved in something meaningful, without the usual stressors that come along with a full-time commitment. This supports the notion that retirees are willing to become involved, on a limited basis, with their former organization. These results have important implications for organizations since retirees may provide an excellent resource for creative staffing approaches (Hirshron & Hoyer, 1994; Rosen & Jerdee, 1988; Taylor et al., 2005).

Hypothesis 5, which dealt with the predictors of post-retirement behaviors, was partially supported. While perception of retirement was the only significant factor at the p < .05 level in the cross-validated model, all were significant at the p < .10 level. Complex factor loadings at the measured variable level may suggest more underlying organizational influence, as well as individual motivations to work, than this model depicts.

While three paths were significant at p < .10, one was significant in the opposite direction than predicted. We predicted those retirees who had a more positive perception of the organization would be more likely to return to the organization. It was disconcerting that this relationship was negative, indicating just the opposite. Logically, we would assume a more amicable relationship would foster reciprocity, not only does this seem consistent with human nature, but has been demonstrated in organizational theory and studies (Eisenberger et al., 1986; Konovsky & Pugh, 1994; Shore & Wayne, 1993). However, there could be some unique behavior going on in this particular retiree sample since this organization had a large-scale early retirement offer and many of the retirees in this sample may have left the organization during that early retirement offer. This large-scale early retirement could be affecting the relationships in this study, in particular this negative relationship between perception of the organization and post-retirement behaviors. It may be the individuals who took this early retirement offer did so to leave the organization that they had negative perceptions of. Maybe one of the only reasons why they would want to return to the organization is for part-time work, to perhaps obtain additional money. This way, they could return on a limited basis, make some money, without having to deal with all of the stressors of being a full-time employee.

Another explanation for the negative relationship between perception of the organization and post-retirement behaviors could be that the individuals may have negative perceptions of the organization because of the early retirement offer (e.g., having to make quick decisions to retire, feelings of involuntariness, lack of retirement planning/preparedness), but for purely personal reasons (e.g., financial, activity, generativity) they would consider returning if it was on their terms (quite different than full-time employment and obligations of a full-time employee).

While we do not know for sure who and how many retirees in our sample took this early retirement offer, we can estimate by age that the majority of retirees were under 60 years old (the employees had to be at least 47 years old with 10 years tenure at the organization to be eligible) at the time of the offer, constituting "early retirement." With that in mind, we performed some additional analyses. We found that for those retirees who retired when they were less than 60 years old, there were negative correlations between age retired and interest in volunteering at or on behalf of the organization ($-.186$, N = 586, $p < .01$), age retired and interest in working part-time or seasonal ($-.212$, N = 589, $p < .01$), and age retired and interest in working full-time ($-.305$, N = 585, $p < .01$). Conversely, for those retirees who retired when they were 60 years old and older, there was no correlation between age retired and volunteering at or on behalf of the organization ($-.007$, N = 303, NS), age retired and interest in working part-time or seasonal (.006, N = 304, NS), and age retired and interest in working full-time (.084, N = 301, NS). Therefore, it appears as though the younger retirees in this sample were driving the negative correlations.

Additionally, we performed cross-tabulations between retirees who were less than 60 years old when they retired versus retirees who were 60 years old or older when they retired. We found that 56.7% of those who retired before age 60 were interested in returning to work on a part-time or seasonal basis versus 24.4% of those who retired after age 60. This also suggests that it may be those early retirees demonstrating a greater influence by tipping the correlations in a negative direction. In addition, this suggests that younger people are more likely to be interested in returning to the organization to work part-time or seasonal. So, is it these younger retirees who have the negative perception of the organization as well? We are not entirely comfortable attributing this phenomenon to age alone, in that it may be some type of period or cohort effect (Atchley, 2000).

In addition, we correlated age and age retired with satisfaction with retirement health/activities to determine if there was a similar relationship (as noted earlier in terms of age) occurring. We found satisfaction with retirement health/activities to be negatively correlated with age, when considering those retirees greater then 60 years old ($-.115$, N = 647, $p < .01$), but not with those retirees less than 60 years old ($-.081$, N = 293, NS). However, when satisfaction with retirement health/activities was correlated with age retired, for those retirees greater then 60 years old there was no correlation (.005, N = 295, NS), but with those retirees less than 60 years old there was a negative correlation ($-.114$, N = 591, $p < .01$). Therefore, again, age retired may be driving satisfaction with retirement health/activities.

Given our findings with regard to Hypothesis 5–perception of the organization, perception of retirement, and meaning of work predict post-retirement behaviors–it is important to take note of a few critical issues. First, while we attained a CFI value of .903 for the structural model on the hold-out sample, which is typically considered a reasonable fit (Ullman, 1996), the structural model correlations (standardized coefficients with post-retirement behaviors) are low to moderate and in the opposite direction as predicted for one of the three predictors. In addition, only 8.2% of the variance in post-retirement behaviors is accounted for by our three predictor constructs. Although these figures are not as large as we would have liked (or expected), we believe it is a reasonably good first attempt to better understand and predict these here-to-fore unstudied organizationally relevant predictors of post-retirement behaviors.

LIMITATIONS

First, this research data was gathered from one organization only, a southern California utility, and therefore due to its uniqueness some researchers may question its generalizability to other retiree populations. This is a valid concern, as cross-sectional data from a variety of organizations would have made the results more generalizable. However, we also believe that other organizations may be experiencing similar issues regarding early retirement and loss of organizational knowledge and experience due to retirement and therefore may find this information useful and applicable to them. A second issue is related to the number of young (or early) retirees in this sample. This unusually young sample of retirees deems generalizability to other retiree samples an important and valid caution.

A third limitation to this study has to do with parameters established by the utility company when selecting the retiree sample for collection of the survey data. We did not have access to survey the large number of retirees who are currently engaged in work activities for the utility because of certain organizational restrictions. Access to these retirees would have allowed us to gain more insight regarding the underlying reasons why retirees actually return to the organization. Instead, the majority of our findings rely on the retirees' interest in becoming engaged in these activities and the reasons why they say they would participate in post-retirement work behaviors.

A final limitation was our inability to test our model for possible differences by important demographic variables such as gender, ethnicity, and education level. As noted by one of the reviewers, our results may have been somewhat different for men versus women or those with college educations versus those with less than a college education. However, given the need to cross-validate our results, our results could not be tested separately for each subgroups. However, future studies that employ much larger and diverse samples are strongly encouraged to examine for possible difference among subgroups.

CONCLUSION

While some of the results were unexpected, we believe this new model opens the door for more research examining the phenomena of the aging workforce and post-retirement work behaviors. It will become critical for organizations to examine creative means for staffing as well as accomplishing other important organizational goals such as knowledge transfer, succession planning, and community presence and involvement (Shultz et al., 2003). While not every organization is in a position to utilize its retirees–and not every organization would want to–the model developed here does provide an excellent resource and opportunity for continuing to develop relationships and meet needs.

REFERENCES

Adams, G.A., & Beehr, T. A. (Eds.) (2003). *Retirement: Reasons, processes, and results.* New York, New York: Springer Publishing.

Ajzen, I. (1991). The theory of planned behavior. *Organizational Behavior and Human Decision Processes, 50,* 179-211.

Ajzen, I., & Fishbein, M. (1980). *Understanding attitudes and predicting social behavior.* Prentice Hall, Englewood Cliffs, NJ.

Alley, D., & Crimmins, E. (in press). The demography of aging and work. In K. S. Shultz and G. A. Adams (Eds.), *Aging and work in the 21st century.* Mahwah, NJ: Lawrence Erlbaum Publishers.

Ashforth, B. E., & Mael, F. A. (1989). Social identity theory and the organization. *Academy of Management Review, 14,* 20-39.

Atchley, R. C. (1971). Retirement and leisure participation. Continuity or crisis? *The Gerontologist, 11,* 13-17.

Atchley, R. C. (2000). *Social forces and aging: An introduction to social gerontology* (9th ed.). Belmont, CA: Wadsworth Publishing Company.

Barnes-Farrell, J. L. (2003). Beyond health and wealth: Attitudinal and other influences on retirement decision making. In G. A. Adams and T. A. Beehr (Eds.), *Retirement: Reasons, processes, and results* (pp. 159-187). New York, New York: Springer.

Blau, P. M. (1964). *Exchange and power in social life.* New York: Wiley.

Census Bureau (1995). *Sixty-five Plus in the United States.* Statistical Brief, Economics and Statistics Administration, United States Department of Commerce.

Dennis, H. (1988). Retirement planning. In H. Dennis (Ed.) *Fourteen steps in managing an aging workforce* (pp. 215-229). Lexington Book: Lexington, MA.

Dorfman, L. T., Kohout, F. J., & Heckert, D. A. (1985). Retirement satisfaction in the rural elderly. *Research on Aging, 7,* 577-599.

Drucker, P. F. (2001, November 1). The next society. *The Economist.* Retrieved from http://www.economist.com/printedition/PrinterFriendly.cfm?Story_ID = 770819

Eisenberger, R., Huntington, R., Hutchinson, S., & Sowa, D. (1986). Perceived organizational support. *Journal of Applied Psychology, 71,* 500-507.

Eisenberger, R., Fasolo, P., & Davis-LaMastro, V. (1990). Perceived employee support and employee diligence, commitment, and innovation. *Journal of Applied Psychology, 75,* 51-59.

Feldman, D.C. (1994). The decision to retire early: A review and conceptualization. *Academy of Management Review, 19,* 285-311.

Fischer, L. R., & Schaffer, K. B. (1993). *Older volunteers: A guide to research and practice.* Newbury Park, CA: Sage Publications.

Fishbein, M., & Ajzen, I. (1975). *Belief, attitude, intention and behavior: An introduction to theory and research.* Reading, MA: Addison-Wesley.

Floyd, F. J., Haynes, S. N., Doll, E. R., Winemiller, D., Lemsky, C., Murgy, T. M., Werle, M., & Heilman, N. (1992). Assessing retirement satisfaction and perceptions of retirement experiences. *Psychology and Aging, 7,* 609-621.

Forteza, J. A., & Prieto, J. M. (1994). Aging and work behavior. In H. C. Triandis, M. D. Dunnett, and L.M. Hugh (Eds.), *Handbook of Industrial and Organizational Psychology,* (2nd. ed., vol. 4, pp. 447-483). Palo Alto, CA: Consulting Psychologists Press

Fretz, B. R., Kluge, N. A., Ossana, S. M., Jones, S. M., & Merilangas, M. W. (1989). Intervention targets for reducing preretirement anxiety and depression. *Journal of Counseling Psychology, 36,* 301-307.

Hansson, R. O., DeKoekkoek, P. D., Neece, W. M., & Patterson, D. W. (1997). Successful aging at work: Annual review, 1992-1996: The older worker and transitions to retirement. *Journal of Vocational Behavior, 51,* 202-233.

Hayward, M. D., Crimmins, E. M., & Wray, L. A. (1994). The relationship between retirement life cycle changes and older men's labor force participation rates. *Journals of Gerontology: Social Science, 49B,* S219-230.

Hedge, J. W., Borman, W. C., & Lammlein, S. E. (2006). *The aging workforce: Realities, myths, and implications for organizations.* Washington, DC: American Psychological Association.

Hirshorn, B. A., & Hoyer, D. T. (1994). Private sector hiring and use of retirees: The firm's perspective. *The Gerontologist, 34,* 50-58.

Konovsky, M. A., & Pugh, S. D. (1994). Citizenship behavior and social exchange. *Academy of Management Journal, 37,* 656-669.

Lindbo, T. L., & Shultz, K. S. (1998). The role of organizational culture and mentoring on mature worker socialization toward retirement. *Public Productivity and Management Review, 22,* 49-59.

Lublin, J. S. (1998, March 2). Companies send intrepid retirees to work abroad. *Wall Street Journal,* p. B1-B5.

Mael, F. A., & Ashforth, B. E. (1992). Alumni and their alma mater: A partial test of the reformulated model of organizational identification. *Journal of Organizational Behavior, 13,* 103-123.

Mael, F. A., & Ashforth, B. E. (1995). Loyal from day one: Biodata, organizational identification, and turnover among newcomers. *Personnel Psychology, 48,* 309-333.

Mael, F. A., & Tetrick, L. E. (1992). Identifying organizational identification. *Educational and Psychological Measurement, 52,* 813-824.

Mor-Barak, M. E. (1995). The meaning of work for older adults seeking employment: The generativity factor. *International Journal of Aging and Human Development, 41,* 325-344.

Mor-Barak, M. E., Scharlach, A. E., Birba, L., Garcia, G., & Sokolov, J. (1992). Employment, social networks and health in retirement years. *International Journal of Aging and Human Development, 35,* 143-157.

Oken, M. A., Barr, A., & Herzog, A. R. (1998). Motivation to volunteer by older adults: A test of competing measurement models. *Psychology and Aging, 13,* 608-621.

Rosen, B., & Jerdee, T. H. (1985). *Older employees: New roles for valued resources.* Chicago: Dow-Jones Irwin.

Rosen, B., & Jerdee, T. H. (1988). Managing older workers careers. *Research in Personnel and Human Resource Management, 6,* 37-74.

Satorra, A., & Bentler, P. M. (1988). Scaling corrections for chi-square statistics in covariance structural analysis. *Proceedings of the American Statistical Association,* 308-313.

Settoon, R. P., Bennett, N., & Linden, R. C. (1996). Social exchange in organizations: Perceived organizational support, leader-member exchange, and employee reciprocity. *Journal of Applied Psychology, 81,* 219-227.

Shore, L. M., & Wayne, S. J. (1993). Commitment and employee behavior: Comparison of affective commitment and continuance commitment with perceived organizational support. *Journal of Applied Psychology, 78,* 774-780.

Shultz, K. S. (2001). The new contingent workforce: Examining the bridge employment options of mature workers. *International Journal of Organizational Theory and Behavior, 4,* 247-258.

Shultz, K. S., & Adams, G. A. (Eds.). (In press). *Aging and work in the 21st century.* Mahwah, NJ: Lawrence Erlbaum Publishers.

Shultz, K. S., Morton, K. R., & Weckerle, J. R. (1998). The influence of push and pull factors in distinguishing voluntary and involuntary early retirees' decision and adjustment. *Journal of Vocational Behavior, 52,* 45-57.

Snel, J., & Cremer, R. (Eds.). (1994). *Work and aging: A European perspective.* London, UK: Taylor and Francis.

Spiegel, P. E., & Shultz, K. S. (2003). The influence of pre-retirement planning and transferability of skills on naval officers' retirement satisfaction and adjustment. *Military Psychology, 15,* 284-306.

Sterns, H. L., & Kaplan, J. (2003). Self-management of career and retirement. In G.A. Adams and T. A. Beehr (Eds.), *Retirement: Reasons, processes, and results* (pp. 214-241). New York, New York: Springer.

Taylor, M. A., & Doverspike, D. (2003). Retirement planning and preparation. In G. A. Adams and T.A. Beehr (Eds.) *Retirement: Reasons, processes, and results* (pp. 53-82). New York, New York: Springer.

Taylor, M. A., & Shore, L. M. (1995). Predictors of planned retirement age: An application of Beehr's model. *Psychology and Aging, 10,* 76-83.

Taylor, M. A., Shultz, K. S., & Doverspike, D. (2005). Academic perspectives on recruiting and retaining older workers. In P.T. Beatty and R. M. S. Visser (Eds.), *Thriving on an aging workforce: Strategies for organizational and systemic change.* Malabar, FL: Krieger Publishing Company.

Thompson, W. E. (1958). Preretirement anticipation and adjustment in retirement. *Journal of Social Issues, 14,* 35-45.

Ullman, J. B. (1996). Structural Equation Modeling. In B. G. Tabachnick and L. S. Fidel (Eds.) *Using Multivariate Statistics* (3rd ed. pp. 709-810). New York: Harper Collins College Publishers.

Powerful Tools for Caregivers Online: An Innovative Approach to Support Employees

Daniel Kuhn
Linda Hollinger-Smith
Judith Presser
Jan Civian
Nicole Batsch

INTRODUCTION

Several national studies have described the enormous impact of family caregiving on the ability of employees to effectively manage their work and personal responsibilities. The National Alliance for Caregiving and AARP (2004) conducted a nationally representative survey and estimated that there are 44.4 million caregivers age 18 and older in the U.S. who provide unpaid care to an adult family member or friend. The survey showed that almost 6 in 10 caregivers (59%) either work or have worked while providing care and 62% of caregivers report having had to make some work-related adjustments ranging from going in late and leaving early to having to give up work entirely. More than 40% had to reduce their work hours or responsibilities, or leave the work force altogether. The MetLife Juggling Act Study: Balancing Caregiving with Work (1999) showed that employed caregivers incur significant losses in career development, salary and retirement income, and substantial out-of-pocket expenses as a result of caregiving obligations. Moreover, caregiving responsibilities seriously affect the productivity of caregivers, particularly because of altered work schedules. Both male and female children of aging parents make significant changes at work in order to accommodate caregiving responsibilities (MetLife Mature Market Institute, 2003).

The economic impact of family caregiving on business is also substantial, although cost estimates vary. The MetLife Juggling Act Study (1997) revealed that U.S. businesses lose as much as $29 billion annually due to family caregiving. The Alzheimer's Association estimates that the cost of Alzheimer's disease alone is $36.5 billion annually in terms of caregivers' lost productivity, absenteeism, and turnover (Koppel, 2002). The costs of family caregiving to employees and their employers are high and will grow dramatically in the coming decades with the "graying of America." Caring for relatives with chronic illnesses not only adversely affects workers and the workplace, it also induces significant levels of stress. Although the caregiver role can be rewarding, it has also been linked with numerous physical and mental health, financial, and social problems as well as an increased risk of mortality (Beach et al., 2000; Ory et al., 1999; Vitaliano et al., 2003).

In the United States, the Internet has become the primary source of health information for individuals with health care needs and their family caregivers. According to a survey by the Pew Internet and American Life Project (2005), 8 in 10 Internet users or about 95 million American adults have investigated a variety of health information on average of 16 topics per search, and most of these individuals have also researched a medical condition on behalf of a loved one. The National Alliance for Caregiving and AARP (2004) survey found that the Internet is the leading source of health information for caregivers (29%), compared to doctors (28%) and other health professionals (10%). The Internet has also spawned an ever-increasing number of online support groups and electronic message boards for individuals with chronic illnesses and their family caregivers (White & Dorman, 2001; Glueckauf, 2005).

In spite of the growing trend toward using the Internet for health related information and support, few studies have examined the utility of the Internet for caregiver information and education. Researchers documented positive results in web-based interventions involving parents of sick children (Gray et al., 2000; Krishna et al., 2003) and family caregivers of heart transplant recipients (Dew et al., 2004), traumatic brain injury patients (Rotondi et al., 2005), and persons suffering from Alzheimer's disease, Parkinson's disease, and stroke (Bass et al., 1998; Beauchamp et al., 2005; Marziali et al., 2005). These studies suggest that web-based education and support may also improve the effectiveness of caregivers in managing the health of chronically ill relatives and may improve confidence in the caregiving role. This article describes a web-based program for employed caregivers aimed at improving their self-care and reducing the negative work-related outcomes associated with family caregiving.

BACKGROUND OF PROGRAM

The American Business Collaboration (ABC) for Quality Dependent Care , a groundbreaking corporate initiative comprised of eight major companies, was launched in 1992 in response to the increased number of employees who must arrange care for family members in order to be fully productive at work. These companies have made significant investments in communities where their employees live and work in order to improve the quality and supply of child and elder care programs and services. In ABC company focus groups and surveys conducted by WFD Consulting which administers the ABC, employees identified support groups as a means of assisting them in their caregiver role. However, the ABC companies found out through experience that on-site support groups often do not work for a variety of reasons: employees cannot commit the time, do not feel comfortable identifying themselves as a caregiver, or may not be located at their company's workplace due to telecommuting or working offsite with clients.

In 2004, three companies of the ABC (Exxon Mobil Corporation, IBM and Texas Instruments) funded Mather LifeWays, a nonprofit organization based in Evanston, Illinois, to create an online version of its caregiver education program, *Powerful Tools for Caregivers* (PTC). In its original format, PTC is a community-based education program aimed at providing family caregivers with the skills necessary to better care for themselves while caring for a relative or friend with a chronic medical condition. PTC is presently taught by trained class leaders in limited areas of 18 states. Research conducted examining hundreds of caregivers participating in PTC in Oregon and Illinois demonstrated a variety of positive outcomes including decreased depression, improved self-confidence, and increased engagement in relaxation and exercise activities (Boise et al., 2005; Kuhn et al., 2003; Edelman et al., 2006).

The traditional PTC classes are held weekly over a period of six weeks in groups of 10 to 15 participants at locations such as churches, senior centers, and civic centers. Classes are two and a half hours in length and are typically led by professionals in fields of health and human services using a standardized curriculum. Table 1 is a synopsis of the content covered in each of the six classes. Participants learn how to: (1) locate community resources; (2) better manage their stress; (3) communicate more effectively; (4) cope with their emotions; and, (5) take steps to care for themselves through weekly action plans. Each participant receives a supplemental guide, *The Caregiver Helpbook*, written especially for the course (Schmall et al., 2000).

The overall goal of PTC Online is to enable participants to better care for themselves while caring for their older relatives with chronic medical conditions such as stroke, Alzheimer's disease, or Parkinson's disease. PTC is rooted in Bandura's social cognitive theory (1977, 1987, and 1997) that posits that a high degree of self-efficacy will increase the frequency of certain behaviors, particularly personal health promoting behaviors. Self-efficacy is related to one's belief that new attitudes and behaviors can be achieved. These expectations and beliefs affect one's personal choices that may be modified by skills training. Self-efficacy principles have been successfully applied to patients with chronic diseases such as arthritis (Lorig et al., 1998; Mendes de Leon et al., 1996; O'Leary, 1985), as well as other diseases, through the Chronic Disease Self-Management Program developed at Stanford University (Lorig et al., 2001). PTC applies these same principles with activities specifically suited to the self-care needs of family caregivers.

TABLE 1. Synopsis of PTC Classes

Class 1–Taking Care of You: Principles of self-care and responsibility are introduced. Caregivers identify tools and resources to meet their self-care goals. Challenges of caregiving and the significance of self-care are dramatized through a video. Caregivers identify ways to locate community resources including information about one's family member with a medical condition. A personalized plan for self-care during the coming week is written and shared.

Class 2–Identifying and Reducing Personal Stress: Steps are presented for effective stress management. Caregivers learn how to change negative self-talk to positive self-talk and practice relaxation exercises. An action plan for the coming week is written and shared.

Class 3–Communicating Feelings, Needs and Concerns: Caregivers learnhow to communicate feelings, needs and concerns more effectively by using "I" messages. Through dramatizations, caregivers experience the impact of "you" messages. Progressive muscle relaxation is practiced. An action plan for the coming week is written and shared.

Class 4–Communicating in Challenging Situations: Caregivers learn three communication tools: assertiveness, Aikido, and DESC. With Aikido, caregivers learn to find "common ground" with another person. With DESC (Describe, Express, Specify, Consequence), caregivers further learn how to set limits. Another progressive muscle relaxation is practiced and an action plan for the coming week is developed.

Class 5–Learning from our Emotions: The focus is on identifying and applying constructive tools for dealing with difficult feelings, especially depression and anger. Another progressive muscle relaxation is practiced and an action plan for the coming week is developed.

Class 6–Mastering Caregiving Problem-Solving: The focus is on the internal emotional process caregivers go through when they experience a life role change. Tools for dealing with changes and for making tough decisions are discussed, including a seven-step decision-making model and family meetings. "Tools of optimism" are presented. Caregivers acknowledge their accomplishments and develop a long-term action plan.

ABC asked Mather LifeWays to develop, implement, and evaluate an online version of PTC for 200 employees of the three sponsoring companies. PTC Online was seen as an innovative means of supporting employees who have little or no time to take part in traditional support groups in the workplace or other community settings. The online format–available 24 hours a day, seven days a week–was thought to fit the needs of employed caregivers who needed the convenience of participating in PTC at any time and from any place. Moreover, the self-help focus of PTC in an educational format might prove attractive to employees who otherwise might not take part in support groups.

METHODOLOGY

Design and Intervention

Similar to the community-based format, PTC Online is six weeks in length. Online material consists of text, graphics, video, audio, and interactive exercises. Aside from a computer with Internet access, no special software or hardware is required for participation, and no technological expertise is necessary. Prior to the course, each participant logs on to a password-protected website. An online tutorial and manual are offered prior to the six-week course to learn how to use the simple navigational tools. For 1 to 2 hours weekly, participants read the course content, watch a video that dramatizes the importance of self-care, and listen to relaxation tapes. At the end of each class, participants can view or download selected chapters of *The Caregiver Helpbook* to supplement online coursework. Participants interact with each other and a trained facilitator in a discussion board; as many as 25 participants are enrolled at a time in order to foster interaction. In the pilot program, two-weekly live optional web chats and telephone conferences were offered to promote interaction. Following completion of the course, for one year participants receive monthly electronic newsletters that contain brief articles that reinforce the use of self-care tools and address other aspects of caregiving.

Like many work-life programs, PTC Online was made available to employees of the three sponsoring companies on a private, confidential basis through a vendor; in this case, Mather LifeWays. Hoping to target employee caregivers, and recognizing that many caregivers do not self-identify, e-mail messages and posters at worksites asked employees if they helped an older relative or friend with errands, personal care, or transportation, or if they provided companionship, emotional or financial support to a relative living either nearby or at a distance. These promotional materials directed employees to the ABC web site to enroll in the free course, where they were assured that their participation would remain confidential.

Participants were asked to complete web-based surveys with standardized measures examining the impact of the course on their well-being and on work-related outcomes at three points in time: pre-course; post-course; and, six-months post-course. Participants were also asked to complete a qualitative evaluation of the course to find out which components of the course were most useful and which parts required improvement. Participation in the evaluation was strictly voluntary. All participants were assured of confidentiality and informed that results of the evaluation would only be shared in aggregate form. Informed consent procedures for this exploratory study were approved by the Institutional Review Board of Mather LifeWays.

Sample

A total of 217 employees of the three sponsoring companies requested to register for PTC Online through the ABC website. Those expressing interest were then sent an e-mail outlining details of PTC Online (i.e., length of the course, estimated number of hours to dedicate, voluntary evaluation component, overview of content, etc.). Of those, 176 employees (81%) accepted the invitation to participate in the program evaluation component and completed a baseline (pre-course) web survey. Of those who completed a baseline survey, 21 employees un-enrolled from the course (12%) typically due to lack of time (i.e., job/home commitments. increased caregiving responsibilities, etc.) rather than lack of interest in the course itself. Of the 155 employees who participated in the course, 49 (31.6%) completed follow-up surveys (immediate post-course and 6-month post-course). On average, participants completed 4 of the 6 weekly sessions.

Measures

A web survey was developed using E-Listen software and was comprised of several standard measures. Wellness-focused measures examined exercise, resilience, self-efficacy, and self-reported health status. *Involvement in exercise and relaxation activities* was assessed by a 3-item instrument and measured on 5-point scales (from "never" to "more than five times a week"). Internal consistencies for this measure in the present study exceeded 0.85 at all data points (baseline, post, 6-months post). *Resilience* was measured by a 4-item instrument developed by WFD Consulting, Inc. targeting aspects of a healthy lifestyle scored on 5-point scales (from "always" to "never"). Internal consistencies in the present study exceeded 0.68 for this measure. *Self-efficacy* was assessed by the 5-item General Perceived Self-Efficacy Scale (Schwarzer & Jerusalem, 1995) measuring global aspects of one's self-confidence to manage problems, find solutions, and accomplish goals, and scored on 5-point scales (from "strongly agree" to "strongly disagree"). Internal consistencies for this measure exceeded 0.74, similar to published studies across various populations (Scholz et al., 2002).

Self-reported health status was measured on a single 5-point scale (from "excellent health" to "poor health").

Key work-related measures were also examined. *Work productivity interference* was evaluated by a 10-item instrument (WFD Consulting, Inc.) that assesses how frequently personal or family demands interfere with aspects of work responsibilities. Those items employ 5-point scales (from "very often" to "never"). Internal consistencies for this measure in the present study were very high, exceeding 0.95 at all data points. *Job stress and burnout* were evaluated on a 7-item instrument and measured on 5-point scales ranging from "strongly agree" to "strongly disagree." This instrument was developed and validated by WFD Consulting, Inc. (Richman et al., 1998). Internal consistencies for this measure are in excess of 0.80, similar to previous workforce studies by WFD Consulting.

A third set of measures addressed the impact of caregiving related to one's role as a caregiver and psychological aspects of caregiving. Pearlin's *Caregiver Self-Concept Scales* measure three dimensions of one's self-concept as a caregiver including gain, loss, and competence as well as overall feelings about caregiving (Skaff & Pearlin, 1992). The subscales of caregiver gain consist of 4-items, caregiver loss involves 2-items, caregiver competence includes 2-items, and overall feelings about caregiving consist of 3-items. The items employ 4-point scales ranging from "very much" to "not at all." Internal consistencies for the present study were in excess of 0.76, similar to published reports of reliability. Depression was assessed with the *Center for Epidemiologic Studies Short Depression Scale* (CES-D10; Radloff, 1977), a well-validated 10-item instrument with a 4-point scale (from "rarely or none of the time" to "all of the time"). Internal consistencies for the present study exceeded 0.83, comparable to published reliability data for caregiver samples (Lorig et al., 2001)

Dose Effects

Participation in various PTC Online activities was examined to determine if taking part in a high, moderate, or low level of activities influenced outcomes. The number of weekly lessons, asynchronous discussions, live chats, and telephone conference calls were combined into a "Total Dosage" score ranging from 0 to 24 (one point for each activity per week: 4 activities/week $\times$ 6 weeks = maximum of 24). Total Dosage was categorized as Low Dose (0-3), Moderate Dose (4-8), and High Dose (9-24) based on cut-points for three equal groups from the sample.

Analysis

We first compared baseline scores between participants who completed only pre-course surveys and those who completed post-course surveys, followed by comparing baseline scores of those who un-enrolled during the course to those who participated. Repeated measures analyses of variance were calculated to assess changes in the study measures over time. Correlations were then calculated among dosage effects for each PTC activity (i.e., weekly lessons, discussions, chats, and conference calls) and change scores on each measure to assess if the degree of participation in PTC activities was related to change scores. Finally, stepwise multiple regressions were performed to identify factors predictive of healthy outcomes defined as measures of resilience, self-reported health, and exercise/relaxation activities.

RESULTS

Demographics

Demographic characteristics of participants and their care recipients are summarized in Table 2. The majority of participants were 45 to 54 years of age (54.3%), female (71%), Caucasian (83%), and caring for elderly parents or in-laws (89%). About 95% of participants worked full-time, and 47% had a spouse or partner also working full-time. Thirty-six percent of participants also reported caring for children living at home. About one-third of participants were relatively new to caregiving, having provided care to their older relatives for less than one year. Over 40% provided one to five hours of direct care weekly, while 27% provided eleven or more direct hours of care weekly. Over 12% of participants indicated they provided no direct care hours weekly to their older relatives. These participants may have been "long distance" caregivers or may have hired help, either at the home or through a senior living residence. There were no statistically significant differences on baseline measures between the "no direct care provided" respondents and those providing some degree of direct care, so further analyses combined all respondents.

Nearly 50% of care recipients were 80 years of age or older and 73% was female. Over 30% of care recipients lived alone, 25% lived with a spouse, and 23% lived with the caregiver participating in PTC Online. Arthritis, Parkinson's disease, dementia, and diabetes were the top four

TABLE 2. Demographic Characteristics of Caregivers and Care Recipients

Caregivers	N	%	Care Recipients	N	%
Age			Age		
25-34 years of age	6	3.4	18-49 years of age	6	3.4
35-44 years of age	32	18.3	50-59 years of age	6	3.4
45-54 years of age	95	54.3	60-69 years of age	14	8.0
55-64 years of age	39	22.3	70-79 years of age	63	35.8
65 years of age or older	3	1.7	80 years of age or older	87	49.5
Employment			Relationship		
Full-time	164		Parent or in-law	154	89.0
Part-time	9	5.2	Spouse	4	2.3
Years caregiving			Other	15	8.7
Less than one year	60	34.3	Living arrangements		
One to less than 3 years	47	26.9	Lives with caregiver	41	23.4
Three to less than 5 years	32	18.3	Lives with spouse	44	25.1
Five or more years	36	20.6	Lives alone in home	53	30.3
Hours per week caregiving			Lives in retirement home	8	4.6
None	22	12.6	Lives in assisted living	16	9.1
One to 5 hours	72	41.1	Lives in retirement home	12	6.9
Six to 10 hours	34	19.4	Diagnoses		
Elevn to 20 hours	25	14.3	Arthritis	66	37.5
More than 20 hours	22	12.6	Heart disease	58	33.0
Gender			Dementia	50	28.4
Femaie	125	71.0	Diabetes	48	27.3
Male	51	29.0	Stroke	27	15.3
Race			Cancer	22	12.5
Caucasian	146	83.0	Respiratory disease	22	12.5
African-American	12	6.8	Blindness	19	10.8
Hispanic	12	6.8	Parkinson's disease	15	8.5
Asian/Pacific Islander	6	3.4	Memory Problems		
Other Race	5	2.9	None		
			At times	38	21.6
			Most of the time/all of	89	50.6
			the time	49	27.8

medical conditions of care recipients, according to caregivers. Half of care recipients reportedly had some degree of memory loss and 28% experienced memory loss "most or all of the time."

Preliminary Analyses

Baseline scores were compared between participants who completed only pre-course surveys (n = 106) and those who completed post-course surveys (n = 49). There were no significant differences between mean baseline scores of these two groups on wellness measures, job stress and burnout, and caregiver measures. There was a significant difference between mean baseline scores of the two groups related to caregiving responsibilities interfering with work productivity.

Participants who completed only pre-course surveys reported that caregiving responsibilities interfered with work productivity more often than enrollees who also completed post-course surveys ($t = 2.24, p = 0.004$). Comparing baseline scores of those who dis-enrolled (n = 21) during the course to those who participated, there were no significant differences between mean baseline scores on any measures.

Changes in Measures Over Time

Wellness, work-related, and caregiver measures were examined by univariate analyses of variance with time of measurement (pre-course versus immediate post-course versus 6-months post-course) as a within-subjects factor. Multivariate tests for the main effect of time of measurement were conducted for each measure using Pillai's Trace, as this calculation is most robust to violations of assumptions to normality of data. For all statistically significant differences discussed below, Mauchly's tests confirming sphericity assumptions were met. Post-hoc comparisons were performed using the Bonferroni adjustment for multiple pair wise comparisons. Table 3 summarizes results of repeated measures analyses with effect size indicated by partial eta squared.

Wellness measures. The PTC Online course was effective in improving participants' *involvement in exercise and relaxation activities, resilience, self-efficacy, and self-reported health status.* Exercise and relaxation activity scores increased from a mean of 7.76 at baseline to a mean of 8.76 immediately following the course to mean of 9.59 at 6-months post-course (main effect $F = 8.152, p = 0.001$). Pair wise comparisons of exercise and relaxation measures revealed no differences between baseline and post-course means ($p = 0.081$) or post-course and 6-months post-course means ($p = 0.161$). The 6-month post-course mean was significantly greater than the baseline mean ($p = 0.011$).

Resilience scores increased from a mean of 14.00 at baseline to a mean of 14.47 post-course to a mean of 15.35 at 6-months post-course (main effect $F = 4.939, p = 0.014$). Pair wise comparisons of resilience scores revealed no differences between baseline and post-course means ($p = 0.869$) or post-course and 6-months post-course means ($p = 0.207$).

TABLE 3. Repeated Measures Analyses of Variance for Wellness, Work-Related, and Caregiver Measures (N = 49)

Measure	Baseline Mean (SD)	Post-Course Mean (SD)	6-month Follow Up Mean (SD)	F	p value	Partial eta squared
Exercise/relaxation activities	7.76 (3.032)	8.76 (2.251)	9.59 (2.002)	8.152	0.001	0.419
Resilience	14.00 (1.620)	14.47 (1.281)	15.35 (1.498)	4.939	0.014	0.387
Self-efficacy	18.59 (2.551)	20.12 (2.027)	19.41 (3.465)	5.817	0.013	0.437
Self-reported health status	3.47 (0.717)	3.53 (0.514)	3.59 (0.712)	0.485	0.620	ns
Work interference/ productivity	35.41 (6.295)	34.47 (7.787)	36.06 (7.965)	0.347	0.709	ns
Job stress/burnout	3.93 (1.168)	3.00 (1.690)	2.87 (1.767)	5.347	0.011	0.390
Overall feelings about caregiving	9.35 (1.730)	10.06 (1.819)	10.82 (1.380)	5.702	0.008	0.413
Caregiver competencies	6.35 (1.169)	6.65 (0.862)	7.06 (0.899)	4.983	0.013	0.428
Caregiver gains	11.29 (2.201)	12.24 (2.682)	10.76 (2.905)	2.889	0.070	ns
Caregiver losses	5.71 (2.229)	5.88 (1.764)	6.29 (1.687)	1.538	0.230	ns
Caregiver depression	30.12 (4.386)	31.53 (5.234)	32.12 (4.986)	2.304	0.116	ns

The 6-month post-course mean was significantly greater than the baseline mean ($p = 0.018$).

Self-efficacy scores increased from a mean of 18.59 at baseline to a mean of 20.12 post-course and somewhat decreased to a mean of 19.41 at 6-months post-course (main effect $F = 5.817$, $p = 0.013$). Pair wise comparisons of self-efficacy scores found the post-course mean was significantly greater than baseline mean ($p = 0.009$). There were no differences between baseline and 6-month post-course means ($p = 0.916$) or post-course and 6-months post-course means ($p = 0.980$).

There was an improvement in self-reported health status scores from baseline to 6-months post-course, but the change was not statistically significant ($p = 0.620$).

Work-Related measures. PTC Online was effective in reducing participants' *job stress and burnout.* Job stress and burnout scores decreased from a mean of 3.93 at baseline to a mean of 3.00 post-course to a mean of 2.87 at 6-months follow up (main effect $F = 5.347$, $p = 0.011$). Pair wise comparisons of job stress and burnout scores revealed significant increases from baseline to post-course means ($p = 0.045$) and from baseline to 6-months post-course means ($p = 0.040$). There were no differences between post-course and 6-month post-course means ($p = 0.980$).

There was an increase in work productivity scores from baseline to 6-months post-follow up, but the change was not statistically significant (p = 0.709).

Caregiver measures. PTC Online was also effective in increasing both participants' *overall feelings about caregiving* and *competencies as a caregiver.* Overall feelings about caregiving scores increased from a mean of 9.35 at baseline to a mean of 10.06 post-course to a mean of 10.82 at 6-months post-course (main effect $F = 5.702$, $p = 0.008$). Pair wise comparisons of feelings about caregiving scores revealed no differences between baseline and post-course means ($p = 0.353$) or post-course and 6-months post-course means ($p = 0.308$). The 6-month post-course mean was significantly greater than the baseline mean ($p = 0.012$).

Caregiver competency scores increased from a mean of 6.35 at baseline to a mean of 6.65 post-course to a mean of 7.06 at 6-months post-course (main effect $F = 4.983$, $p = 0.013$). Pair wise comparisons of caregiver competency scores found no differences between baseline and post-course means ($p = 0.708$) or post-course and 6-months post-course means ($p = 0.269$). The 6-month post-course mean was significantly greater than the baseline mean ($p = 0.010$).

Changes over time in measures of caregiver gain (p = 0.070), caregiver loss (p = 0.230), and depression (p = 0.116) demonstrated some improvements, but results were not statistically significant.

Relationships Among Dosage Effects and Change Scores

Kendall's tau correlation coefficients were calculated among dosage effects for each PTC activity (i.e., weekly lessons, Bulletin Board discussions, live chats, and conference calls) and change scores on each measure to assess if the degree of participation in PTC activities was related to change scores. Respondents who participated more often in live chats had significantly lower change scores for depression ($r = 20.350$, $p = 0.036$). Although not statistically significant, a tendency was noted for Moderate/High Dosage participants to report better outcomes across all measures (p = 0.090).

Predictors of Healthy Outcomes

Stepwise multiple regression was performed to identify factors predictive of healthy outcomes, measured by self-reported health and resilience. This analysis was based on Pearlin's theoretical model of caregiving and the stress process (Pearlin et al, 1990). Pearlin's model links the effects of caregiver characteristics and resources to stressors and potential effects or outcomes. Caregiver characteristics, past experiences with caregiving, coping skills, and external resources influence how caregivers deal with stress in their lives. Pearlin identified various dimensions and sources of caregiver role strain that produce stressful outcomes. Occupation and other external responsibilities often produce cross-pressures between work and caregiver roles. Mediating conditions may explain why individuals exposed to similar stressors may respond differently. In the case of working caregivers, types and sources of work interference and job stressors and how workers react to these job stresses (i.e., resilience factors) may act as mediating factors. Pearlin's model examines the effects or outcomes of caregiving in terms of health-related measures.

In the present study, a model was tested that examined predictors of self-reported health, caregiver competencies, exercise/relaxation activities, and self-efficacy as predictor (independent) variables as PTC Online content and activities target these concepts. Resilience, work productivity interference, job stress/burnout, and depression were treated as mediating factors in the analysis.

As shown in Figure 1, increased caregiver competencies and exercise/relaxation activities directly predicted improved self-report of health status. Decreased job stress/burnout, reduced work interference due to family responsibilities, and increased resilience were also medi-

FIGURE 1. Multiple Regression Model of Factors Predicting Caregivers' Self-Reported Health (standardized beta coefficients indicate relative importance of variable as predictor or mediator of self-reported health)

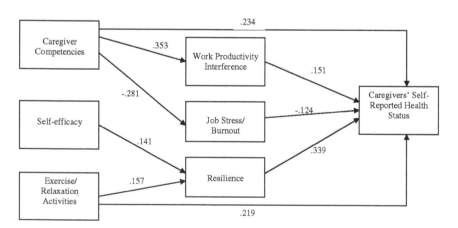

ating factors for the effect of increased caregiver competencies on improving self-reported health status (adjusted r squared = 0.291, F = 19.996, $p = 0.001$).

DISCUSSION

The evaluation of PTC Online provides strong evidence about the benefits of a web-based, self-care education program for employed caregivers of older adults. Regarding wellness outcomes, participants reported greater involvement in exercise and relaxation activities, improved resilience, and increased self-efficacy after participating in PTC Online, and these results were sustained 6-months post-course. With regard to work-related outcomes, participants experienced continued reductions in job stress and burnout as a result of participating in the program. Additionally, participants reported more positive feelings about their caregiving roles and increased competencies as caregivers over time. The overall effect size was moderate for outcomes of the program evaluation.

In support of the benefits of PTC Online, caregiver competencies, self-efficacy, and exercise/relaxation activities predicted improvements in self-reported health status and caregiver resilience. Caregivers reported increased resilience in meeting daily life challenges as well as reductions in work productivity interference due to caregiving, job stress/burnout, and depression. These four factors mediated the positive impact of PTC Online in improving caregiver competencies and perceived self-efficacy.

Because of the small number of participants who completed post-course surveys, the sample size was inadequate to determine the impact of "dosage effects." Due to the relatively low level of participation in the weekly live web chats and phone conferences, these features are not likely to contribute to the effectiveness of PTC Online. On average, participants completed four of the six weekly web sessions, indicating that full participation in the educational program is not necessary to benefit.

Limitations of this intervention study are noteworthy. Results may not be generalizable because participants in PTC Online were motivated help-seekers and they may not be representative of employed caregivers in non-corporate settings. Other limitations include the relatively small number of participants and lack of a comparison group. A delayed intervention group or wait list group would have been ideal but this option was not feasible in light of the objectives of this service-oriented project. Attrition is also a key limitation, yet not surprising given the hectic pace of work reported by participants and their caregiving demands. In the future, some type of incentive might improve retention in both the course and the evaluation.

Further cost-benefit analysis in terms of outcomes for employees and care recipients would be useful. For example, it is conceivable that PTC Online may play a role in lowering healthcare costs of caregivers. The potential financial benefits of PTC Online require additional study, and in light of the growing number of caregivers in the workplace, such effort will become increasingly important.

Participants in PTC Online derived many of the same benefits reported by participants in two populations of caregivers in Oregon and Illinois who took part in the community-based version of PTC (Boise, Congleton & Shannon, 2005; Edelman et al., 2006). This finding is important in that many PTC Online participants would not likely take part in the community-based version of PTC due to heavy work and family obligations. Compared to adult children caregivers who took part in the community-based version of PTC, the PTC Online participants were younger, had more minor children living at home, and worked more hours per week.

Although PTC Online may be an attractive alternative to the community-based version of PTC, attrition is a challenge in both venues, with about one in five participants unable to complete four or more classes within the allotted six weeks. However, PTC Online participants have access to the course for a full year following their initial registration, enabling them to continue at their own pace or to revisit lessons. About 30 percent of registrants logged back in at a later date to further examine and utilize the course materials and tools. This opportunity for extended participation obviously does not exist in the time-limited, community- based option.

PTC Online is an effective and first-of-its kind course that uses computer technology to address some of the practical problems of caregiving. The web-based format attracts employees who otherwise might not be able to attend PTC classes held in the community and allows for participation from remote locations at any time. PTC Online may also be attractive to employers because it can be delivered to a diverse and scattered workforce. PTC Online may be suitable for work-life programs, employee-assistance providers, and employers interested in improving the health and well-being of family caregivers in the workplace.

The initial development of PTC Online was fostered by a collaboration of ABC companies in partnership with Mather LifeWays. As a result of the initial success of PTC Online, the partnership continues as the ABC companies and others have contracted with Mather LifeWays to offer the course to a substantial number of their employees. PTC Online is seen as a work-life benefit that adds to a company's benefits package. Potential effectiveness of PTC Online among other groups of family caregivers such as elderly spouses deserves further study.

REFERENCES

Bandura, A. (1977). *Social Learning Theory.* Englewood Cliffs, NJ: Prentice Hall.

Bandura, A. (1987). *Social Foundations of Thought and Action: A Social Cognitive Theory.* Englewood Cliffs, NJ: Prentice Hall.

Bandura, A. (1997). *Self-Efficacy: The Exercise of Control.* New York: W. H. Freeman and Company.

Bass, D. M., McLendon, M. J., Brennan, P. F., & McCarthy, C. (1998). The buffering effect of a computer support network on caregiver strain. *Journal of Aging and Health, 10*(1), 20-43.

Beach, S. R., Schulz, R., Yee, J. L., & Jackson, S. (2000). Negative and positive health effects of caring for a disabled spouse: Longitudinal findings from the caregiver health effects study. *Psychology and Aging, 15*, 259-271.

Beauchamp, N., Irvine, A. B., Seeley, J., & Johnson, B. (2005). Worksite-based Internet multimedia program for family caregivers of persons with dementia. *The Gerontologist, 45*(6), 793-801.

Boise, L., Congleton, L., & Shannon, K. (2005). Empowering family caregivers: The Powerful Tools for Caregiving program. *Educational Gerontology, 31,* 573-586.

Edelman, P., Fulton, B. R., Woolridge, P., Kuhn, D., & Lindeman, D.A. (2006, in review). Longitudinal evaluation of a self-care education program for caregivers: Powerful Tools for Caregivers.

Dew, M. A., Goycoolea, J. M., Harris, R. C., Lee, A., Zomak, R., Dunbar-Jacob, J., Rotondi, A., Griffith, B. P., & Kormos, R. L. (2004) An Internet-based intervention to improve psychosocial outcomes in heart transplant recipients and family caregivers: Development and evaluation. *Journal of Heart and Lung Transplantation, 23*(6), 745-58.

Glueckauf, R. L. (2006, in press). Telehealth and family caregiving: Developments in research, education, and health care policy. In D. Hagler, D. Monahan & R. Toseland (Eds.), *Education, Training and Support Programs for Caregivers.* New York: Oxford University Press.

Gray, J. E., Safran, C., Davis, R. B., Pompilio-Weitzener, G., Stewart, J. E., Zaccagnini, L., & Pursley, D. (2000). Baby CareLink: Using the internet and telemedicine to improve care for high-risk infants. *Pediatrics, 106*(6), 1318-24.

Koppel, R. (2002). *Alzheimer's Disease: The Cost to U.S. Businesses in 2002.* Chicago, IL: Alzheimer's Association.

Kuhn, D., Fulton, B. R., & Edelman, P. (2003). Powerful Tools for Caregivers: Improving self-care and self-efficacy of family caregivers. *Alzheimer's Care Quarterly, 4*(3), 189-203.

Krishna, S., Francisco, B. D., Balas, E. A., Konig, P., Graff, G. R., & Madsen, R. W. (2003). Internet-enabled interactive multimedia asthma education program: A randomized trial. *Pediatrics, 111*(3), 503-10.

Lorig, K. R., Ritter, P, & Stewart, A. L. (2001). Chronic disease self-management program: 2-year health status and health care utilization outcomes. *Medical Care, 39*, 1217-23.

Lorig, K. R., Sobel, D. S., Ritter, P. L., Laurent, D., Hobbs, M. (2001). Effects of a self-management program for patients with chronic disease. *Effective Clinical Practice, 4*, 256-262.

Marziali, E., Donahue, P., & Crossin, G. (2005). Caring for others: Internet health care support intervention for family caregivers of persons with Alzheimer's, stroke or Parkinson's. *Families in Society: The Journal of Contemporary Social Services, 86*(3), 375-383.

Mendes de Leon, C., Seeman, T. E., Baker, D. I., Richardson, E. D., & Tinetti, M. E. (1996). Self-efficacy, physical decline, and change in functioning in community-living elders: A prospective study. *Journals of Gerontology: Psychological Sciences and Social Sciences, 51B*, S183-S190.

MetLife Mature Market Institute. (1997). *The MetLife Juggling Act Study of Employer Costs for Working Caregivers.* Retrieved October 5, 2005 from www.metlife.com/ Applications/Corporate/WPS/CDA/PageGenerator/0,1674,P8895,00.html.

MetLife Mature Market Institute (1999). *The MetLife Juggling Act Study: Balancing Caregiving with Work.* Retrieved October 5, 2005 from www.metlife.com/Applications/Corporate/WPS/CDA/PageGenerator/0,1674,P8895,00.html.

MetLife Mature Market Institute (2003). *The MetLife Study of Sons at Work: Balancing Employment and Eldercare,* Retrieved October 5, 2005 from www.metlife. com/Applications/Corporate/WPS/CDA/PageGenerator/0,1674,P8895,00.html.

National Alliance for Caregiving & AARP. (2004). *Family Caregiving in the U.S.: Findings from a national survey.* National Alliance for Caregiving: Bethesda, MD and AARP: Washington, DC.

O'Leary, A. (1985). Self-efficacy and health. *Behavioral Research and Therapy, 12*:437-451.

Ory, M. G., Hoffman, R. R., Yee, J. L., Tennestedt, S., & Schulz, R. (1999). Prevalence and impact of caregiving. A detailed comparison between dementia and nondementia caregivers. *The Gerontologist, 39*, 177-185.

Pearlin, L. I., Mullan, J. T., Semple, S. J., & Skaff, M. M. (1990). Caregiving and the stress process: An overview of concepts and their measures. *The Gerontologist, 30*, 583-594.

Pew Internet & American Life Project (2005). *Health Information Online.* Retrieved December 1, 2005 from http://www.pewinternet.org/PPF/r/156/report_display.asp

Radloff, L.S. (1977). The CES-D scale: A self-report depression scale for research in the general population. *Applied Psychological Measurement, 1*: 385-401.

Richman, A., Crawford, B., Rodgers, C., & Rogers, E. S. (1998). *Workplace Survey Validation Study.* Newton, MA: WFD Consulting, Inc.

Rotondi, A.J., Sinkule, J., & Spring, M. (2005). An interactive Web-based intervention for persons with TBI and their families: Use and evaluation by female significant others. *Journal of Head Trauma & Rehabilitation, 20* (2), 173-85.

Schmall, V. L., Cleland, M., & Sturdevant, M. (2000). *The Caregiver Helpbook*. Portland, OR: Legacy Health System.

Spector, W. D., Fleishman, J., Pezzin, L., & Spillman, B. (2000). *The Characteristics of Long-Term Care Users*. (AHRQ Publication No. 00-0049). Agency for Healthcare Research and Policy, Rockville, MD.

Scholz, U., Gutiérrez-Doña, B., Sud, S., & Schwarzer, R. (2002). Is perceived self-efficacy a universal construct? Psychometric findings from 25 countries. *European Journal of Psychological Assessment, 18*, (3), 242-251.

Schwarzer, R. & Jerusalem, M. (1995). Generalized Self-Efficacy scale. In J. Weinman, S. Wright, & M. Johnston (Eds.), *Measures in health psychology: A user's portfolio. Causal and control beliefs* (pp. 35-37). Windsor, UK: NFER-NELSON.

Skaff, M. M. & Pearlin, L. I. (1992). Caregiving: role engulfment and the loss of self. *The Gerontologist, 32*(5): 656-664.

Vitaliano, P. P., Zhang, J., & Scanlon, J. M. (2003). Is caregiving hazardous to one's physical health? A meta-analysis. *Psychological Bulletin, 129*, 946-972.

White, M. & Dorman, S. M. (2001). Receiving social support online: Implications for health education. *Health Education Research, 16*(6), 693-707.

Will the Types of Jobs Being Created Enable Older Workers to Keep Working?

Geri Adler

Don Hilber

INTRODUCTION

The prevalence of elderly workers in the economy is constantly changing. It is now expected that the number and proportion of workers older than 65 will expand greatly during the next decade or more; the trend towards earlier retirement among men having reversed itself during the last twenty years, and the cohort of women with higher participation in the work force soon reaching elderly status (Purcell, 2000;

Quinn, 1997; Toosi, 2005; Vanderhart, 2003). It is also now recognized that retirement does not necessarily mean leaving the labor force entirely, as a majority of near-elderly workers retire, take a private and/or public pension and continue working in some capacity (Gustman & Steinmeier, 2005; Purcell, 2005). There has been much research conducted on the supply of older workers–their financial needs, their desires to work, and their socio-economic characteristics–and emerging research into alternative employment arrangements for this age group. But there is a dearth of research on whether the future demands of the economy will enable these workers to continue in the same or similar jobs if they so desire. This paper suggests an approach for gauging that likelihood and discusses its implications for older workers, their employers, and policy makers.

LITERATURE REVIEW

Factors Impacting the Future Supply of Older Workers

The supply of older workers is influenced by a number of factors that can both raise and lower work force participation. Determinants that might keep workers on the job longer include less generous Social Security provisions (Gustman & Steinmeier, 2005), a shift away from defined pension plans to age-neutral private pensions creating greater variability in financial wealth (IMF, 2005), a less physically demanding job mix (Johnson, 2004), optimism about future ability to remain working (Hendrickson, 2005), and workplace practices that reduce average hours worked, but retain participation by part-time work, self-employment, contracting, and consulting (Cahill et al., 2005; Pennar, 2002). Factors that contribute towards fewer elderly in today's job market are job displacement (Chan & Stevens, 2001; Koeber & Wright, 2001; Korczyk, 2004), disability (Bernstein, 2005; Johnson, 2004), lack of respect accorded older workers (McEvoy & Blahna, 2001), greater net worth among those now nearing typical retirement age (Batrica & Ucello, 2004), and greater confidence about managing finances in retirement (Taylor, 2005).

When it comes to the work-retirement decision, studies repeatedly have shown that financial needs and economic incentives matter most in raising work force participation (Gustman & Steinmeier, 2005; Purcell, 2005; Quinn, 1997). Social Security provisions exert the major influence in decisions on when to leave the labor force despite expected gains in net worth, primarily in home ownership and house values (Purcell, 2005). Furthermore the increase in retirement age to 67 is predicted to raise participation (Gustman & Steinmeier, 2005). In fact, many retirees will need moderate income from a job to raise their financial income replacement ratio from 68% to the generally-desired level of 80% (Batrica & Ucello, 2004; Elmeskov, 2004; Johnson, Smeeding, & Torrey, 2005).

There have also been vast changes in how private accounts are structured. While the percentage of workers participating in defined contribution plans have remained steady near 40%, those with defined benefit plans have fallen to 20% (U.S. Census Bureau, 2005). These changes represent a major shift of risk from institutions to households, exacerbated by a poorly developed system for converting lump-sum assets to annuities and greater need for retirees to cover more of their health care expenses (IMF, 2005). Defined benefit plans have been shown to offer a powerful incentive to workers to retire early, typically after 30 years of service (Penner et al., 2002). However, as these plans dissipate, given the problematic way they are now impacting corporate finances and state-local government budgets, more would-be retirees may remain working in some fashion, keeping the nascent rise in labor force participation among the elderly on an upward trajectory.

Aside from stricter private and public pensions, changes in workplace arrangements will prompt additional older workers to remain in the labor force in new and different ways (Drucker, 2001). While three-fourths of all men take Social Security benefits before age 65, half of these retirees will remain in the work force as part-time employees (Gustman & Steinmeier, 2005; Purcell, 2004). Many will take on bridge jobs, positions that span the time between leaving a career job and full withdrawal from the work force (Quinn, 1997). Critically, the decision to retire and to take a bridge job typically occurs among the younger "older workers," and well before the "standard" retirement age (Cahill et al., 2005).

The rising trend in partial retirement will persist if the desires of the baby boom generation are fulfilled. Over three-fourths of boomers intend to either cycle between work and leisure, work part-time, or start their own business (Hendrickson, 2005). Most boomers will opt for part-time employment, as primarily only those with sufficient assets are likely to become self-employed business owners (Karoly & Zissimo-poulos, 2005). Generating a larger share of part-time opportunities will hinge on work practices changing (Krantz-Kent, 2005; Phillips, 2004). Only one-quarter of all full-time employees aged 51 to 65 are allowed to reduce work hours with their present employer as few companies have installed a formal phased retirement program (Penner et al., 2002). While near-elderly employees welcome reduced schedules, they become wary of phased retirement programs that might alter their pension contributions or payouts (Brown, 2005). Thus, given workplace and personal realities, most boomers will not start their own business or continue work for their present employer at reduced hours and benefits. Instead, many will retire and contract back with their former employer or seek work at similar settings.

With rising net worth predominantly tied up in housing and confidence about finances tied to work continuance, two factors remain that will limit any rapid rise in older labor force participation: disability and displacement. In fact, 40% of workers retired earlier than planned largely because of poor health or job loss (Helman et al., 2005).

Health problems and functional limitations are important factors in the work-retirement decision. With increasing age, the proportion of workers unable to work because of a job-limiting disability increases (Atchley & Barusch, 2004). Disability accounts for 12% of all adults age 55-64 being unemployed (Bernstein, 2005). The causes of disability vary but circulatory problems, mental conditions, and joint disorders are common problems experienced by older workers (Atchley & Barusch, 2004; Johnson, 2004).

The extent of permanent job loss in the economy is also crucial to work force participation decisions. The incidence of displacement rises for the 55 to 64 age group, forcing many near-elderly into an earlier than expected retirement, particularly those who work in the goods-producing sector of the economy where cost savings on the part of employers are greater (Koeber & Wright, 2001). In comparison to displaced younger workers, older adults remain unemployed longer, are often paid less at subsequent positions, and are more likely to become discouraged and leave the workforce altogether (Atchley & Barusch, 2004; Chan & Stevens, 2001). As long as permanent job displacement remains a feature of the economy, a significant share of older workers will be at risk of involuntarily exiting the work force.

What is the end result of these various factors that determine the supply of elderly work force participants? From 2004 to 2014, overall labor force participation for those aged 55 to 64 is projected to rise from over 62% to over 65%, while for those aged 65 to 74 it will increase from almost 22 to 27% (Toosi, 2005). The major deterrents to keep working, worsening health and worker dislocation, will not fully offset the incentives to keep working–the scheduled rise in full benefits for Social Security, the decline of defined benefit plans, the uncertainty of both defined contribution payouts and health care costs, and some partial retirement options remaining available.

Future Demands of Jobs

The prevalence of older workers is predominantly seen as supply-driven, though their decision to work might be governed in indirect ways by employer practices regarding hiring, layoffs, workplace environment and their benefits structure. There is comparatively little research about employer needs for particular skills possessed by older workers.

Neither chronological age nor typical losses in physical ability due to aging necessarily decrease the collective working ability of the elderly (Yazaki, 2002). In the 1990s, the share of older workers facing virtually no physical demands on the job increased significantly, from 25 to 40% (Johnson, 2004). The proportion is expected to rise further, as the mix of jobs in the United States will continue to shift towards knowledge work (Hecker, 2005).

The openness of professional and managerial jobs to older workers remains daunting. Age discrimination, outlawed in 1967 after the passage of the Age Discrimination in Employment Act, is still considered pervasive (Atchley & Barusch, 2004). Substantial entry barriers, often in the form of negative stereotypes, must be surmounted. For example, Hirsch and colleagues (2000) reported that occupations requiring computer use employed and hired fewer older workers. Examining the willingness to use computers and adopt other technological changes, Friedburg (2003) found that perceived length of time to retirement rather than age influenced usage. This suggests that older workers who expect to remain in the work force will keep up their skills. They will more likely continue working in some fashion for their present employer, who will best recognize skill attainment, than for other employers, who may base hiring decisions on outdated perceptions about such skills.

Need for Research on Supply-Demand Match

A continuation of employment after retirement will be increasingly common, though it will more likely be on a part-time or contract basis. While many individuals express the desire to launch an entirely new career, staying connected to a past employer or continuing to work within the same industry is the more likely scenario. Even short-tenured displaced workers, who have a harder time becoming re-employed, minimize financial risk by contracting back with their present employer rather than embarking on a bridge job with another organization (Chan & Stevens, 2001).

This rising participation, in combination with greater numbers of older workers, is causing a groundswell of change in the workplace. By 2014, over 20% of the labor force is expected to be at least 55 years old, up from 15% in 2004 and almost 12% in 1994 (Toosi, 2005). Some researchers speculate that shortages of labor are likely either because of slowing productivity growth or because participation among the elderly will not rise fast enough to meet the demand for skills (Nyce & Schieber, 2004; Rix, 2002). Others believe that demographic forces cannot cause an overall labor shortfall, but that spot shortages might develop as small businesses needs do not always align with older worker needs in terms of hours, benefits, location and skills (Capelli, 2004; Phillips, 2004). Still, all arrive at the same general conclusion that there will be labor market mismatches involving older workers.

The ability of the job market to generate opportunities suitable for older workers is of increasing concern. What these workers crave, and what will keep an increasing proportion of them employed in their late 50s to late 60s, is the income and respect that comes from contributing their acquired skills and being rewarded for it. For older worker employment to occur, job growth will primarily need to be in industries that near-elderly workers are now gainfully employed in, either to allow their present employer to retain them in some fashion, or to enable a similar employer to more readily hire them.

Our research formulates a general framework that provides insight into how likely it is that older workers can continue to work in the industries in which they are now employed. Staying within an industry enables an older adult to remain in their present job, to use their acquired skills with reduced hours for their current employer, or to work for a similar employer. These are more lucrative and more assured options for them than taking a job that does not reward them for built-up experience or engaging in a potentially frustrating job search in another industry.

METHODOLOGY

Procedure

In order to examine whether there is a good match between workers and expected jobs, we focused on the job market by industry for persons aged 55 to 64, when the decision to fully retire or to take a bridge job largely occurs. We will analyze the current prevalence of these older workers in specific industries along with the future expectations for overall job growth in these industries.

There are three aspects to the framework. First, we will calculate the present proportion of older workers aged 55 to 64 in 20 major industry groups to the total of all workers in those groups, using a representative sample of states.

Second, we will compare these proportions against the expected rate of job growth between 2004 and 2014 for these same industry groups, determining how strong of a relationship exists between older worker prevalence and future job growth by using correlation coefficients. This will also enable us to isolate industries likely to face shortages of workers as well as any industries likely to have an abundance of workers who are older. Stark differences among industries will depict which types of older workers might need to be courted by employers to remain on the job and which might be seen as expendable.

Finally, we will compute the overall degree of relative shortages or surplus generated by any such mismatches, taking into account industry size, the need to find workers for new jobs, and the need to replace those workers now aged 55 to 64. This will show whether potential labor market mismatches are of minor concern, are pervasive across many industries, or are liable to be concentrated in a few particular industries.

Data Sources

Data used in this research comes from two sources. The future number of jobs is derived from the 2004 to 2014 projections of industry employment published every two years by the U.S. Bureau of Labor Statistics (Berman, 2005). The number of workers by age and industry stems from the Longitudinal Employer-Household Dynamics (LEHD) program, a relatively new partnership between the federal government and State Employment Security Agencies. The main advantages of this data set are that no other source collects current employment information from employers with the desired age and industry detail, and that the data aligns with employment projections by time period and industry classification. The major limitations of this data are that only certain types of employment are included (wage and salary jobs covered by state unemployment insurance) and only 32 states currently participate.

To surmount LEHD's lack of complete national data we created a synthetic proxy using a sample of states that best approximate the U.S. totals for three important, current and known characteristics. These are: (1) industry mix–the share of total jobs in each of the 20 industry groups in 2004; (2) the proportion of older adults aged 55 to 64 in 2004; and (3) expected job growth between 2002 and 2012. This data was available for the U.S., all 50 states and the District of Columbia, thus states were ranked by each of these indicators according to how much they deviated from the nation. For industry mix, the overall deviation was calculated as the sum of the absolute value of the 20 separate industry job share deviations. The sum of the three ranks determined a score, with a lower score designating a state more like the U. S. aggregate in all three respects. States in two regions, the Pacific Northwest and the Upper Midwest clustered with low scores, so to create a more reasonable proxy, the lowest scoring state in each of the four, major Census regions was selected.

The resulting set-of-states used in this research are all LEHD partners: Minnesota, New Jersey, North Carolina and Washington. Together, they truly approximated the U. S. aggregate. Their combined proportion of workers aged 55 to 64 was 10.17%, close to the 10.10% for the nation as a whole. Their projected job growth was 14.9%, nearly identical to the 15.1% sum-of-states estimate and closer than any single state. Their combined industry mix showed far less overall deviation than any single state. Table 1 shows how closely the four-state sample approximates the nation in terms of industry mix. While some industry groups were slightly over and under represented by this sample, the only industry group with an atypical share of jobs was mining, which contains only a small proportion of jobs in the economy (one half of one percent). This industry, prevalent only in those few states with abundant supplies of coal, metals, oil and/or natural gas, was excluded from subsequent analysis.

TABLE 1. Percent of Employment by Industry

NAICS		United States	Four-State Sample	Percentage Pt Difference
11	Agriculture, forestry, fishing and support	0.59%	0.58%	-0.01%
21	Mining	0.50%	0.13%	-0.37%
22	Utilities	0.35%	0.28%	-0.07%
23	Construction	6.10%	5.98%	-0.12%
31-33	Manufacturing	8.90%	9.54%	0.64%
42	Wholesale trade	3.70%	4.24%	0.53%
44-45	Retail trade	11.23%	11.25%	0.02%
48-49	Transportation and warehousing	3.21%	3.26%	0.06%
51	Information	2.12%	2.18%	0.06%
52	Finance and insurance	4.82%	4.78%	-0.04%
53	Real estate and rental and leasing	3.76%	3.67%	-0.09%
54	Professional and technical services	6.46%	6.39%	-0.07%
55	Management of companies and enterprises	1.06%	1.39%	0.33%
56	Administrative services	6.16%	5.75%	-0.41%
61	Educational services	2.06%	1.90%	-0.16%
62	Health care and social assistance	10.10%	10.18%	0.08%
71	Arts, entertainment, and recreation	2.07%	1.98%	-0.09%
72	Accommodation and food services	6.87%	6.40%	-0.47%
81	Other services	5.78%	5.49%	-0.29%
91	State and local public administration	14.16%	14.63%	0.47%

RESULTS

There is a large variation among the 19 industry groups as to their shares of workers aged 55 to 64, as depicted in Table 2. For example, Educational Services has proportionally three times as many older workers as Accommodation and Food Services. There is also great variation in projected employment change between 2004 and 2014, with some industries expecting to shrink while others create jobs more than twice as fast as the all-industry average. There is no pattern between older worker preponderance and job growth. The industries with high or very high percentages of workers currently aged 55 to 64 are expected to grow at an average rate or decline, while those with low or very low shares of such workers run the gamut from decline to very high job growth rates. The three industries that will be adding new jobs much faster than the others, (1) Administrative Services; (2) Professional and Technical Services; and (3) Health Care and Social Assistance, all staff their operations with an average or near-average share of older workers.

TABLE 2. Industry Share of Older Workers and Expected Job Growth

Industry	Percent Age 55-64 2004	Projected Job Change 2004 to 2014	Relative Share of Older Workers	Relative Growth Rate
Accommodation and food services	5.8%	16.5%	very low	average
Arts, entertainment, and recreation	9.3%	25.1%	low	high
Agriculture, forestry, fishing and support	9.7%	-10.7%	low	decline
Construction	9.7%	11.4%	low	average
Information	9.9%	11.6%	low	average
Administrative services	10.0%	31.0%	low	very high
Retail trade	10.1%	11.0%	low	average
Finance and insurance	11.2%	8.3%	average	low
Professional and technical services	11.5%	28.4%	average	very high
TOTAL, ALL INDUSTRIES	**12.2%**	**14.0%**		
Management of companies and enterprises	12.2%	10.6%	average	average
Other services	12.3%	11.8%	average	average
Wholesale trade	12.7%	8.4%	average	low
Health care and social assistance	12.9%	28.3%	average	very high
Real estate, rental and leasing	13.0%	16.9%	average	average
Transportation and warehousing	14.1%	12.4%	high	average
Manufacturing	14.2%	-5.4%	high	decline
State and local public administration	15.7%	11.1%	very high	average
Utilities	16.2%	-1.3%	very high	decline
Educational services	18.3%	16.6%	very high	average

The lack of a statistically significant relationship is shown more clearly in Figure 1. Future employment change is associated negatively with current older worker share, but with a weak correlation coefficient of 2.18. The results reinforce the underlying assumption embedded in the industry employment projections that there will be no generalized labor shortages of older workers, but do imply that there could be labor mismatches, which are the simultaneous occurrence of shortages in some industries and surpluses in others.

Table 3 presents crude estimates of these potential mismatches among industries by 2014, under the premise that those aged 55 to 64 reduce their participation in the workforce equally across industries, as they become members of the 65 to 74 age group ten years later. This as-

FIGURE 1. Expected Job Growth Among Select Industries Compared to Their Share of Older Workers

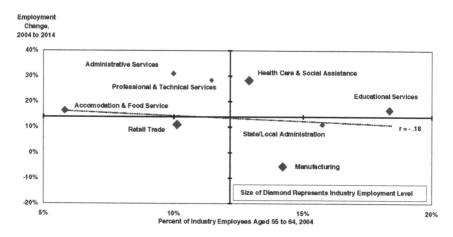

sumption is necessary because the projections for all industries have already built in an overall labor force participation rate, with rising participation among the elderly, that allows for the job market to clear without generating overall shortages or surpluses (Berman, 2005). Our estimates are derived by adding the percent change in net jobs (growth demand) to the percent of older workers (replacement demand), subtracting the overall growth plus replacement rate for the economy, and multiplying by the expected size of that industry's employment in 2014. For the majority of industries, retirements will not be a major issue one way or the other–their overall need to add new employees and replace retiring ones will not be so large that older workers are likely to be especially courted or shunned by them.

DISCUSSION

This paper has sought to determine how amenable the future job market will be for older workers as they make the decision whether or not to leave the work force entirely. Starting from the premise that there will be no general labor shortages as the older worker supply expands gradually; the results suggest that there will be severe labor mismatches in only a few industries. Most industries are either a minor part of the U.S. economy, have small replacement needs, or are growing slowly enough

TABLE 3. Estimated Potential Labor Market Mismatches by Industry, 2014

Industries Facing a Large Potential Worker Shortage	Number (Million)	Industries Facing a Large Potential Worker Surplus	Number (Million)
Health Care & Social Assistance	2.9	Manufacturing	2.4
Administrative Services	1.5	Retail Trade	0.9
Educational Services	1.3		
Professional & Technical Services	1.2		
Industries Facing a Negligible Potential Worker Shortage	**Number (Million)**	**Industries Facing a Negligible Potential Worker Surplus**	**Number (Million)**
Arts, Entertainment & Recreation	0.2	Agriculture, Forestry, Fishing	0.5
Real Estate, Rental & Leasing	0.1	Accommodation & Food Services	0.5
State & Local Public Administration	0.1	Finance & Insurance	0.4
Transportation & Warehousing	0.0	Construction	0.4
		Wholesale Trade	0.3
		Information	0.2
		Other Services	0.1
		Management of Companies	0.1
		Utilities	0.1

Estimates based on industry projected employment growth to 2014 relative to the all-industries average, plus replacement of workers aged 55 to 64 in 2004, presuming these workers all reduce labor force participation at the same, expected rate by 2014.

so neither shortages or surpluses of older workers are likely. Four other industries will desperately need all types of workers, including their present near-elderly ones. With the exception of manufacturing, the economy is generally creating the right types of jobs for older workers to remain employed in some fashion.

A strong positive correlation between the supply of workers aged 55 to 64 and projected job growth might have suggested a strict polarization of all industries between (a) those with a double need to recruit lots of workers for new jobs while retaining more workers to mitigate replacement demand; and (b) those with so few potential retirees that they have to lay off many workers to help mitigate the net loss of jobs. A strong negative correlation would have implied more traditional retirements as slow job expansion among those with higher proportions of older workers lessens the need to retain such workers. As it turns out, the almost random association means that we will likely see a variation of industry-specific responses–a mix of active retention and recruiting of older workers in some industries concurrent with the imperative to retire these workers in others, without necessarily rehiring them.

Four industries, health care and social assistance, professional and technical services, administrative services, and educational services, have a combination of job growth and replacement needs that gives them a strong incentive to retain or rehire older workers. Together, these account for 36% of jobs in 2014, providing opportunities for many older workers. Two industries, manufacturing and retail trade, face the opposite situation of having too few slots into which retiring older workers might be re-employed. For retail, however, with positive job growth and high turnover rates, the situation is not as dire for older workers as in manufacturing, where a predicted loss of net jobs will result in meager new employment opportunities. So although manufacturing is an industry with high replacement needs due to a proportionately large older work force, its growth is declining to the extent that its companies are more likely to continue displacing their older workforce than seeking to retain them.

IMPLICATIONS

The main implication for older workers is that their success at remaining in the workforce depends upon their current industry. Workers aged 55 to 64 will face better odds of being retained, rehired, or contracted for if they are employed in health care, professional services, administrative services or education than those working at other kinds of organizations. Older adults need to be aware of this situation and will find it advantageous to bargain aggressively with their present employers for a good post-retirement arrangement. On the other hand, employees of manufacturers will find that landing suitable work after retirement is more difficult than other older workers. They might want to reconsider voluntary early retirement or at least ensure their finances are in fine shape before making that decision. The majority of older workers should explore the job market thoroughly before making a retirement decision. This means maintaining or acquiring transferable skills and knowing if their occupation is prevalent and in a faster-growing industry. It may also be advisable for them to start the job search process, which could be lengthy, well before an anticipated retirement date. Finally, it might require consideration of working for a temporary help agency, as these types of firms are the major sub-category within the fast-growing administrative services industry (Berman, 2005).

The main implication for employers is that even without overall labor shortages, the competition for workers will intensify thanks to labor mismatches among industries. The proportion of employees who are aged 55 to 64 will keep expanding throughout the next decade. This age group will be actively pursuing new work arrangements, and some industries will be so short-handed to both expand and replace retirees that a bargaining war could erupt among them. Recruiting older workers with transferable skills could possibly spread to encompass other industries, too. Thus most employers, but particularly those in the four industries with anticipated shortfalls, need to be more attentive to the particular needs of older workers in order to retain them. This generally means granting greater autonomy, providing more flexible work arrangements, maintaining a suitable benefit package if work hours are reduced, and being attentive to the respect given them by younger workers and managers (McEvoy, 2001). Savvy employers in fast-growing industries might also wish to actively recruit workers in their 50s, before their retirement and post-retirement work decisions are made. Companies in manufacturing and retail trade do not have the same imperatives to retain or court older workers to fill workforce needs. Their challenge is that they surmount a reputation as an eventual "dead-end" place to work and hence cannot attract recruits that typically bring new ideas and skills to the work place.

There are several implications for policy-makers. Industry differences warrant a micro approach to policy–one that pinpoints assistance or incentives to particular groups–rather than sweeping macro changes that impact all alike. While a broad set of recommendations to keep workers employed longer would help fast-growing industries in need of workers, it would hamper those in decline who rely on voluntary retirements to reduce their workforce rather than resort to permanent layoffs. It might be wiser for public policy-makers to devote more attention towards those who desire a job, but are trapped in declining industries, particularly manufacturing and some of its smaller counterparts like utilities and agriculture. Targeted retraining, relocation assistance and pension portability would help reduce the inequities inherent in mismatches. They would also attack one of the two main barriers to increased older worker supply–job displacement.

Poor health is the other situation that keeps older-worker supply scarce and hence another policy area suited for a micro approach. More attention is warranted for the 55 to 64 age group where health risks are rising and public benefits coverage is low compared to those aged 65 and older (Bernstein, 2005). Better health among this age group would expand the pool of workers available to meet the needs of growing industries. Targeting health programs to this age group would help industries with larger replacement demand and mitigate mismatches.

CONCLUSION

Despite continued displacement and disability, there will a projected rise in the supply of older workers, given past changes in public and private pensions and the entrenched option to retire and take bridge jobs. Detailed industry projections suggest that the future demands of the economy will enable most of these workers to continue in the same or similar jobs if they so desire, but that labor mismatches will occur in several prominent industries. This has varying implications for older workers and their employers, depending on which industry they are in, and for policy makers to consider targeted approaches to assist them.

REFERENCES

Atchley, R. C. & Barusch, A. S. (2004). *Social forces and aging: An introduction to social gerontology* (10th ed.). Belmont, CA: Wadsworth/Thomson Learning.

Batrica, B., & Ucello, C. (2004). In brief: How will boomers fare at retirement (PPI Issue Paper, 2004-05)? Washington, DC: AARP Public Policy Institute.

Berman, J. M. (2005). Industry output and employment projections to 2014. *Monthly Labor Review, November*, 45-69.

Bernstein, A. B. (2005, December). Health, United States, 2005: With chartbook on trends in the health of Americans with special feature on adults 55-64 Years. Washington, DC: National Center for Health Statistics. Retrieved December 12, 2005, from http://www.cdc.gov/nchs/hus.htm

Brown, S. K. (2005). Attitudes of individuals 50 and older towards phased retirement. Washington, DC: AARP. Retrieved November 1, 2005, from http://research.aarp.org

Cahill, K. E., Giandrea, M. D., & Quinn, J. F. (2005). Are traditional retirements a thing of the past? (Working Paper 384) Washington, DC: Bureau of Labor Statistics.

Cappelli, P. (2004). Will there really be a labor shortage? *Public Policy and Aging Report, 14*(3), 1, 3-6.

Chan, S., & Stevens, A. H. (2001). Job loss and employment patterns of older workers, *Journal of Economics, 19*(2), 484-521.

Drucker, P. (2001, November 1). The next society. *Economist.* Retrieved December 1, 2005, from http:www.economist.com/surveys/PrinterFriendly.cfm?story_id = 770819

Elmeskov, J. (2004). Aging, public budgets and the need for policy reform. *Review of International Economics,* 12(2), 233-242.

Friedberg, L. (2003). The impact of technological change on older workers: Evidence from data on computer use. *Industrial and Labor Relations Review,* 56(3), 511-529.

Gustman, A., & Steinmeier, T. L. (2005). Retirement effects of proposals by the President's commission to strengthen Social Security. *National Tax Journal,* LVIII(1), 27-49.

Hecker, D. (2005). Occupational employment projections to 2014. *Monthly Labor Review, November,* 70-81.

Helman, R., Salisbury, D., Paladino, V., & Copeland, C. (2005). Encouraging workers to save: The 2005 retirement confidence survey (EBRI Issue Brief No. 280). Washington, DC: Employee Benefit Research Institute.

Hendrickson, E. (2005, February 22). "The new retirement survey" from Merrill Lynch reveals how baby boomers will transform retirement. Retrieved October 20, 2005, from http:www.ml.com/cms/templates/so/print.asp?id = 7695_7696_8149_ _46503_46635

Hirsch, B. T., MacPherson, D. A., & Hardy, M. A. (2000). Occupational age structure and access for older workers. *Industrial and Labor Relations Review,* 53(3), 401-419.

IMF (June, 2005). Household balance sheets. *Global Financial Stability Report.* Retrieved on October 20, 2005, from http://www.imf.org/external/pubs/ft/gfsr/2005/01/

Johnson, D. S., Smeeding, T. M., & Torrey, B. B. (2005). Economic inequality through the prisms of income and consumption. *Monthly Labor Review, April,* 11-24.

Johnson, R. (2004). Trends in job demands among older workers, 1992-2002. Monthly Labor Review, *July,* 48-56.

Karoly, L. A., & Zissimopoulos, J. (2003). Self-employment trends and patterns among older U.S. workers (Working Paper, WR-136). Santa Monica, CA: Rand.

Koeber, C., & Wright, D. W. (2001). W/age bias in worker displacement: How industrial structure shapes the job loss and earnings decline of older American workers. *The Journal of Socio-Economics,* 30, 343-352.

Korczyk, S. M. (2004). Is early retirement ending (PPI Issue Paper, 2004-10)? Washington, DC: AARP Public Policy Institute.

Krantz-Kent, R. (2005). Variations in time use at stages of the life cycle. *Monthly Labor Review, September,* 38-45.

McEvoy, G. M., & Blahna, M. J. (2001). Engagement or disengagement? Older workers and the looming labor shortage. *Business Horizons, September-October,* 46-52.

Nyce, S. A., & Schieber, S. J. (2004). Demographics matter: The economic reality of an aging society. *Public Policy and Aging Report, 14*(3), 11-15.

Penner, R., Perun, P., & Steuerle, E. (2002). Legal and institutional impediments to partial retirement and part-time work by older workers. Washington, DC: The Urban Institute. Retrieved October 20, 2005, from http://www.urban.org/Uploaded PDF/410587_SloanFinal.pdf

Phillips, B. D. (2004). The future small business workforce: Will labor shortages exist? *Business Economics, October*, 19-27.

Purcell, P. J. (2000). Older workers: Employment and retirement trends. *Monthly Labor Review, October*, 19-30.

Purcell, P. (2005). Older workers: Employment and retirement trends. In O. S. Mitchell, R. L. Clark (Eds.), *Reinventing the Retirement Paradigm* (Chapter 4). New York: Oxford University Press.

Quinn, J. F. (1997). Retirement trends and patterns in 1990s: An end of an era? *Public Policy and Aging Report, Summer*, 10-14.

Rix, S. E. (2002). The labor market for older workers. *Generations, Summer*, 25-30.

Taylor, P. (2005). From the age of Aquarius to the age of responsibility. Washington, DC: Pew Research Center. Retrieved December 8, 2005, from http://pewresearch.org/socialtrends/socialtrends-boomers120805.pdf

Toosi, M. (2005). Labor force projections to 2014: Retiring boomers. *Monthly Labor Review, November*, 25-44.

U.S. Census Bureau (2005). Social Insurance and Human Services. Retrieved January 6, 2006, from http://www.census.gov/prod/2004pubs/04statab/socinsur.pdf

Vanderhart, M. J. (2003). Labor supply of older men: Does Social Security matter? *Economic Inquiry*, 41(2), 250-263.

Yazaki, Y. (2002). Assessing the suitability of the elderly for employment. *The Geneva Papers on Risk and Insurance*, 27(4), 534-539.

Retirement Transitions
Among Married Couples

Angela L. Curl
Aloen L. Townsend

INTRODUCTION

According to Haynes et al., (1987), "the word 'retirement' can refer to a life event, a transition or crisis state, a process, or a social role or status." This definition highlights the complex nature of the term 'retirement.' Despite this complexity, retirement has traditionally been defined as working until age 65 and then completely withdrawing from paid employment, deriving income primarily from retirement sources, and viewing oneself as retired, ignoring those who do not fit into the traditional model, such as those who experience disability (Gibson, 1988), Tibbitts, as early as 1954, described retirement as a continuum, beginning with "separation or withdrawal from one's principal or career occupation in gainful employment" or gradual retirement (including shifting to part-time work), to "complete or final separation from the workforce," and ending with the cessation of all productive activity (e.g., community service, arts and crafts, gardening, and home maintenance) "beyond that of mere self-maintenance." This highlights the processual nature of retirement, where more than one type of transition can occur in the course of retiring.

This study examined the patterns of retirement transitions evidenced by married couples in the Health and Retirement Study (described in the Methodology section; Willis, 2004) over an 8-year period. These transitions could be a one-time transition from full-time work to zero employment, some type of gradual retirement, a period of physical disability or unemployment or other reasons for being out of the labor force, a re-entry into paid employment, or some combination of these patterns.

MEASUREMENT OF RETIREMENT

There are subjective and objective ways to measure retirement. Subjective measurements of retirement generally ask individuals whether they consider themselves retired. These types of questions ask respondents to give their personal definition of retirement and their retirement status or whether they consider themselves retired using fixed response categories (e.g., retired [answered with yes or no]; or not retired, partially retired, completely retired). The advantage of subjective retirement measures is that they reveal the self identification of individuals and their possible future employment decisions. Subjective measures also can capture aspects of work that are difficult to measure, such as "retiring" to work only 40 hours per week instead of 80 hours or "retiring" to self-employment (Gustman & Steinmeier, 2000). Commonly used "objective" measures of retirement include the acceptance of Social Security and/or pension benefits, the complete withdrawal from paid employment, and hours worked per week below an arbitrary cut-off (Quinn et al., 1990). Researchers have also used departure from a long-held job or career or sudden reduction of wages or hours worked as objective measures.

Gustman and Steinmeier (2000), using various measures of retirement with longitudinal data from the Health and Retirement Study, found that the percentage of those retired depended on the definition of retirement. They concluded that each of the examined subjective and objective measures had its strengths and weaknesses. For example, measurement of retirement as a complete withdrawal from employment has appeal because it is easy to measure and does not have the appearance of an arbitrary cut-off point; however, this measure excludes everyone who works for any amount of pay. Measuring retirement by hours worked includes more workers, but cut-points are arbitrarily determined. Gustman and Steinmeier concluded that the best measure of retirement (subjective or objective) depends on the purpose of the study.

GENDER, MARRIAGE, AND RETIREMENT

On average, women have shorter paid work histories (Coile, 2003), are less positive about retirement (Crawford, 1972), plan less for retirement (Ekerdt et al., 1996), accumulate less individual retirement wealth (Coile, 2003), and experience more involuntary layoffs during late middle age (Flippen & Tienda, 2000) than men. Fewer women retire at either age 62 or age 65 (important ages for eligibility for Social Security) compared to men, and instead spread their retirement out over a longer age range (Blau, 1998; Gustman & Steinmeier, 2000).

Retirement Among Married Couples

For married individuals, retirement is a couple-level event where the retirement of one spouse affects the life circumstances of both. For instance, retirement by either spouse can have consequences for the household's total income, household routines and coordination of schedules, health insurance coverage, marital satisfaction and conflict, and the timing of retirement for the other spouse (Crawford, 1972; Henretta et al., 1993; Johnson & Favreault, 2001; Kelley, 1981; Moen et al., 2001). A study conducted by Favreault and Johnson (2002) found that unmarried men are more likely to retire before age 62, while married men are more likely to retire between the ages of 63 and 65. In addition, men married to significantly younger women tend to delay their retirement (but they still tend to retire before their wives, rather than jointly) compared to men married to women about the same age or older. They also found that married women at any age are more likely than unmarried women to retire.

Retirement Transitions

There are a number of different types of retirement transitions, as the definition and measurement of 'retirement' highlights. An individual can go from work to complete retirement (i.e., no paid employment), or can gradually retire by transitioning from full-time work to part-time work or partial retirement. This individual may continue working part-time for the rest of his or her life, or may later transition to a state of complete retirement. Individuals can also transition to a state of "less retirement" by re-entering the labor force after complete retirement, by going from partial retirement to working full-time, or by subjectively no longer considering himself or herself to be retired. Thus the process of retirement can be nonlinear (i.e., not necessarily becoming increasingly more retired). Retirement transitions can also be more complex if individuals exit the labor force for other unplanned reasons, such as disability, unemployment, or to provide caregiving assistance. These exits out of the labor force for other reasons represent many different life-course trajectories (Choi, 2003). They can reflect an alternative route to retirement (Dahl, Nilsen, & Vaage, 2000), an interim status until reaching a certain age or becoming eligible for pension benefits (Gibson, 1988), a temporary status (e.g., returning to work after being unemployed or temporarily disabled; Choi, 2003), or a continuation of a lifetime pattern of discontinuous labor force involvement.

A great number of studies on retirement transitions have already been conducted. However, these studies have focused primarily on the factors that predict a work or retirement transition (e.g., Berkovec & Stern, 1991; Blau, 1998; Favreault & Johnson, 2002; Mutchler et al., 1999). Other studies have examined the impact of a retirement transition on some other outcome, such as depressive symptomatology (Kim & Moen, 2002; Szinovacz & Davey, 2004), retirement satisfaction (Szinovacz & Davey, 2005), or marital quality (Moen et al., 2001).

In contrast, Gustman and Steinmeier (1986) used data from the Retirement History Study (data collected 1969-1975) to document the transitions (of men only) between the states of full-time work, part-time work, and full-time retirement over a four-year period. Gustman and Steinmeier (2000) have also documented the amount of transition evident in the Health and Retirement Study, using self-defined retirement status, but only looked at transitions for adjoining measurement periods, referred to as waves (four waves, each two years apart).

This study extends the knowledge base by examining retirement transitions over an eight-year period using data from a large, nationally-representative longitudinal survey (Health and Retirement Survey; Willis, 2004). It focuses specifically on retirement transitions (numbers, types, and patterns), similarities and differences by gender, and the correspondence of retirement transitions between spouses. In addition to the lengthy duration, the utilization of five data points, each approximately two years apart, permits finer-grained modeling of the complex nature of retirement. Also, this study operationalizes retirement using a combination of an objective work measure (hours worked) and self-identified retirement status. Restricting the sample to married couples focuses on an important demographic group (middle-aged dual-earner couples) and emphasizes the interdependence of retirement in married couples. Requiring data from both spouses allows for examination of gender similarities and differences in retirement transitions.

METHODOLOGY

Sample

The sample participants were interviewed face-to-face in their homes for the first wave (1992) of the Health and Retirement Survey (HRS) and then over the phone for the subsequent waves of data collection (Institute for Social Research [ISR], 2002; Willis, 2004). The HRS utilized a nationally-representative sample of adults aged 51 to 61 (born between 1931 and 1941) and their spouses (regardless of age), with over-sampling of Blacks, Hispanics, and residents of Florida. The present study utilized data from the first five waves of Version D of the HRS prepared by the RAND Corporation (www.rand.org/labor/aging/).

A total of 12,654 respondents, in 7,608 households, were interviewed at wave 1 for the HRS (ISR, 2002). Over time, additional respondents were added to the sample due to marriage/cohabitation with an HRS respondent. The sample selection criteria for the present study excluded individuals who were not married at wave 1, who had more than one spouse over the eight-year study span, or who divorced or separated from their spouse during the study. The study also excluded individuals who did not identify their race as White or Black, did not report the same race as their spouse, or who were of Hispanic origin. This criterion was imposed to reduce racial and ethnic heterogeneity within the sample (characteristics associated with retirement transitions), in order to concentrate on similarities and differences by gender. This study focused on the retirement transitions of married couples, so both spouses were required to be interviewed at wave 1. The couple was retained in the sample if at least one spouse was interviewed at each subsequent wave (since one spouse could provide proxy retirement data for the other). The three couples where both spouses died before the end of the study were retained in the sample until their deaths. Finally, in order to be included in the sample, both the husband and wife had to be working full-time or part-time at wave 1, and at least one of them had to report not being self-employed, as those who are self-employed have different characteristics than wage and salary workers (Karoly & Zissimopoulos, 2004). Final sample size for this study was 2,236 individuals (1,118 couples).

Measures

Demographics. The demographic variables included were gender (female = 1), age at baseline (in years), self-identified race (Black/African American = 1), years of education at baseline, total annual household income in dollars, and total household wealth in dollars. As this is a study of heterosexual married couples, the marital role labels of "husband" and "wife" are used interchangeably with gender labels. Household income was computed by RAND by summing all the income obtained by both spouses through earnings and other sources such as government transfers (e.g., Social Security Supplemental Income, worker's compensation), retirement earnings, and capital income (St. Clair et al., 2004). Total household wealth was computed by RAND by summing the value of assets (including housing and savings) and subtracting all debts (e.g., mortgages, credit card balances, loans from relatives, medical debts), which resulted in negative wealth for some households.

Labor Force/Retirement Transitions. A single measure has been created by the RAND Corporation that summarizes labor force/retirement status at each wave in terms of both subjective and objective criteria. This measure combines information from many questions that ask respondents whether they are working for pay, their employment status, whether they consider themselves retired, usual hours worked per week and usual weeks worked per year, whether they have a second job, hours per week and weeks per year worked on the second job, and whether they are looking for work. The RAND measure of labor force/retirement status has seven response categories: working full-time, working part-time, unemployed, partly retired, retired, disabled, or not in the labor force. For details on how individuals were assigned to one of these seven statuses, see St. Clair et al., (2004). For this study, these seven categories were collapsed into four: working full-time or part-time, partly retired, completely retired, and not in the labor force. This last category combines those who are disabled, unemployed, or not in the labor force (i.e., those who do not work for pay or who are homemakers).

The number and type of transitions reported by husbands and wives were determined by examining the labor force/retirement status at each wave. This study required that all husbands and wives were actively working (full-time or part-time) at the beginning of the study. From the original working state, they could transition to being partly retired, completely retired, or "not in the labor force" (e.g., disabled, unemployed, homemaker). A transition was considered to have occurred if the status at a subsequent wave differed from the status at the previous wave. For example, if a husband indicated that he was working at wave 1 (baseline) and at wave 2, and subsequently reported being partly retired at wave 3, he was coded as experiencing one transition. As evident in this example, the transitions could occur at any subsequent wave of the study. On the other hand, if a wife reported working full-time or part-time for every wave, zero transitions were considered to have occurred. Since this study used five waves of data, up to four transitions could occur per person. This study determined how many transitions occurred for each person, as well as the type of transition pattern he or she experienced. Figure 1 portrays all possible transition patterns that hypothetically could have occurred over the eight-year (five-wave) study.

Analysis Plan

The number and types of retirement transitions experienced by the sample are described through figures that summarize the data separately for husbands and wives, as well as through frequencies and percentages. In addition, paired *t*-tests were used to test for significant gender differences in means for demographic characteristics and the number of transitions experienced by husbands and wives. To determine the magnitude and direction of the relationship between the number of transitions of husbands and wives, Pearson's correlation was used. A couple-level pattern variable was used to summarize how many couples

FIGURE 1. All 81 Possible Work and Retirement Transitions

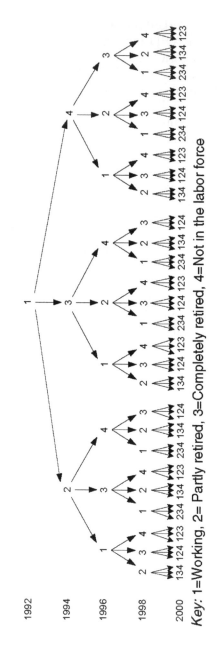

1992

1994

1996

1998

2000

Key: 1=Working, 2= Partly retired, 3=Completely retired, 4=Not in the labor force

experienced the same *number* of transitions, and, if the couple did not experience the same number, which spouse had the greater number of transitions. Another couple-level pattern variable summarizes how many couples experienced exactly the same *type* (number and pattern) of transitions over the eight years.

RESULTS

Demographics

The average age of husbands (M = 55.49 years, SD = 4.20, range 26 to 73), was significantly older than the average age of their wives (M = 51.84 years, SD = 5.19, range 31-65), paired $t(1117)$ = 25.87, p < .01. The majority of husbands (n = 967, 86.5%) were between the ages of 51 and 61 in 1992, with the remainder almost equally divided between those younger than 51 and older than 61. In comparison, only 61.5% (n = 688) of wives were between the ages of 51 and 61 in 1992, and 37.9% (n = 424) were younger than 51. By 2000, 50.9% (n = 569) of husbands and 28.3% (n = 316) of wives were age 65 or older. The racial composition of the sample was predominantly White (n = 1,996; 89.3%), with 240 Black respondents (10.7%). On average, husbands and wives both completed 13 years of education (M = 12.96, SD = 2.87 and M = 13.10, SD = 2.25, respectively), or approximately one year of college. Mean education levels of husbands and wives were not significantly different, paired $t(1117)$ = -1.81, p = .07. However, 18.8% (n = 210) of husbands and 12.5% (n = 140) of wives had less than a high school diploma, while 14.8% (n = 166) of husbands and 12.1% (n = 135) of wives had some post-college education. In 1992, couples in this sample had a mean annual household income of $63,683 ($SD$ = $41,496) and a mean household wealth of $205,134 ($SD$ = $315,541).

Retirement Transitions by Gender

Figures 2 and 3 present the most common transition patterns of husbands and wives, arrayed according to the number of transitions experienced. About 500 husbands and wives experienced zero transitions from employment (husbands: n = 486, 43.5%; wives: n = 501, 44.8%). Among respondents who did experience one or more transitions, the two most common transition patterns were identical for husbands and wives: transitioning from work to partial retirement and transitioning

FIGURE 2. Retirement Transitions of Husbands and Wives

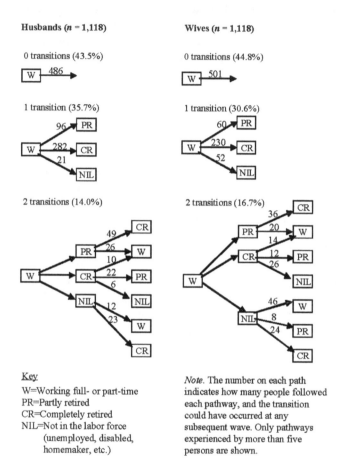

from work to complete retirement. By the end of the eight-year period, 63.6% (*n* = 750) of husbands and 53.6% (*n* = 599) of wives transitioned to complete retirement as a final state. One hundred and fourteen husbands (10.2%) and 92 wives (0.8%) transitioned from a state of greater retirement (complete retirement) to lesser retirement (partial retirement), or from retirement (complete or partial) to working, at least once during the study. For example, 47 husbands and 40 wives transitioned from complete retirement to partial retirement (but may have transitioned again afterwards).

FIGURE 3. Work and Retirement Transitions for Husbands (n = 1,118) and Wives (n = 1,118)

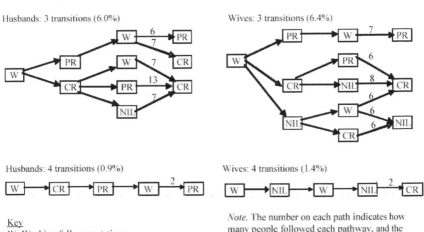

Key
W=Working full- or part-time
PR=Partly retired
CR=Completely retired
NIL=Not in the labor force (unemployed, disabled, homemaker, etc.)

Note. The number on each path indicates how many people followed each pathway. and the transition could have occurred at any subsequent wave. Only pathways experienced by more than five persons are shown (except for the 4-transitions pathway), but the percentages count all transition pathways (including those less frequently experienced).

Of the 81 transition patterns that were hypothetically possible for this study (Figure 1), 41 different patterns were observed for husbands and 49 patterns were observed for wives (Figures 2 and 3). This highlights the greater diversity in retirement experiences of wives. For husbands and wives who experienced at least one transition, more husbands (45.0%, *n* = 503) than wives (37.3%, *n* = 417) transitioned from work to complete retirement and remained completely retired throughout the study. Husbands were less likely than wives to report being "not in the labor force" (i.e., disabled, unemployed, homemaker) for one or more waves (14.9% vs. 34.0%, respectively). On the other hand, husbands were more likely than wives to report being partly retired for one or more waves of the study (40.4% vs. 30.3%, respectively).

Retirement Transitions of Couples

The data in Figures 2 and 3 summarize patterns for individual husbands and wives, not joint patterns for couples. Four different methods were used to examine the correspondence of retirement transitions of husbands and wives. First, the mean number of retirement transitions were compared to see if there was a significant difference between those of husbands and wives, but none was found, paired $t(1117) = 1.08$, $p = .28$. The mean number of transitions for husbands was .85 ($SD = .83$), while the mean for wives was .89 ($SD = 1.00$). Second, the number of transitions of husbands and wives were correlated, and a positive correlation was found, $r = .17$, $p < .01$. Because these are dyadic data and partners are distinguishable (by gender and marital role), this is equivalent to an intra-class correlation (Gonzalez & Griffin, 1997). Seventeen percent shared variance between partners in the number of transitions is thus considered a moderate-size effect. Third, a variable was created to examine the couple-level pattern in the number of transitions. Nearly half the couples ($n = 522$, 46.7%) experienced the same number of transitions; in 304 couples (27.2%), the wife experienced more transitions than her husband, and in 292 couples (26.1%), the husband experienced more transitions than his wife, $\chi^2(1, N = 1,118) = 147.60$, $p < .01$.

Fourth, another couple-level pattern variable was created to examine how many couples experienced exactly the same retirement transition pattern (excluding 83 couples where one or both spouses died during the study; husbands were statistically more likely to die than wives, $z = -1.95$, $p = .05$). Using this method, 421 couples (40.7%) were found to have experienced exactly the same retirement pattern over the eight years of the study. Two hundred and ninety-nine couples (28.9%) experienced zero transitions (i.e., remained employed) during the course of the study. For 107 couples (10.3%), the husband and wife experienced the one transition of going from work to complete retirement, while eight couples (0.8%) transitioned from work to partial retirement (and stayed partly retired). The remaining seven couples who shared the same work/retirement pattern had other transitions (e.g., they both experienced 3 transitions: going from work to partial retirement and then complete retirement).

DISCUSSION

This study found evidence of both similarities and differences in the retirement transitions of husbands and wives. The most common retirement pattern, regardless of gender, was the single transition from work to complete retirement. A sizable number of husbands and wives also made the single transition to partial retirement (and stayed partially retired throughout the remainder of the study). In this sample, husbands and wives had approximately the same mean number of work/retirement transitions. One major gender difference was that wives were more likely than husbands to report being not in the labor force (for reasons other than retirement) for one or more waves. Another difference was that more husbands than wives became "less retired" (e.g., by transitioning from complete retirement to partial retirement) at least once during the study.

This study also found evidence that supports the life-course concept of the "linked lives" of married couples (Kim & Moen, 2002; Moen et al., 2001). The number of transitions of husbands and wives was positively correlated, and almost 50% of individuals experienced the same number of transitions as their spouse. Even more striking is the finding that individuals in 421 couples (40.7%) experienced the same transition pattern as their spouse. Previous research has documented that retirement of one spouse affects the lives of both, through its potential impact on such aspects as the amount of time spent together and the marital context (e.g., household income and wealth, time for leisure activities; Blau, 1998; Moen & Kim, 2001), as well as the timing of the other spouse's retirement (Blau, 1998). Our study documents that one partner's pattern of retirement also can affect the other partner's pattern, in terms of both the number and type(s) of retirement transitions.

Policy Implications

Data for this study were collected during a time of changing Social Security policies. Concern about the financial solvency of these government programs has resulted in major programmatic changes, such as raising the minimum age of eligibility for full Social Security benefits from 65 to 67 (Social Security Administration [SSA], 2004). In addition, since 2000, beneficiaries who have reached this age of full retirement no longer have to withdraw from the labor force in order to qualify for Social Security benefits (SSA, 2005). These changes are designed to encourage older adults to remain in the workforce longer, and thus continue paying Social Security taxes, even while collecting benefits.

According to an AARP study, about 80% of Baby Boomers expect to work for pay during their retirement, some because of the stimulation, enjoyment, or sense of accomplishment that they get from work and others because of economic necessity (Rix, 1999). This highlights the fact that many might choose to work longer if they had the choice, and increased flexibility in terms of work and retirement options may increase the numbers of people that stay economically active. In order to make retirement policies more flexible, the United States could adopt plans that allow workers to take partial Social Security benefits while continuing to work. Sweden has successfully used this strategy to keep workers in the labor market longer (SSA, 2004), partly because of the availability of part-time positions in Sweden (Naegele, 1999).

Another strategy would be to encourage more formal gradual retirement options, such as part-time positions and job-sharing. A working group formed by the Advisory Council on Employee Welfare and Pension Plans (Employee Benefits Security Administration, 2000) has identified three types of barriers in the United States to gradual retirement (also called phased retirement): the design of private pension plans, the potential loss of health care coverage, and legal concerns, such as potential violations of the Age Discrimination in Employment Act (ADEA) of 1967. The working group's recommendations to address these barriers include changing the way pensions are calculated so that benefits are not reduced if pay decreases due to gradual retirement, allowing individuals to purchase Medicare coverage between the ages of 55 and 65, and reviewing the ADEA and providing written guidance concerning age discrimination as it relates to designing gradual retirement programs. If adopted, these policy reforms may increase the number of transitions that individuals and couples experience in middle and late-adulthood.

Practice Implications

Work and retirement transitions involve potentially stressful changes. There is a need for mental health practitioners (e.g., social workers, psychologists, marriage and family counselors) to help married couples as they approach retirement. Planning for the transition(s) between work and retirement–including strategies to meet social, emotional, and financial needs–has been shown to have a positive influence on retirement outcomes such as adjustment to the new role, perceived quality of life, and psychological well-being (Anderson & Weber, 1993; Lo & Brown, 1999; Richardson, 1993; Rosenkoetter & Garris, 1998). In addition to encouraging clients to plan for retirement, there is a need to help clients (individually and as a couple) during and after retirement. The initial two years after retirement has been linked with a decline in marital quality for both husbands and wives (Moen et al., 2001; Szinovacz & Davey, 2005). The complexity and nonlinearity of the retirement patterns revealed in our study, including transitions to "lesser retirement," argue for a need to increase awareness among practitioners that the traditional linear model of retirement (i.e., going from work to full retirement and staying fully retired) does not represent the current experience of many individuals. As Riley and Riley (1994) noted, policies and social structures often lag behind changes in individuals' everyday experiences wrought by changing age structures. Retirement is currently a prime example, and practitioners can be advocates for social change regarding retirement policies and options.

Study Limitations and Strengths

Our results emphasize the growing complexity of retirement and the need for extended longitudinal studies that examine work and retirement transitions. This study utilizes data from five waves of measurement, which permits the examination of patterns of *stability* and up to four *changes* in labor force status. The longer the study period and the more numerous the data collection points, the more change is evident. Between-wave transitions might have also occurred; thus this study may still underestimate the number of transitions experienced. Complete work-history data that tracks all work and retirement transitions could provide greater precision in future studies.

In order to study retirement transitions at the couple level, a four-category measure was created that distinguished between working, partial retirement, complete retirement, and out of the labor force status. Using the original seven categories of labor force status provided in the RAND HRS dataset was beyond the scope of this descriptive study, as each category exponentially increases the number of retirement transition patterns possible and creates challenges for summarizing the data. Although disability, unemployment, and being out of the labor force due to other reasons were grouped together into a category called "not in the labor force," there is great heterogeneity in the experiences of individuals within and between these labor force statuses (Choi, 2003). Further in-depth research is needed to explore the retirement transitions of those who are "not in the labor force" for one or more waves.

This study focused exclusively on the impact of gender and marriage on retirement transitions; however, other aspects of people's lives (e.g., race/ethnicity, social class) are likely to also be important. Numerous studies have found evidence of disadvantaged work patterns (e.g., lower paying jobs, more involuntary labor market exits and disability, longer periods of unemployment) for racial or ethnic minorities (e.g., Bound et al., 1995; Flippen & Tienda, 2000; Gibson, 1988). In addition, income and education are structural factors that work independently and in conjunction to produce retirement disparities (Brown et al., 1996; Bound et al., 1995; Dahl et al., 2000; Flippen & Tienda, 2000). Future research should examine the relationship between race/ethnicity or social class and retirement transitions in married couples. Husbands' and wives' patterns of retirement transitions, over the eight-year period covered by our study, were complex. Even more complex patterns may appear if both gender and race are considered, a possibility we plan to investigate in future research.

Despite its limitations, this study contributes to previous literature about retirement transitions in several ways. First, this study uses nationally-representative and current (1992 to 2000) data from the Health and Retirement Survey, which extends previous research that is often based on smaller numbers, convenience sampling, or older data. Second, this study uses data from a total of five separate time points to highlight the potential complexity of retirement patterns, while most of the previous research on transitions has relied on data from only two or three time points. Third, this study focuses on retirement transitions of dual-earner married couples, where both spouses provided data about their work and retirement status, while the majority of prior studies focus on the retirement experiences of individuals (Ekerdt, 2002). As the Baby Boomer generation ages and the number of married couples facing retirement decisions grows, there is a pressing need for empirical evidence to provide a solid basis for policy and practice.

REFERENCES

Anderson, C., & Weber, J. (1993). Preretirement planning and perceptions of satisfaction among retirees. *Educational Gerontology, 19*, 397-406.

Berkovec, J., & Stern, S. (1991). Job exit behavior of older men. *Econometrica, 59*(1), 189-210.

Blau, D. M. (1998). Labor force dynamics of older married couples. *Journal of Labor Economics, 16*(3), 595-629.

Bound, J., Schoenbaum, M., & Waidmann, T. (1995). Race and education differences in disability status and labor force attachment in the Health and Retirement Survey. *Journal of Human Resources, 30*(Suppl.), S227-S267.

Brown, M. T., Fukunaga, C., Umemoto, D., & Wicker, L. (1996). Annual review, 1990-1996: Social class, work, and retirement behavior. *Journal of Vocational Behavior, 49*, 159-189.

Choi, N. G. (2003). Determinants of stability and changes in self-reported work disability among older working-age populations. *Journal of Aging & Social Policy, 15*(1), 11-31.

Coile, C. (2003, March). *Retirement incentives and couples' retirement decisions* (Working Paper No. 2003-04). Chestnut Hill, MA: Center for Retirement Research at Boston College.

Crawford, M. P. (1972). Retirement as a psychosocial crisis. *Journal of Psychosomatic Research, 16*, 375-380.

Dahl, S. A., Nilsen, O. A., & Vaage, K. (2000). Work or retirement? Exit routes for Norwegian elderly. *Applied Economics, 32*, 1865-1876.

Ekerdt, D. J. (2002). The fruits of retirement research. *Contemporary Gerontology, 9*(2), 35-39.

Ekerdt, D. J., DeViney, S., & Kosloski, K. (1996). Profiling plans for retirement. *Journal of Gerontology: Social Sciences, 51B*(3), S140-S149.

Favreault, M. M., & Johnson, R. W. (2002). The family, Social Security, and the retirement decision. In M. M. Favreault, F. J. Sammartino, & C. E. Steuerle (Eds.), *Social Security and the family: Addressing unmet needs in an underfunded system* (pp. 295-329). Washington, DC: Urban Institute Press.

Flippen, C., & Tienda, M. (2000). Pathways to retirement: Patterns of labor force participation and labor market exit among the pre-retirement population by race, Hispanic origin, and sex. *Journal of Gerontology: Social Sciences, 55B*(1), S14-S27.

Gibson, R. C. (1988). The work, retirement, and disability of older black Americans. In J. S. Jackson (Ed.), *The Black American elderly: Research on physical and psychosocial health* (pp. 304-324). New York: Springer Publishing.

Gonzalez, R., & Griffin, D. (1997). The statistics of interdependence: Treating dyadic data with respect. In S. Duck (Ed.), *Handbook of personal relationships: Theory, research, and interventions* (2nd ed., pp. 271-302). New York: Wiley.

Gustman, A. L., & Steinmeier, T. L. (1986). A structural retirement model. *Econometrica, 54*(3), 555-584.

Gustman, A. L., & Steinmeier, T. L. (2000). Retirement outcomes in the Health and Retirement Study. *Social Security Bulletin, 63*(4), 57-70.

Haynes, S. G., McMichael, A. J., & Tyroler, H. A. (1987). Stress research in the evaluation of illness and death around normal, involuntary retirement: A review. In L.

Henretta, J. C., O'Rand, A. M., & Chan, C. G. (1993). Joint role investments and synchronization of retirement: A sequential approach to couples' retirement timing. *Social Forces, 71*(4), 981-1000.

Institute for Social Research. (2002). *Overview of the Health and Retirement Study*. Retrieved August 20, 2003, from http://hrsonline.isr.umich.edu/intro/sho_uinfo. php?hfyle = overview&xtyp = 2

Johnson, R. W., & Favreault, M. M. (2001, March). *Retiring together or working alone: The impact of spousal employment and disability on retirement decisions* (Working Paper No. 2001-01). Chestnut Hill, MA: Center for Retirement Research at Boston College.

Karoly, L. A., & Zissimopoulos, J. (2004, March). *Self-employment and the 50 + population* (Working Paper #2004-03). Washington, DC: AARP. Retrieved April 26, 2004, from http://research.aarp.org/econ/2004_03_self_employ.pdf

Kelley, H. H. (1981). Marriage relationships and aging. In R. W. Fogel, E. Hatfield, S. B. Kiesler, & E. Shanas (Eds.), *Aging: Stability and change in the family* (pp. 275-300). New York: Academic Press.

Kiefer, K. M. (with Summer, L., & Shirey, L.). (2001, February). *What are the attitudes of young retirees and older workers?* (Data Profiles: Young Retirees and Older Workers Profile No. 5). Washington, DC: National Academy on An Aging Society.

Kim, J. E., & Moen, P. (2002). Retirement transitions, gender, and psychological well-being: A life-course, ecological model. *Journal of Gerontology: Psychological Sciences, 57B*(3), P212-P222.

Lo, R., & Brown, R. (1999). Stress and adaptation: Preparation for successful retirement. *Australian and New Zealand Journal of Mental Health Nursing, 8,* 30-38.

Moen, P., Kim, J. E., & Hofmeister, H. (2001). Couples' work/retirement transitions, gender, and marital quality. *Social Psychology Quarterly, 64*(1), 55-71.

Mutchler, J. E., Burr, J. A., Massagli, M. P., & Pienta, A. (1999). Work transitions and health in later life. *Journal of Gerontology: Social Sciences, 54B*(5), S252-S261.

Naegele, G. (1999, August). *Active strategies for an ageing workforce.* Conference Report of the Turku Conference: European Foundation for the Improvement of Living and Working Conditions.

Quinn, J. F., Burkhauser, R. V., & Myers, D. A. (1990). *Passing the torch: The influence of economic incentives on work and retirement.* Kalamazoo, MI: W. E. Upjohn Institute for Employment Research.

Richardson, V. E. (1993). *Retirement counseling: A handbook for gerontology practitioners.* New York: Springer Publishing Company, Inc.

Riley, M. W., & Riley, J. W. (1994). Structural lag: Past and future. In M. W. Riley, R. L. Kahn, A. Foner, & K. A. Mack (Eds.), *Age and structural lag: Society's failure to provide meaningful opportunities in work, family, and leisure* (pp. 15-36). Oxford, England: John Wiley & Sons.

Rix, S. E. (1999). *Update on the older workers: 1998–Employment gains continue.* Retrieved August 8, 2001, from www.research.aarp.org/econ/dd42_worker98.html

Rosenkoetter, M. M., & Garris, J. M. (1998). Psychosocial changes following retirement. *Journal of Advanced Nursing, 27,* 966-976.

Social Security Administration. (2004). *Social Security programs throughout the world: Europe, 2004.* Retrieved December 21, 2004, from www.ssa.gov/policy/docs/progdesc/ssptw/2004-2005/europe/ssptw04euro.pdf

Social Security Administration. (2003). *Social Security programs throughout the world: The Americas, 2003.* Retrieved December 21, 2004, from www.ssa.gov/policy/docs/progdesc/ssptw/2002-2003/americas/ssptw03americas.pdf

St. Clair, P., Bugliari, D., Chien, S., Haider, S., Hayden, O., Hurd, M., Ilchuk, S., Lopez, G., Loughran, D., Panis, C., Pantoia, P., Reti, M., & Zissimopoulos, J. (2004, April). *RAND HRS data documentation: Version d.* Retrieved November 13, 2004, from http://hrsonline.isr.umich.edu/meta/rand/randhrsd/randhrsd.pdf

Szinovacz, M. E., & Davey, A. (2004). Retirement transitions and spouse disability: Effect on depressive symptoms. *Journal of Gerontology: Social Sciences, 59B*(6), S333-S342.

Szinovacz, M. E., & Davey, A. (2005). Retirement and marital decision making: Effects on retirement satisfaction. *Journal of Marriage and Family, 67,* 387-398.

Tibbitts, C. (1954). Retirement problems in American society. *American Journal of Sociology, 59*(4), 301-308.

Willis, R. J. (2004, April). *The Health and Retirement Study: A longitudinal study of health, retirement, and aging, 1992-2000* [Computer file]. Conducted by the University of Michigan, Survey Research Center. ICPSR ed. RAND Corporation, HRS Version D, prepared for the Social Security Administration. Ann Arbor, MI: Inter-university Consortium for Political and Social Research [producer and distributor].

Strategic Human Resource Management and the Older Worker

Jerry W. Hedge

INTRODUCTION

The number of older individuals in the United States is increasing rapidly. Shifts in the age composition of the U. S. labor force mirror those of the population, as members of the baby boom cohort (those born between 1946 and 1964) grow older, and are followed in the labor force by a declining percentage of younger individuals born between 1965 and 1983. The number of older workers will grow substantially in the next several decades. According to the Bureau of Labor Statistics (BLS), 12.9% of the workforce was 55 + in 2000, and by the end of the decade will comprise 16.9% of the workforce. This represents a 46% increase for that age group during the first decade of the 21st century. As the baby boomers swell the ranks of those in their "pre-retirement" years, the average age of the working population will increase substantially.

The aging workforce presents organizations with numerous challenges that will become more pronounced over the next several decades. Definitions of what constitutes "old" or "older" have shifted over the years due to increasing life expectancies and more active and productive lifestyles. Workers over the age of 45 were considered "older" not too many years ago, but now with a large number of the baby boom cohort in the 45 to 64 age group, these workers will become central to the economy as a whole, and more specifically to human resources planning. In addition, recent surveys (e.g., AARP, 2003) have suggested that many of today's older workers may delay retirement, or work well into it. If organizations are to adapt successfully to this workforce transformation, they will need to ensure that their organizational policies and actions are designed in ways that will encourage and promote continued investment in older employees.

ORGANIZATIONAL POLICIES AND PROCEDURES

As organizations grapple with this aging workforce, a strategic human resource management challenge will be to offer new and attractive opportunities that capture the desire of older workers to continue to contribute to organizational life in significant ways. Organizations will need to create structures, policies, and procedures that cultivate an environment supportive of older workers' performance, work attitudes and motivation, and physical and psychological well-being. Unfortunately, most organizations are ill-prepared to meet the challenges associated with older workers.

Corporate Culture

In addition, while HR management systems can be adopted that offer opportunities for challenging job responsibilities for older workers, these systems are influenced by an organization's norms and stereotypes toward older workers (Farr et al., 1998). In turn, an organization's culture affects its policies and practices. Age-related stereotypes abound within organizations, and may influence decisions regarding pay, promotions, assignments, and training opportunities. Indeed, there are probably far more policies and decisions that are implicitly age-based than those which are explicitly so (Marshall, 1998). It is the implicit ones that are the most difficult to detect and change.

Combating Age Stereotyping

False and demeaning stereotypes of older workers are quite common. Research summarized by McCann and Giles (2002) identified widely held perceptions that still persist in society at large, such as the "elderly" are: physically debilitated, cognitively restricted, unable to effectively cope with changes, and overly focused on retirement. In addition, they discussed examples of ageism in the workplace, including ageist jokes and barbs ("over the hill"), and expressed ageist attitudes ("You can't teach an old dog new tricks"). In perhaps no work context is this "old dog/new trick" perception more striking than in the area of training, where numerous studies (e.g., Maurer et al., 2003) have found a persistent belief that older people are not worth training because they will not be around long, learn too slowly, do poorly in the classroom, and are computer illiterate. When applied to a workplace context, these generalizations may play a part in stereotypical expectations by management and co-workers, and may serve as a precursor for ageist communication and discriminatory practices toward older workers.

Changing long-held stereotypes is not an easy process. Indeed, they are the foundation for age discrimination and underutilization of older workers, and dispelling them is an essential part of any organization's efforts to better utilize this population of workers. In part, it requires changing the perspectives and mechanisms on which age stereotypes operate. The myths and stereotypes about aging workers are often so ingrained in an organization's psyche that a strong commitment and follow-through from top management is critical. It is also important that management emphasize reasons other than legal compliance for this initiative, such as the fact that better utilization of older employees makes good business sense (Hedge et al., 2005).

Such widely held societal stereotypes are detrimental to individual and organizational productivity, and while legislation can mandate particular organizational policies, it cannot dictate attitudes or behaviors. If managers do not "buy into" the Age Discrimination in Employment Act (ADEA) law and amendments they are likely to comply only so far as to avoid the potential for lawsuits. Without a commitment to the ADEA and an understanding of the law from an HR perspective, managers may never truly change their decision-making or behaviors that affect older employers (Dennis, 1988).

Although the corporate culture regarding older workers cannot be changed overnight, over time an organization's human resource policies and practices can begin to alter culture, aging stereotypes, norms, and values. Because managers influence an organization's cultural values, they can play a critical role in moving the organization to one that supports age-neutral policies and practices.

Managerial Training

The capabilities and needs of older workers are poorly understood, and managerial training can help to ensure a broader understanding of the older worker. Training can also be an important tool for combating stereotypes and age norms.

The aging process and the workplace. It is an important task of training to identify myths, stereotypes, and age norms, and correct them with the realities of aging. An accurate understanding of the characteristics of older workers and relationships between age and variables such as performance is essential. For example, while research on aging suggests that physical and cognitive abilities do decline with age, these declines tend not to generalize particularly well to deficits in on-the-job performance (see, for example, McEvoy & Cascio, 1989). Managers must also be trained to recognize the potential of bias (both in themselves, and in others), and how to prevent it before it impacts decisions (Liebig, 1988). Thus, these managerial training programs should be based on an assumption that, given comparable qualifications, older workers have the same potential, and should be developed and supported in the same way organizations invest in their younger employees.

Knowledge of legal issues. Managers, at all organizational levels, may struggle when dealing with age issues because they lack clear information concerning the laws related to age discrimination and how these laws are applied in the workplace. Because of the intricacies of these laws, and constantly evolving court interpretations, meeting the requirements of the ADEA can seem difficult, so providing fundamental training on ADEA issues is crucial. An understanding of discrimination law and the various prescriptions for managers that result from the law are essential (see Sterns et al., 2005).

Generational differences. A number of years ago, Rosen and Jerdee (1985) recommended training managers on the value differences between older and younger employees. They noted, for example, that the values of the older members of the workforce were shaped by the post-depression, World War II, and 1950s eras, and may include a strong work ethic, and an emphasis on job and financial security, family solidarity, respect for authority figures, and patriotism. Conversely, Christensen (1990) suggested that younger members of the workforce may have grown up in homes that lacked traditional family structures and authority, may place more value on leisure, and may be more suspicious of authority figures and structures.

Our aim here is not to suggest stereotypic views of different generations, but rather to point out that different generations are influenced by unique forces that have helped to shape them. Zemke, Raines, and Filipczck (2000) argued that as unique as an individual's experiences may be, a generational cohort is a product of its time – economic, social, sociological, demographic. Thus, a generation, to a certain degree, is defined by common tastes, attitudes, and experiences. The three generations that comprise today's workforce, and a fourth generation that is entering it, share a place in history with their generation. Managers need to be aware of these differences; understanding generational differences is critical to making them work for the organization and not against it. Consequently, it is important that training address not only the existence of potential generational conflicts, but processes for dealing with them.

HUMAN RESOURCES MANAGEMENT STRATEGIES AND THE OLDER WORKER

The late-career years present numerous opportunities and challenges for individuals and organizations. A number of authors have suggested that many workers nearing 50 years of age may prefer increased flexibility of schedule and varied work opportunities. Also, middle age and older workers often begin to place more emphasis on intrinsic rewards from work–such as a feeling of accomplishment, of learning and experiencing new things, and of doing something worthwhile–and less of a focus solely on hierarchical advancement in the organization. The result is that they often want to continue working, but on different terms–with more flexible work arrangements, and jobs and work environments more responsive to their interests and needs (Barth et al., 1995; Shultz, 2003).

Thus, the availability of creative career management practices may be particularly important to members of the baby-boom generation who are now beginning to be classified as older workers. As Morris and Venkatesh (2000) suggested, management strategies that treat the "workforce" as a monolithic entity, with no real appreciation of differences across age groups, are likely to fail.

Organizations need to have a better understanding of their workforce profile, including its current age structure, and how that might impact various organizational policies and practices. Yet, a recent survey of senior HR executives found that 66% of respondents reported that their companies had no age profile of their workforce, and thus, a real lack of hard data about how retirements will affect their businesses (Munson, 2003). Indeed, an organization might make very different decisions about its career development practices and succession planning activities for a relatively old workforce compared to a relatively young workforce. At a time when new human resources management software is available for producing and monitoring the demographic profile of a workforce, such data would seem relatively easy for organizations to capture.

Alternative Work Arrangements

A variety of human resource management strategies have been suggested that offer older workers opportunities for flexible work scheduling, developing new knowledge and skills, or utilizing their current skills and abilities set differently.

Flexible Work Scheduling. Work schedule adjustments may be a relatively simple method of keeping older workers motivated and productive. Many work-schedule innovations have been used to address the needs of younger workers, most notably linked to child care issues. Such HR practices may involve small additional monetary costs relative to the payoffs. In fact, Sparks, Faragher, and Cooper (2001) suggested that arrangements with flexible hours can result in lowered job stress, reduced absenteeism and tardiness, improved job satisfaction and productivity, and better work-family balance.

Phased Retirement. The concept underlying the use of phased retirement is that workers can "phase" into retirement gradually rather than work full-time until the day they retire (Paul, 1988). Phased retirement is typically used as an employment option for full-time employees who are several years away from retirement. These employees are permitted to reduce their work hours gradually–through shorter workdays or fewer days per year–to some minimum schedule, until retirement. Penner et al. (2002) noted that phased retirement can be a very attractive option for older workers, although Greller and Stroh (2003) questioned whether such programs amount to anything more than a way to turn veteran employees into a contingent workforce.

Job Transfer and Special Assignments. Job transfers allow workers to gain some variety in work activities, and work with different coworkers. They may include such temporary personnel activities as job rotation, where employees are allowed to move to different jobs with similar levels of responsibility. Some organizations have also adopted strategies where older employees are given special assignments that require a high level of organization-specific knowledge these workers have gathered over the years. These job placement practices can be very useful ways of utilizing older workers, because older employees can be given assignments that match their particular interests and talents. For example, Beehr and Bowling (2002) noted that older workers may make excellent mentors for newer employees or serve as valuable advisors and sounding boards for decision makers in the organization.

Training

Training is another important element of a strategic human resource policy for older workers. Generally, skill obsolescence may be particularly problematic for workers, especially in certain technologically intensive occupations. Keeping skills fresh through training throughout the career life cycle is critical, but some studies have suggested that older workers may be less likely to participate in training programs than younger workers, either because employers may not encourage them to participate or because they may be more hesitant to do so. Indeed, as noted by Farr, Tesluk and Klein (1998), the pace of change of the work environment may set off a negative spiral for older workers related to their self-efficacy around the development of new knowledge and skills (e.g., keeping pace with new work practices, developing new knowledge and skills, and their subsequent job performance).

Pay and Benefits

A re-thinking of HR strategy related to existing pay and benefits can make a big difference to older workers. Certainly, evidence indicates that older workers have different preferences than younger workers in the areas of compensation and benefits (Hale, 1990). Some older employees may be particularly attracted to improved health insurance, or other medical benefits. In fact, they may want to work beyond normal retirement age in order to keep their health insurance coverage. Although older people are healthier than they used to be, certain chronic conditions become more common with age. Consequently, HR professionals who seek older workers to fill part-time and consulting positions (which often do not come with health care benefits) may need to consider adding health care as a major incentive (Wellner, 2002).

It should be mentioned, however, there are certain legal and regulatory difficulties for employers who wish to provide more flexible formal benefit plans to encourage older workers to continue working, and for workers who wish to work part-time. Requirements of uniformity built into the laws governing pensions and benefits make it difficult to set up separate formal programs for older employees. Penner et al., (2002) discuss various alternatives under existing laws, and while there are challenges to be confronted when establishing such systems, these alternatives can be beneficial to both organizations and employees, and certainly worth considering.

Investing in the Older Worker

An organization's personnel practices often are driven by its human resources philosophy. This philosophy may view older workers as "goods" with a limited usefulness, or it may view workers as "assets" that will continue to grow if managed properly. According to Yeatts, Folts, and Knapp (2000), the former embraces a depreciation model approach, where an individual's value to an organization is seen as peaking early in a career, leveling off at mid-career, and steadily declining until retirement. In this model, investment in older workers is viewed as cost-prohibitive. Consequently, older employees would be expected to receive little help in adapting to workplace changes. They even may be offered incentives to leave the organization.

The alternative approach is the conservation model, which views employees of all ages as renewable assets that will yield a high rate of return over long periods of time, if they are adequately educated, trained, and managed. In contrast to the depreciation model, the conservation HR philosophy would be expected to result in age-neutral personnel practices that assist employees in maintaining an acceptable fit with their jobs.

All too often organizations yield to the temptation to "retire" older workers, and replace them with younger, cheaper labor. Because wages and salaries tend to increase up until age 50 or so and then level off, older workers are more costly than younger workers from a straight compensation perspective. Thus, during mergers and periods of corporate downsizing, the potential of saving dollars by reducing the numbers of highly paid older workers has considerable (albeit, short-sighted) appeal. Those who argue in favor of divesting their work force of older employees tend to overlook the costs of recruiting and training new workers. The costs of retraining (rather than retiring) older workers should be balanced against replacement costs, which include recruitment, relocation, and training of new workers. According to Rosen and Jerdee (1985), companies rarely attempt to systematically analyze the costs and benefits of supporting "late career employees."

Simpson, Greller, and Stroh (2002) noted that the only consensus that has emerged across the social science and public policy literature is that employers are reluctant to train older workers; offering them less on-the-job training than their younger co-workers. Rationale for such thinking and acting is of three sorts: (1) *opportunity costs* (experienced older workers are too valuable to allow them "down time" to devote to training); (2) *wage rates* (older workers are usually at the high end of the wage scale, so "down time" for training incurs higher cost in wages than it does for younger persons); and (3) *expected payback period* (compared to younger employees, older employees have fewer remaining years of employment with the firm).

The opportunity cost and wage rates arguments seem to have some legitimacy as far as on-the-job training is concerned. A more comprehensive perspective that includes all work-related educational activity (on-the-job, at-the-job, or off-the-job) does not support this belief. Simpson et al. (2002) suggest that the notion of pay-back period is both arbitrary and unrealistic, noting that few investments produce returns over the entire remainder of a person's career. More realistically, if the pay-back period is the 3 to 5 years that human resource management professionals generally use to evaluate training investments, then a 55-year-old and a 25-year-old both can expect to be employed for the full period.

Certainly, it makes considerable sense for organizations to adopt HR strategies that actively address the needs and desires of older segments of the workforce. In the face of increasing needs for technical, administrative, executive, professional, and service workers in most fields, and with projected shortages of younger people over the next 25 years, organizations should begin to focus more attention on developing and implementing strategies to foster continued utilization of older employees (Hedge et al., 2005).

Career Progression, Career Management, and the Older Worker

The *classic* idea of a career involved working full-time in a primary occupation, often for one employer, until retirement. Much of the body of knowledge in vocational counseling is based on this model, and a large percentage of older workers have spent much of their careers embracing this model (Sterns & Miklos, 1995). The reality of the current work environment is that organizations can no longer promise steady upward mobility or life-long employment. The competitive pressures of the global economy, the switch from a manufacturing to a service-based economy, the rapid pace of technological change, and changing social systems have given rise to a new career model.

Hall and Mirvis (1995) have suggested that careers no longer belong to organizations, but to individuals, and that organizations will be unable to meaningfully plan a person's career. Thus, career ownership takes on new meaning: workers now must assume responsibility for their own career management, with a new strategic focus on adaptability to change, and on self-directed and continuous learning of new skill sets. This new career model generally involves working in multiple occupations, for multiple organizations, and in a more competitive job market. Career success is being defined differently, in terms of adaptability and mobility across occupations and organizations rather than upward mobility within an organization (Howard, 1998).

These ever-changing work conditions require employees to be continually adapting to the demands of novel situations and continually learning new knowledge and skills. Consequently, Farr et al., (1998) suggested that the career of the future will involve periodic cycles of skill learning, mastery, and "reskilling" in order to transition into new positions, jobs, and assignments. Career growth becomes a function of continuous development and use of new skills and abilities that equip individuals to assume new assignments and positions as needs arise. In addition, Hall and Mirvis (1995) see this idea of career flexibility and autonomy as ideal for the older worker because many of the external constraints (e.g., children's education) and internal drives (e.g., advancement) are less likely to dictate behavior. As long as health care and other basic needs are met, the older worker may be freer to pursue more flexible career options than many younger workers.

Sterns and Mikos (1995) suggested that workers have the potential for growth and change at anytime in their work-lives. In addition, an individual's vocational potential, at any point in his/her career, reflects a unique combination of age-related and non-age-related influences–biological and environmental determinants, history-relevant influences which affect most members of a cohort in similar ways, and unique career and life changes. An organization's human resources policies and procedures should reflect an understanding of both these normative and non-normative influences on an individual's development and abilities. In fact, because these multiple factors affect behavioral change during the course of a career, it is important to recognize that individual differences become more, not less pronounced with increasing age. Consequently, the organization's focus should be on a worker's ability and expertise rather than on stereotypic, age-related expectations.

Although the responsibility for career management may be coming to rest more with individual workers, it is in the best interests of organizations to assist with the process, because better career management can lead to less obsolescence and more motivated and satisfied workers (Sterns & Kaplan, 2003). Indeed, it is incumbent on firms to make sure that both younger and older employees are exposed to a variety of challenging work assignments. From an organizational viewpoint, strategic career management programs based on careful HR planning can help organizations keep valued employees.

From a long-term perspective, HR practices can play a critical role in determining the types of experiences individuals accumulate over the course of their careers. By exposing employees to a variety of situations and responsibilities, continual learning of critical knowledge and skills help ensure continued motivation to learn, positive work attitudes, and effective job performance (Hedge et al., in press).

CONCLUSIONS

As the baby boom cohort moves rapidly toward retirement age, concepts such as "productive aging" and "active aging" receive more frequent mention in the popular press. Certainly, there is a growing realization of the integral role these workers will play in the labor force of the future. Older adults want to continue to stay involved in work-life in meaningful roles. They wish to utilize their potential, contribute to their families and communities, and preserve their health and well-being (Feinsod et al., 2005).

In recent years, Federal legislation has been enacted to allow individuals to work beyond traditional retirement ages. Social Security regulations have been re-written to encourage delay of labor force withdrawal, and to reduce financial incentives for early retirement, because of the expected drop in the ratio of workers to retirees when the baby-boom generation retires. In addition, age discrimination laws have been extended to protect workers from mandatory retirement at any age. Nonetheless, many organizations continue to be enamored with downsizing and re-structuring activities, actions that tend to impact older workers disproportionately (Shea, 1991). Corporate policies that for decades encouraged workforce turnover to permit early retirement of older people, and recruitment of younger talent, have been good for employers (and sometimes good for employees as well). But, they run counter to the policies and practices that are needed to cope with future shortages of talent and experience.

In fact, Schetagne (2001) argued convincingly that HR strategies and practices which support the transfer of knowledge and skills between generations of workers are critical, yet suggested that only a small part of knowledge and skills are transmitted from older to younger workers before they leave the organization. Of special concern should be the burgeoning retirement of baby boomers over the next few years, which may exacerbate this loss of institutional knowledge, since they will be leaving in greater numbers and in rapid succession.

Although labor force participation rates drop sharply when individuals enter their early 60s, particularly at ages 62 and 65, a substantial minority do work beyond 65. While there is some evidence suggesting that the trend toward earlier retirement has leveled off, it is still likely that a significant amount of early retirements will continue in the decades ahead. For HRM strategists looking for ways to increase participation rates among individuals who are beyond retirement age, much remains to be learned about why some workers remain at work through their late sixties and into their 70s, and others choose to leave. Certainly, no one standard policy can hope to encourage labor force participation equally for all groups, but a greater understanding of why different groups work beyond the typical age of retirement would help to provide a basis for developing policies targeted toward each group (Williamson & McNamara, 2001).

Regardless of the changes organizations make in the structure and functioning of the workplace of the future, almost certainly the older worker will play a crucial role. Organizations need to make it worthwhile for the older employee to continue to be productive and to gain satisfaction from their work activities, in order for it to result in a positive outcome for both older employees and their organizations (Shea, 1991). For their part, older workers will need to improve their work skills through education and training. The likely result of such commitment might be lifelong retraining so as to combat skill obsolescence (Peterson & Wendt, 1995).

The development and implementation of effective human resource management practices for the aging workforce are critical. The ability of organizations to incorporate innovative hiring strategies, flexible work schedules, training, imaginative compensation arrangements, and new workplace technologies will all contribute to retaining key talent. Organizations that have developed flexible and positive policies and practices for the management of older employees should have a decided marketplace advantage.

REFERENCES

AARP (2003). *Staying ahead of the curve 2003: The AARP working in retirement study*. Washington, D. C.: AARP, Knowledge Management.

Barth, M. C., Mcnaught, W., & Rizzi, P. (1995). Older Americans as workers. In S. A. Bass (Ed.), *Older and active: How Americans over 55 are contributing to society* (pp. 263-294). New Haven, CT: Yale University Press.

Christensen, K. (1990). Bridges over troubled water: How older workers view the labor market. In P. B. Doeringer (Ed.), *Bridges to retirement: Older workers in a changing labor market* (pp. 175-207). Ithaca, NY: ILR Press.

Dennis, H. (1988). Management training. In H. Dennis (Ed.), *Fourteen steps in managing an aging work force* (pp. 141-153). Lexington, MA: Lexington Books.

Farr, J. L., Tesluk, P. E., & Klein, S. R. (1998). Organizational structure of the workplace and the older worker. In K. Schaie & C. Schooler (Eds.), *Impact of work on older adults* (pp. 143-185). New York: Springer Publishing.

Feinsod, R., Davenport, T., & Arthurs, R. (2005). *The business case for workers age 50 +: Planning for tomorrow's talent needs in today's competitive environment*. Washington, D. C.: AARP, Knowledge Management.

Greller, M. M., & Stroh, L. K. (1995). Careers in midlife and beyond: A fallow field in need of sustenance. *Journal of Vocational Behavior, 47*, 232-247.

Hale, N. (1990). *The older worker: Effective strategies for management and human resource development*. San Francisco: Jossey-Bass Publishers.

Hall, D. T., & Mirvis, P. H. (1995). The new career contract: Developing the whole person at midlife and beyond. *Journal of Vocational Psychology, 47*, 269-289.

Hedge, J. W., Borman, W. C., & Lammlein, S. L. (2005). *The aging workforce: Realities, myths, and implications for organizations*. Washington, D. C.: APA Books.

Hedge, J. W., Borman, W. C., & Bourne, M. J. (in press) Developing a system for career management and advancement in the U. S. Navy. *Human Resources Management Review* (Special issue on Large Scale Interventions in Government and DoD).

Howard, A. (1998). Commentary: New careers and older workers. In K. W. Schaie and C. Schooler (Eds.), *Impact of work on older adults* (pp. 235-245). New York: Springer Publishing Company.

Liebig, P. S. (1988). The work force of tomorrow: Its challenge to management. In H. Dennis (Ed.), *Fourteen steps in managing an aging work force* (pp. 3-21). Lexington, MA: Lexington Books.

McCann, R., & Giles, H. (2002). Ageism in the workplace: A communication perspective. In Nelson, T.D. (Ed.), *Ageism: Stereotyping and prejudice against older persons* (pp. 163-199). Cambridge, MA: The MIT Press.

Marshall, V. W. (1998). Commentary: The older worker and organizational restructuring: Beyond systems theory. In K. W. Schaie and C. Schooler (Eds.), *Impact of work on older adults* (pp. 195-206). New York: Springer Publishing Company.

McEvoy, G. M., & Cascio, W. F. (1989). Cumulative evidence of the relationship between employee age and job performance. *Journal of Applied Psychology, 74,* (pp.11-17).

Morris, M. G., & Venkatesh, V. (2000). Age differences in technology adoption decisions: Implications for a changing work force. *Personnel Psychology, 53,* (pp. 375-403).

Munson, H. (2003, March). *Valuing experience: How to motivate and retain mature workers* (Report # 1329-03-RR). New York: The Conference Board.

Paul, C. E. (1988). Implementing alternative work arrangements for older workers. In H. Dennis (Ed.), *Fourteen steps in managing an aging work force* (pp. 113-119). Lexington, MA: Lexington Books.

Penner, R. G., Perun, P., & Steuerle, E. (2002). *Legal and institutional impediments to partial retirement and part-time work by older workers.* Washington, D. C.: The Urban Institute.

Peterson, D., & Wendt, P. A. Training and education of older Americans as workers and volunteers. In S. A. Bass (Ed.), *Older and active: How Americans over 55 are contributing to society* (pp. 217-237). New Haven, CT: Yale University Press.

Robson, W. B. P. (2001, October). *Aging populations and the workforce: Challenges for employers.* Winnipeg, Manitoba: British-North American Committee.

Rosen, B., & Jerdee, T. H. (1985). *Older employees: New roles for valued resources.* Homewood, IL: Dow-Jones-Irwin.

Schetagne, S. (2001). *Building bridges across generations in the workplace: A response to aging of the workforce* (Report # 702). Vancouver, BC: Columbia Foundation.

Schultz, K. S. (2003). Bridge employment: Work after retirement. In G. A. Adams & T. A. Beehr (Eds.), *Retirement: Reasons, processes, and results* (pp. 214-241). New York: Springer Publishing.

Shea, G. F. (1991). *Managing older employees.* San Francisco: Jossey-Bass.

Simpson, P. A., Greller, M. M., & Stroh, L. K. (2001). Variations in human capital investment activity by age. *Journal of Vocational Behavior, 61,* 109-138.

Sparks, K., Faragher, B., & Cooper, C. L. (2001). Well-being and occupational health in the 21st century. *Journal of Occupational and Organizational Psychology, 74,* 489-510.

Sterns, H. L., & Miklos, S. M. (1995). The aging worker in a changing environment: Organizational and individual issues. *Journal of Vocational Behavior, 47,* 248-268.

Sterns, H. L., & Kaplan, J. (2003). Self-management of career and retirement. In G. A. Adams & T. A. Beehr (Eds.), *Retirement: Reasons, processes, and results* (pp. 188-213). New York: Springer Publishing.

Sterns, H. L., Doverspike, D., D., & Lax, G. A. (2005). The Age Discrimination in Employment Act. In F. Landy (Ed.), Employment discrimination litigation: Behavioral, quantitative, and legal perspectives (pp. 256-293). San Francisco: Jossey-Bass.

Wellner, A. S. (2002, March). Tapping a silver mine. *HR Magazine, 47(3)*, (pp. 26-32).

Yeatts, D. L., Folts, W. E., & Knapp, J. (2000). Older workers' adaptation to a changing workplace: Employment issues for the 21st century. *Educational Gerontology, 26*, 566-582.

Zemke, R., Raines, C., & Filipczak, B. (2000). *Generations at work*. New York: American Management Association.

Working in Old Age: Benefits of Participation in the Senior Community Service Employment Program

Ronald H. Aday
Gayle Kehoe

INTRODUCTION

As the American population ages, so too does the workforce. Expectations are that the older worker will become the fastest growing segment of the working population, with workers age 55 and over growing at four times the rate of the overall workforce (Toossi, 2004). More than 23 million persons aged 55 and older were in the labor force in 2004, an increase of nearly one million over the previous 12 months alone (Holbrook, 2004). Recent trends in workforce participation patterns indicate that even as many older workers remain continually employed throughout their adult years, more workers will be likely to transition in and out of the workforce, between retirement and work, and between fulltime and part-time employment (AARP 2004). Among others, this trend will require new opportunities for training, education, workplace accommodations, and career development.

This study examines the impact of employment in the Senior Community Service Employment Program (SCSEP) on the older adults participating in programs in California and Tennessee. SCSEP is a federal program subsidizing the part-time employment of qualifying low-income adults 55 years of age and older in locally based community service employment opportunities. The purpose of the present study was to examine the relation between program participation and several social and mental health indicators of successful aging. This research aids our understanding of the needs of older workers, especially those who have become "discouraged" from seeking needed employment. Furthermore, adding the results of this study of economically disadvantaged older workers to the findings of other categories of older workers will add to our understanding of how remaining productive past normal retirement ages can contribute to successful aging.

REVIEW OF THE LITERATURE

Work is positively related to increased physical and mental health, and paid employment is directly related to life satisfaction (Morrow-Howell, 2000). Work organizes daily life by offering temporal distinctions between work and leisure, grants the worker a sense of purpose, and confers social status (Moore, 1996). The meaning of work is a complex concept encompassing much more than the need to meet economic requirements. Recent research in sociology and psychology stresses the centrality of work to a generalized sense of well being (Gill,

1999; Moore, 1996; Morrow-Howell, 2003) and more specifically to meeting workers' needs for social identity (Gill, 1999) and personal identity (Finch & Robinson, 2003). Older workers expect their occupations to provide them with opportunities to escape isolation (Gill 1999) and build their self-worth (AARP, 2002). Simultaneously, work must be satisfying and meaningful (Sullivan et al., 2003), fulfilling, productive, and contribute to society (AARP, 2002).

Finding employment at older ages is oftentimes difficult due to age discrimination grounded in negative beliefs about older workers (Gross, 2002). Moreover, transitioning from one career to another may require an introduction to technologies that may be unfamiliar to some older workers (Gross, 2002; AARP, 2004; Stein, 2000). Furthermore, when older workers are involuntarily displaced, they experience deeper emotional turmoil than younger workers (Newman, 1995) and may not have the resilience or technological skills to reenter the workforce without assistance (Gross, 2002). An overhaul of current thinking about the aging worker and services to ameliorate barriers to employment are vital (Stein & Rocco, 2001). Combating discouraged workers' negative self-image by improving and updating technology skills (August & Quintero, 2001), renewing a sense of optimism and self-efficacy (Eby & Buch, 1995), and linking potential employees with employers are seen as keys to facilitating the re-entry of older workers into the paid labor force (Gross, 2002).

Commonly circulated myths depict older workers as outdated and incapable of learning new skills, rigid and inflexible, less productive and less motivated than younger workers, and less dependable because of excessive illness (Ray 1991). Unfortunately, these myths are often believed not only by potential employers but also by the older workers themselves (Moore, 1996; Gross, 2002). Younger workers and older supervisors tend to hold more ageist views about older workers than do younger supervisors and older workers (August & Quintero, 2001). Ironically, even as employers should be encouraging retention and recruitment of the older worker as a means of forestalling future worker shortages, AARP (2002) reports a rise in complaints of age discrimination by older workers, noting that age discrimination is now the fastest growing category tracked by the EEOC.

As a result of internalizing negative stereotypes about older workers, emotional or psychological barriers can severely hinder re-employment success. When workers have suffered layoffs and not been able to find immediate reemployment, many begin to doubt their ability to work again, becoming the "discouraged workers" (AARP, 2004; August &

Quintero, 2001; Gross, 2002) in need of assistance to reframe their self-assessed value. For all workers, long periods of unemployment produce a loss of social status and subsequent damage to self-identity that can lead to feelings of worthlessness and insignificance (Moore, 1996). The profound and negative effects of involuntary job loss on older adults' mental health also impacts physical health; however, these effects reverse with reemployment (Gallo et al., 2000).

In contrast to the negative stereotypes of older workers, older workers possess steadier work habits, exhibit less absenteeism and tardiness, demonstrate a greater ability to work unsupervised, and are more responsible and reliable than younger workers (Gross, 2002). Newman (1995) suggests that older workers bring advantages to the job market including well-developed human relations skills and a settled lifestyle. Stein (2000) concludes that older workers are "a rich source of experience, accumulated knowledge, and wisdom."

Yet despite glowing remarks about wisdom and experience and recommendations to promote this valuable resource, the older worker faces challenges in remaining at work and finding new employment when displaced (Moore, 1996). As reported by AARP (2004), if all else is equal, employers hire the younger worker over the older one. Lay-offs (AARP 2004) and unemployment disproportionately affect older workers more than younger workers (Cohen, 2000). Compounding this further, racial minority status contributes to longer unemployment periods and rather than this being a characteristic of the individual, continued unemployment more often reflects physical obstacles to launching a successful job search (Moore, 1996). Furthermore, those who have been displaced and then found new employment had a lowered chance of remaining employed compared to older workers who had never suffered displacement (Chan & Stevens 2001).

Education is the key to re-employment. Better-educated employees have general skills that can transfer to other work environments while less educated workers have fewer transferable skills and remain unemployed longer than better-educated workers (Moore, 1996). A study of human resources personnel referred to in a report given to the Senate Special Committee on Aging (Cohen, 2003), reveals that the most commonly believed disadvantage to hiring older workers is a perception that they possess outdated technological skills. Older workers, on average, receive less than half the training of their younger coworkers and are often most in need of retraining including information technology (Dychtwald et al., 2004).

METHODOLOGY

Data Source

One of the oldest and most widely used programs directed toward older workers is the Senior Community Service Employment Program (SCSEP), which is funded and administered through the U.S. Department of Labor Employment and Training Administration. First authorized in 1965 under the Economic Opportunity Act and implemented in 1973, the program is currently authorized under Title V of the Older Americans Act of 2000. The intention of the program is to help unemployed or underemployed older adults successfully transition into the workforce by assisting them to develop employability skills for today's marketplace while concurrently providing their communities with valuable services until they can move into unsubsidized employment. SCSEP's goal is to transition these workers into unsubsidized employment. Additional to new funding allocations, the revised regulations require local SCSEP delivery systems to be more attuned to providing training that is beneficial to community needs as well as increasing the older adult's future employability.

Program offerings are affected by factors such as size of program, number of participants, funding allocations, and differing needs of participants in rural, urban, and suburban environments. Some programs offer little in the way of pre-employment skills enhancement relying on on-the-job training while others offer extensive classroom experiences. The sites chosen for this study had geographic differences: Modesto, California, is an affluent smaller city, Monterey, California, is more rural, and the Chattanooga, Tennessee site is urban. However, each site had a good reputation for placing older workers into permanent positions. The sites offer training possibilities both on-site and on-the-job. Senior Aides at these sites were placed in non-profit agencies such as senior centers, schools, day-care centers, hospitals, home health agencies, prescription drug counseling programs, Alzheimer's respite programs, and Area Agencies on Aging, to mention a few.

A self-administered questionnaire was used to measure the impact of the three separate SESEP programs on a group of disadvantaged older workers. This research explored the healthy benefits that resulted from older worker participation by focusing on measures of social support, self-esteem, self-efficacy, life satisfaction, empowerment, and job satisfaction. Staff at the 3 sites, chosen for this study, distributed and collected the questionnaires. The questionnaires consisted of mostly closed-ended, but a few open-ended questions provided older workers the opportunity to also voice their opinions on the importance of working in old age.

Study Sample

The mean age of the participants in these programs is 66.0 years of age, with the Modesto and Monterey samples split fairly equally between those 65 and older and those who are younger. The Chattanooga sample is somewhat older with 65.9% of the sample 65 or older. The sample is predominantly female at all three sites (79.5%). This finding is consistent with expectations for SCSEPs nationally (NCOA, 2001). The Modesto site is significantly different from the other two with a much higher proportion of males (38.1%) compared to the other two sites. When looking at the composite sample, the largest portion of the participants are widowed (35.8%), divorced (25.7%), or single (18.3%), while only 20.2% are married. Again, the different sites showed great variability in marital status. The Chattanooga site had the fewest married participants (7%) while the Modesto site had the greatest (35.7%). The racial and ethnic makeup of the three sites, like sex and marital status, varies greatly by site; with the Modesto (57.1%) and Monterey (70.8%) having predominantly Caucasian participants while the Chattanooga site was 80.5% African American. The participants differ greatly in educational attainment between the California sites and the Tennessee site. Both California sites' participants are remarkably well-educated with the majority (61%) of the Modesto participants and nearly half (46.1%) of the Monterey participants having attended college. One third of the Tennessee participants had not finished high school or earned a GED.

STUDY MEASURES

Social Support

A number of questions were also included to identify social support networks that emerged as a result of participating in the older worker program. Questions used to measure perceived and actual supports included asking for a "yes" or "no" response to these questions: "Have you made close friends as a result of the Older Workers Program?" and "Are these friends or acquaintances who you can depend on to help you if you really needed it (i.e., if you were sick or you needed a ride, etc.)?" Two questions attempt to understand the degree of instrumental support given and received: "How frequently have you had to rely on your friends where you work to provide you some type of assistance?" (never, occasionally, pretty often, very frequently) and "How frequently have you provided some type of assistance to a friend you met as a result of your participation in the Older Worker Program?" (never, occasionally, pretty often, very frequently). Other questions measured the emotional depth of these relationships by asking for "yes" or "no" responses about behaviors such as confiding in these friends, feeling personally responsible for their friends' well-being, and feeling emotionally supported by these friendships. Opportunities for strengthening social ties with friends from the program was measured by a set of eight questions that asked participants to check specific activities that they had engaged in outside of the work program such as "go out to eat" or "go shopping together." Responses were summed. These social support variables are also computed into a single, scaled variable used to measure overall social support. Reliability was evaluated using Cronbach's alpha procedure which produced an alpha of .64 indicating a moderately strong internal consistency for this measure.

Self-Esteem

Self-esteem was measured by a modified Rosenberg's Self-Esteem Scale (1965; alpha .77 to .88) using ten statements such as "I am able to do things as well as other people," and "On the whole, I am satisfied with myself." Agreement or disagreement was measured using a seven-point Likert scale with choices ranging from "strongly disagree" (1) to "strongly agree" (7). Negative statements were recoded. An obtained Cronbach's alpha of .84 is consistent with other tests of this assessment tool and indicates strong reliability.

Self-Efficacy

Self-efficacy was measured using a modification of Paulhus' Personal Efficacy Scale, Spheres of Control, Subscale 1 (1983). A series of ten statements such as "It's just chance that makes some people successful" and "I can learn just about anything if I set my mind to it" measured self-efficacy. Agreement or disagreement was measured using a seven-point Likert scale with choices ranging from "strongly disagree" (1) to "strongly agree" (7). Negative statements were recoded. An obtained Cronbach's alpha of .77 is consistent with that obtained by Paulhus (alpha .75).

Life Satisfaction

Life satisfaction was based on Bradburn's Affect Balance Scale (1969). A set of 14 statements indicate overall life satisfaction. Statements included: "These are the best years of my life," "Things seem to be going my way," "At times, I feel I'm being pushed around." Agreement or disagreement was measured using a seven-point Likert scale with choices ranging from "strongly disagree" (1) to "strongly agree" (7). Negative statements were recoded. An obtained Cronbach's alpha of .86 for this scale indicates strong reliability.

Job Satisfaction

Job satisfaction was measured using a modification of Brown's (2004) research. Respondents were asked to agree or disagree with 15 statements such as "I look forward to work each day," "I feel my abilities are valued at work," and "I feel I have a lot of wasted potential." Table 3 lists the statements. Agreement or disagreement was measured using a seven-point Likert scale with choices ranging from "strongly disagree" (1) to "strongly agree" (7). Negative statements were recoded. Reliability was evaluated using Cronbach's alpha procedure. An obtained alpha of .88 indicates a strong internal consistency for this measure.

Participants' Beliefs About the Older Worker

Participants' perceptions of older workers were measured by agreement or disagreement with ten positive or negative statements about older workers. These statements were developed for this study using concepts in common use.

Statements used included, "Older workers make more mistakes than younger workers," "Older workers are more fearful of technology," and "Older workers tend to be more reliable than younger workers." Agreement or disagreement was measured using a seven-point Likert scale with choices ranging from "strongly disagree" (1) to "strongly agree" (7). Negative statements were recoded. An obtained Cronbach's alpha of .59 for this scale indicates modest reliability.

Older Worker Empowerment

Empowerment was measured by requesting the participants to base responses to a series of 15 statements on how much their involvement with SCSEP had changed them. These statements were developed to meet this study's need to measure a broad range of changes within the participants that demonstrate an empowered state of mind. The 15 statements are shown in Table 3. Agreement or disagreement was measured using a seven-point Likert scale with choices ranging from "strongly disagree" (1) to "strongly agree" (7). An obtained Cronbach's alpha coefficient of .95 indicates a very strong measure of internal consistency.

RESULTS

Participants' Beliefs About the Older Worker

Despite major demographic and regional differences in the three study sites, there were no major statistical differences between the three groups. As a whole, the older workers in this study demonstrate a strong sense of awareness of the speciousness of the more common negative stereotypes about older workers. These older workers believe they are not too old to learn (83.2%) and are not more likely to make mistakes (78.6%). They believe they are more motivated (70.3%), more reliable (81.5%), possess the necessary energy to work (64.2%), and can show flexibility (62.2%). Their perceptions about older workers are consistent with known positive attributes of older workers (Gross 2002). Yet, even as these older workers believe in themselves on these attributes, they also recognize that society as a whole may not share these views, with only 40.2% of the sample believing that society does not look down on the older worker. It appears that a majority of these older workers concede that ageism and stereotyping continues to be a concern. A mixed reaction is garnered concerning technology fears, with a third (32.4%) of the sample believing that older adults do fear technology and just under half (45.0%) of the sample not believing older workers fear technology. Overall, when compared to females, males supported a more positive image of the older worker (t = 2.62; p < .03).

A more positive attitude toward oneself as an older worker correlates moderately with a sense of becoming empowered (r = .32; p < .01) (see Table 2). Stronger correlations are seen between positively assessing the values and skills of older workers and having a greater sense of life

satisfaction (r = .40; p < .01), self-esteem (r = .47; p < .01), and self-efficacy (r = .48; p < .01). It would appear that having a higher opinion of
older workers coincides with a better outlook on life and self. Illustrat-
ing this, an 80 year-old woman commented that what she had gained
most from the program was:

> *A feeling that age makes no difference if one is willing to learn,
> new things, new ways. A future is waiting for those who try no mat-
> ter what the age.*

Findings here are consistent with the results from of a large national
sample of employers (Lommel, 2001). Older workers in his study were
also found to have great faith in their motivation and older worker skills.

Health Correlates and Work

The sample is relatively healthy with three-quarters of the group reporting good or excellent health. The majority (68.1%) report maintaining their health status from the previous year and 23.9% believe their
health has improved over the last year. When asked if their health prevented them from engaging in desired activities, well over one-third
(35.5%) admitted that it did. Having fewer physical limitations, as
might be expected, had multiple benefits. As demonstrated in Table 1,
those with fewer limitations in activities had a better sense of life satisfaction (r = .33; p < .01), felt more efficacious (r = .23; p < .05), felt
more empowered by their work experience (r = .26; p < .05), and stayed
on the job longer (r = .22; p < .01). Also, as would be expected, a lack of
limitations correlated rather highly with better overall health (r = .50; p <
.01). Self-rated health status correlates somewhat with life satisfaction
(r = .23; p < .05) but health limiting physical activities is the stronger
correlate to life satisfaction. It would seem that physical limitations impact participants' perceptions of benefit more than their self-rated
health status.

As a result of participating in this program, the majority (68.3%) of
the participants believe their mental health has improved. No one felt
that his or her mental health had deteriorated because of his or her involvement with the program. Participants who felt that program involvement had improved their mental health exhibit a somewhat more
positive attitude about themselves as older workers (r = .21; p < .05).
Improved mental health also correlates moderately with gaining a

greater sense of empowerment ($r = .37$; $p < .01$). Improved mental health did not significantly correlate with any other variables tested.

The older workers participating in this survey were overwhelmingly positive about their overall experience with their Senior Aides program. The majority (92.5%) of these workers are satisfied or very satisfied with their experiences. As might be expected, health status is mildly related to program satisfaction ($r = .19$; $p < .05$) indicating that better health has a positive, if weak, relationship to higher satisfaction. Not surprisingly, those who were most satisfied with the program were also most satisfied with the jobs they held. This relationship remained regardless of how long the participants had held their jobs. Also shown in Table 1, program satisfaction positively correlated to some extent with all the major variables. The more satisfied the participants were with the Senior Aides program the higher their self-esteem ($r = .22$; $p < .05$), the better their feelings about themselves as older workers ($r = .26$; $p < .05$), the higher their satisfaction with their jobs ($r = .34$; $p < .01$), the more empowered they felt ($r = .33$; $p < .01$), the more self-efficacious ($r = .28$; $p < .01$), and the greater their sense of life satisfaction ($r = .43$; $p < .01$).

Older Worker Empowerment

Prior to seeking out the SCSEP program, the majority of participants in this study were currently not in the work force. About one-half (51%)

TABLE 1. Correlations Between Key Variables

Correlates	1	2	3	4	5	6	7	8	9	10
1. Empowerment	---									
2. Job Satisfaction	.41**	---								
3. Self-Esteem	.45**	.52**	---							
4. Life Satisfaction	.64**	.56**	.69**	---						
5. Self-Efficacy	.47**	.60**	.73**	.71**	---					
6. Ageism	.32**	.17	.47**	.40**	.48*	---				
7. Social Support	.24*	.11	.06	.14	.09	.10	---			
8. Health	.18	.03	.12	.23*	-.15	.13	.17	---		
9. Health Limits	.26*	.10	.15	.33**	.23*	.11	-.06	50**	---	
10. Length of Employment	.09	.02	-.07	-.09	-.07	.10	.15	.06	.22*	---

(n = 113) * Correlation is significant at the .05 level
** Correlation is significant at the .01 level

indicated they had been unemployed (laid off) anywhere from several months to more than a year. This is consistent with previous research that has supported the view that it is more difficult for older workers to find reemployment (Chan & Stevens, 2001). Another 8% considered themselves to be underemployed. About one-third (36%) were voluntarily unemployed preceding their program involvement and 4% indicated they had never worked outside the home prior to their SCSEP experience.

Empowering discouraged older workers combines changing attitudes and improving skills. A large part of becoming employable for older workers comes from regaining faith in their worthiness to compete for jobs with other workers (Gross, 2002). Although there was no gender differences on this variable, Senior Aides, as a whole, report improvements in the psychological components of the empowerment variable (see Table 2). The majority (72.2%) of Senior Aides like themselves more now, have more self-respect (80%), look forward to their futures more

TABLE 2. Social Supports Derived from Involvement in the Older Worker Program (N = 113)

Friendship Variables	
Friendship Network	
Made close friends through SCSEP	88.0
Feel personally responsible for friends	53.8
Friends will help when needed	82.0
Friends provide emotional support	81.0
Confide in or ask advice of friends	53.8
Engage in activities outside of work	51.9
Enjoy working with coworkers	84.8
Social skills have improved	73.1
Friendship Activities	
Attend church	23.9
Go out to eat	29.2
Play cards/watch TV	11.5
Go shopping	22.1
Visit on phone frequently	29.2
Participate in social events	31.0
Rely on Friends for Assistance	
Never	25.7
Occasionally	60.0
Pretty Often	10.5
Very frequently	3.8
Provide Assistance to Friends	
Never	9.6
Occasionally	60.6
Pretty often	21.2
Very frequently	8.7

TABLE 3. Frequencies for Job Satisfaction and Empowerment (N = 113)

Statements:	% Agreeing
Job Satisfaction	
1. I find my work boring.	14.5
2. I think I'm a perfect fit for my job.	78.4
3. I look forward to work each day.	78.4
4. I frequently feel overwhelmed at work.	35.5
5. I find it hard to commit to my job.	18.6
6. I feel I have wasted potential.	35.8
7. I feel my abilities are valued at work.	78.4
8. I finish each day satisfied with my achievements.	80.2
9. Most of the things I do at work are interesting.	79.5
10. I enjoy working with my co-workers.	84.8
11. I feel proud when I tell others about my work.	81.3
12. I wouldn't change this job for anything.	58.6
13. This job frustrates me on a daily basis.	18.3
14. This job gives me a chance to be somebody.	63.7
15. I feel very productive in my job.	77.1
Empowerment:	
1. My social skills have improved.	73.1
2. I like myself more now.	72.2
3. I have more confidence in my abilities.	80.4
4. I look forward to the future more.	84.1
5. I'm less afraid of failing now.	69.2
6. I feel more confident I can find and keep a job.	76.9
7. My work skills have improved significantly.	68.5
8. I feel more comfortable working in groups.	71.0
9. I feel more in control of my life.	76.9
10. I find I have more self respect.	80.0
11. I'm less afraid of looking for a job.	63.5
12. My computer skills have improved.	51.0
13. I worry less about the future.	72.9
14. I feel less depressed.	74.3
15. I feel better about living independently.	74.1

(84.1%), and feel that they are more in control of their own lives (76.9%). As well as empowering older workers with renewed self-worth and confidence in their futures, participation in Senior Aides has improved these adults' social skills (73.1%).

Empowerment also includes a sense of confidence that comes from having mastered new skills. Most (68.5%) saw marked improvements in their job skills because of their involvement with SCSEP. A large majority (80.4%) of the Senior Aides felt that their confidence in their skills had been bolstered by their work experience. As is shown in Table 1, increased empowerment has a moderately strong association with increased self-esteem (r = .449; p < .05). Several participants noted they

TABLE 4. Social Supports Derived from Involvement in the Older Worker Program

Friendship Variables	Total Sample % Total	Modesto %	Monterey %	Chattanooga %
Friendship Network				
Made close friends through SCSEP	**88.0**	87.8	80.8	92.7
Feel personally responsible for friends	**53.8**	65.9	40.0	50.0
Friends will help when needed	**82.0**	79.5	82.6	84.2
Friends provide emotional support	**81.0**	85.4	76.0	79.5
Confide in or ask advice of friends	**53.8**	48.8	40.0	67.5
Engage in activities outside of work	**51.9**	56.1	41.7	53.7
Enjoy working with coworkers	**84.8**	93.0	80.8	79.1
Social skills have improved	**73.1**	68.3	73.1	78.0
Friendship Activities				
Attend church	**23.9**	20.9	7.7	36.4
Engage in volunteer work	**16.8**	20.9	15.4	13.6
Go out to eat	**29.2**	30.2	30.8	27.3
Play cards/watch TV	**11.5**	11.6	7.7	13.6
Go shopping	**22.1**	18.6	19.2	27.3
Visit on phone frequently	**29.2**	16.3	30.8	40.9
Participate in social events	**31.0**	46.5	19.2	22.7
Rely on Friends for Assistance				
Never	**25.7**	20.0	26.9	30.8
Occasionally	**60.0**	62.5	61.5	56.4
Pretty Often	**10.5**	15.0	11.5	5.1
Very frequently	**3.8**	2.5	0.0	7.7
Provide Assistance to Friends				
Never	**9.6**	9.8	8.0	10.5
Occasionally	**60.6**	56.1	72.0	57.9
Pretty often	**21.2**	19.5	16.0	26.3
Very frequently	**8.7**	14.6	4.0	5.3

had gained new knowledge or skills from their participation in the program and attributed the positive impact of educational and work experiences encountered in these programs as instrumental in creating higher self-esteem.

> *I'm proud of what I've learned. I have a lot more confidence in myself.*

> *It has given me a sense of worth–learning to do work that prior to my involvement with CSE I was unable to do.*

As well as mastering new skills, older workers must learn to be confident about their own "employability." As is demonstrated in Table 2,

TABLE 5. Frequencies for Job Satisfaction and Empowerment (n = 113)

Statements:	Combined Sites	Modesto	Monterey	Chattanooga
Job Satisfaction				
1. I find my work boring.	14.5	19.5	7.7	14.0
2. I think I'm a perfect fit for my job.	78.4	79.1	80.8	76.2
3. I look forward to work each day.	78.4	85.7	73.1	74.4
4. I frequently feel overwhelmed at work.	35.5	30.2	16.0	53.8
5. I find it hard to commit to my job.	18.6	25.6	11.5	15.9
6. I feel I have wasted potential.	35.8	42.9	26.9	34.1
7. I feel my abilities are valued at work.	78.4	88.4	65.4	76.2
8. I finish each day satisfied with my achievements.	80.2	87.8	69.2	79.5
9. Most of the things I do at work are interesting.	79.5	88.4	73.1	74.4
10. I enjoy working with my co-workers.	84.8	93.0	80.8	79.1
11. I feel proud when I tell others about my work.	81.3	85.7	80.8	77.3
12. I wouldn't change this job for anything.	58.6	69.0	53.8	51.2
13. This job frustrates me on a daily basis.	18.3	20.9	7.7	22.5
14. This job gives me a chance to be somebody.	63.7	72.1	50.0	63.6
15. I feel very productive in my job.	77.1	85.7	61.5	78.0
Empowerment:				
1. My social skills have improved.	73.1	68.3	73.1	78.0
2. I like myself more now.	72.2	73.8	61.5	77.5
3. I have more confidence in my abilities.	80.4	75.6	80.8	85.0
4. I look forward to the future more.	84.1	85.4	76.9	87.5
5. I'm less afraid of failing now.	69.2	77.5	73.1	58.5
6. I feel more confident I can find and keep a job.	76.9	73.2	69.2	85.4
7. My work skills have improved significantly.	68.5	65.9	61.5	75.6
8. I feel more comfortable working in groups.	71.0	78.0	53.8	75.0
9. I feel more in control of my life.	76.9	76.2	69.2	82.5
10. I find I have more self respect.	80.0	78.0	72.0	87.2
11. I'm less afraid of looking for a job.	63.5	63.4	64.0	63.2
12. My computer skills have improved.	51.0	56.4	53.8	43.2
13. I worry less about the future.	72.9	70.7	65.4	80.0
14. I feel less depressed.	74.3	72.5	76.0	75.0
15. I feel better about living independently.	74.1	70.7	73.1	78.0

Header: Percent in Agreement

these workers indicate that they feel more confident that they can find employment and that they can remain employed (76.9%) even though fewer admitted to having lost their fear of looking for a job (63.5%). Despite their fears of looking for a job, slightly more (69.2%) workers report feeling less afraid of failing now than they had before they became Senior Aides. A 58-year-old woman remarked, "I am now able to learn skills without being nervous in a work environment."

Others gave credit to their participation in this program for renewing their sense of self-worth and giving them a positive opinion of the value of their skills.

> *[The program has given me] the opportunity to prove that I can still be a person on whom you can rely and on whom you can count. Everyday I learn something new. I am grateful for the experience of working with people that know what they are doing. Even as a senior there is still the feeling of being treated with respect and dignity. It creates a good feeling in a world where we always seem to be in too much of a hurry.*

> *It has given me new goals and enables me to use my skills and potential to help other seniors.*

> *I now have confidence in knowing that I can still do a job and know I can do well.*

As one might expect, increased empowerment with the social skills to interact with others comfortably, confidence in themselves as able workers, and the self-assurance that they are employable strongly correlates with higher life satisfaction ($r = .64$; $p < .01$). One participant summed up her gains from the program in a global statement of empowerment that might speak for many of the participants in these older worker programs when she stated, "Working has made me realize that I have something to contribute in spite of my age."

Enhanced Social Networks

One important aspect of the overall success of community service employment for older workers is the emotional benefits of a broadened social network. The need to connect and interact with supportive people while workers reconnect with the workforce is elemental to emotional well-being (Eby & Buch, 1995). Moreover, social support has been shown to increase job seeking behavior in older adults (Adams & Rau, 2004). Table 3 illustrates how well these programs are meeting workers' social needs by expanding their friendship circles with an emotionally and instrumentally supportive social safety net. The vast majority of the participants felt they had made close friends through the program (88%) and believed they could rely on these friends if they needed help (82%). Slightly more than one-quarter (25.7%) of the respondents had never asked for help from these friends. A much higher percentage (90.5%) had at least occasionally assisted a friend in the program. The majority of the respondents reported gaining a sense of emotional support from these friendships (81%). Slightly more than half of the participants engaged in outside activities with these friends, most frequently by participating in social events together (31%), going out to eat (29.2%), and visiting on the phone (29.2%). A 67-year-old woman noted that what she valued most from her program experience was the "companionship of coworkers." A 63-year-old man valued most the "opportunity to share my feelings with other coworkers."

Length of employment with the SCSEP program did not significantly impact the development of friendships or the sense of well-being generated by these friendships. Having made close friends through the program is moderately correlated with engaging in outside activities ($r = .31$; $p < .01$) and strongly associated with feeling as if they could depend on these friends for assistance ($r = .54$; $p < .01$). Feeling emotionally supported by these friends is moderately correlated to confiding in them ($r = .37$; $p < .01$) and feeling personally responsible for their well-being ($r = .43$; $p < .01$) regardless of whether or not they had offered or accepted help from their friends or even engaged in activities outside of the workplace. A negative but weak relationship is noted between educational level and making close friendships ($r = 2.19$; $p < .05$). In addition, the more years of school completed, the less likely were the participants to confide in their work-related friends ($r = -.34$; $p < .01$). A moderately strong correlation was found between gaining emotional support from their SCSEP friendships and feeling personally responsible for these friends' well being ($r = .43$: $p < .01$). Some correlation is also seen between satisfaction in the program and a sense of being personally responsible for friends' well-being ($r = .28$; $p < .01$).

CONCLUSIONS

Given that productive activity through work or volunteer work is vital to mental and physical health and a sense of well-being for older adults (Morrow-Howell, 2000); the importance of programming to return older adults to satisfying work should not be minimized. Numerous studies indicate that older adults who are embedded in supportive social networks tend to enjoy better positive emotional affect (Patrick et al., 2001), physical health (Bosworth & Schaie, 1997) and mental health (Chou & Chi, 2001; Krause, 2001) than senior adults who do not maintain close ties with others. Being a viable part of a social network of friends has been established as one of the most dependable predictors of health and longevity (Krause, 2001; Seeman et al., 1993).

Not only are these workers very satisfied with the programs they are involved in and with the jobs they hold through this program, but they are also reporting progress in many areas considered crucial toward re-defining themselves as worthy competitors in the labor force. Results from this study suggest that these workers, while supported by a strong social network, are benefiting from increased self-esteem, greater confidence in their skills, a heightened belief in their ability to find and keep employment, and a greater sense of being in control of their own lives. Like other older adults who need their work to be meaningful (Sullivan et al., 2003) and contribute to society (AARP, 2002), many of those participating in this program have found satisfaction in helping others. Participants are enjoying a renewed sense of purpose through participation in the program.

In particular, one finding from this study seems to emphasize the positive nature of SCSEP: length of involvement in the SCSEP program has no bearing on participants' perceptions of program satisfaction, empowerment, job satisfaction, or friendship development. This suggests that even short-term involvement in program activities fuels positive results. In their study on the enhanced well-being of older adults who engage in volunteer activities, Morrow-Howell et al., (2003), found a similar lack of connection between hours invested and positive outcomes, which they attribute to the benefits of engagement. Some of the positive outcomes from this study are likely to result from engaging older workers' previously unmet needs for meaningful activity.

Despite the glowing reports given by the overwhelming majority of workers in this study, an underlying resentment, or perhaps frustration, emerges when the participants relate their experiences as older workers trying to reenter the workforce. Insights gleaned from this study suggest that many of the older workers are experiencing "structural lag" (Riley, 1987) between their needs and outdated social structures. Several of the workers seemed to have intuitively arrived at this rationale when they question the futility of searching for outside employment believing they will encounter potential employers who see them as undesirable "old-sters" and will deny them employment. Further defining the issue of a structural lag between the needs of older workers and current organizational structure can be seen in the comment made by the older worker who felt that employers would not offer him a part time position. This is indicative of the lag between older workers' desire for modified work schedules (AARP, 2004) and a homogenous employment model consisting of a full-time, permanent workforce that many older workers perceive exists.

In addition, structural lag is reflected in the differences between participants' beliefs about themselves as older workers and the beliefs held by potential employers. Even as these older workers acknowledge a possible shortage of employment opportunities, they look forward to a future when "people can appreciate the skills, knowledge, and experience that seniors have to offer and . . . [are] trying to make our society aware of that fact." The positive attitude held by most of the participants about the work skills and workplace behaviors of older workers denotes a confident self-image juxtaposed against the real world situation of an oftentimes ageist society. Older workers must contend with employers who may believe myths about older workers being outdated and incapable of learning new skills, rigid and inflexible, less productive and less motivated than younger workers, and less dependable because of excessive illness (Ray, 1991; Gross, 2002). Unfortunately, these myths are often believed not only by potential employers but by the older workers themselves (Moore, 1996; Gross, 2002). Yet the older workers in these programs overwhelmingly refused to accept the ageist stereotype of the older worker. Consequently, it may be assumed that programs empowering older workers may also help to negate perceptions of these damaging ageist stereotypes.

Results from this study indicate that these SCSEP programs are successfully meeting many of the needs of the older adults participating in these programs. Prior research (Gallo et al., 2000) indicates some of the negative effects of job loss are reversible through reemployment, and indeed participation in this program has resulted in self-reported improvements in mental health and a high degree of overall life satisfaction. Participation in this program has led to participants' belief in growth in empowerment, self-esteem, self-efficacy, and a concurrently greater sense of satisfaction with their personal and work lives. Impressive strides have been taken in empowering these older workers with skills and knowledge to help them overcome feelings of ageism and low self-esteem.

REFERENCES

AARP. (2002). *Staying ahead of the curve: The AARP work and career study.* Washington, D.C.: AARP.

AARP. (2004). *Aging and work: A view from the United States.* Washington, D.C.: AARP.

Adams, G., & Rau, B. (2004). Job seeking among retirees seeking bridge employment. *Personnel Psychology*, 57, 719-735.

Ardelt, M. (2000). Still stable after all these years: Personality stability theory revisited. *Social Psychology Quarterly*, 63, 392-405.

August, R. A., & Quintero, V. C. (2001). The role of opportunity structures in older women workers' careers. *Journal of Employment Counseling*, 38, 62-82.

Bosworth, H. B., & Schaie, K. W. (1997). The relationship of social environment, social networks, and health outcomes in the Seattle longitudinal study: Two analytical approaches. *The Journals of Gerontology, Series B*, 52, 197-208.

Chan, S., & Stevens, A. H. (2001). Job loss and employment patterns of older workers. *Journal of Labor Economics*, 19, 484-521.

Chou, K., & Chi, I. (2001). Stressful life events and depressive symptoms: Social support and sense of control as mediators and moderators. *International Journal of Aging and Human Development*, 52, 155-172.

Cohen, D. J. (2003). Older Workers. *Senate Special Committee on Aging, Forum on the Older Worker*. Washington, D.C.: U.S. Government Printing Office.

Dendinger, V. M., Adams G. A., & Jacobson, J. D. (2005). Reasons for working and their relationship to retirement attitudes, job satisfaction and occupational self-efficacy of bridge employees. *International Journal of Aging and Human Development*, 61, 21-35.

Doeringer, P., Sum, A., & Tekla, D. (2002). Devolution of employment and training policy: The case of older workers. *Journal of Aging & Social Policy*, 14, 37-60.

Dychtwald, K., Erickson, T., & Morison, B. (2004). It's time to retire retirement. *Public Policy & Aging Report*, 14, 1, 23-27.

Eby, L. T., & Buch, K. (1995). Job loss as career growth: responses to involuntary career transitions. *The Career Development Quarterly*, 44, 26-35.

Finch, J., & Robinson, M. (2003). "Aging and late-onset disability: addressing workplace accommodation." *Journal of Rehabilitation*, 69(2): 38-42.

Gallo, W. T., Bradley, E. H., Siegel, M., & Kasl, S. V. (2000). Health effects of involuntary job loss among Older workers: Findings form the health and retirement survey. *Journal of Gerontology: Series B, Psychological Sciences and Social Sciences*, 55B, 131-140

Gill, F. (1999). The meaning of work: lessons from sociology, psychology, and political theory. *The Journal of Socio-Economics*, 28, 725-747.

Gross, D. (2002). *Different needs, different strategies: A manual for training low-income, older workers*. United States Department of Labor, Employment and Training Administration. Florida Policy Exchange Center on Aging.

Holbrook, D. C. (2004). Breaking the silver ceiling: A new generation of older Americans redefining the new rules of the workplace. Senate Special Committee on Aging. Washington, D.C.

Krause, N. (2001). Social support. In R. H. Binstock & L. K. George (Eds.), *Handbook of aging and the social sciences*, pp. 272-294. New York: Academic Press

Moore, T S. 1996. *The Disposable workforce: Worker displacement and employment instability in America*. New York: Aldine De Gruyter.

Morrow-Howell, Nancy. 2000. *Productive engagement of older adults: Effects on well-being* report. St. Louis Center for Social Development, Washington University.

Morrow-Howell, N., Hinterlong, J., Rozario, J. P., & Tang, F. (2003). Effects of volunteerism on the well-being of older adults. *Journal of Gerontology, Social Sciences,* 58B, S137-S145.

Newman, B. K. (1995). Career change for those over 40: Critical issues and insights. *The Career Development Quarterly,* 44, 64-67.

Patrick, J. H., Cottrell, L. E., & Barnes, K. A. (2001). Gender, emotional support, and well-being among the rural elderly. *Sex Roles,* 45, 15-29.

Ray, S. N. 1999. *Job Hunting After 50: Strategies for Success.* New York: John Wiley and Sons.

Riley, Matilda White. (1987). On the Significance of Age in Sociology. *American Sociological Review,* 52: 1-14.

Seeman, T. E., Berkman, L. F., Kohout, F., Lacroix, A., Glynn, R., & Blazer, D. (1993). Intercommunity variations in the association between social ties and mortality in the elderly: A comparative analysis of three communities. *Annals of Epidemiology,* 3(4), 325-335.

Stein, D. (2000). "The New Meaning of Retirement." ERIC Clearinghouse on Adult Career *and Vocational Education, Columbus, Ohio.*

Sullivan, S. E., Martin, D. F., Carden, W. A., & Mainiero, L. A. (2002). The road less traveled: How to manage the recycle career stage. *Journal of Leadership & Organizational Studies,* 10(2), 34-42.

Sullivan, S. (1999). The changing nature of careers: A review and research agenda. *Journal of Management,* 25: 457-459.

Toossi, M. (2004). Labor force projections to 2012: The graying of the U.S. workforce. *Monthly Labor Review.* U.S. Bureau of Labor Statistics.

Wiatrowski, W. J. (2001). Changing Retirement Ages: Ups and Downs. *Monthly Labor Review.* U.S. Bureau of Labor Statistics.

Making Sense of a Mess:
Phased Retirement Policies and Practices in the United States

Erin L. Kelly
Eric C. Dahlin
Donna Spencer
Phyllis Moen

INTRODUCTION

In the next few decades, the United States will face new challenges and new opportunities because of its aging population and aging workforce. Between 1950 and 2000, the number of Americans aged 65 and older nearly tripled, while the population as a whole doubled. The aging Baby Boom generation and increased longevity mean these trends are likely to continue. In 2000, there were 18.4 million workers over age 55 in the labor force and by 2015 the Bureau of Labor Statistics projects an increase to 31.9 million (General Accounting Office, 2001). In 1990, older workers (ages 55+) comprised 11.9% of the workforce, while fully 20% of the workforce is expected to be over age 55 by 2015 (General Accounting Office, 2001).

How will retirement unfold for today's older workers and the older workers of tomorrow?[1] Most research treats the retirement status passage as an individual event, but this important transition occurs within organizational, public policy, and socio-economic environments that constrain some options and open others. Yet these environments are themselves in flux, producing ambiguities, contradictions, and mismatches for workers making this exit from the workforce. In this article, we investigate the emerging practice of phased retirement and the shifting public policies that surround phased retirement programs in order to assess the prospects for this new alternative path from employment to retirement.

Retirement was institutionalized in the United States as a one-way, one-time exit from full-time work to full-time leisure with the passage of the Social Security Act and related legislation, along with the boom economy of the middle of the 20th century. But the retirement transition is becoming increasingly varied and ambiguous. Several forces are contributing to the growing disarray around retirement: the aging workforce, increasing longevity, technological advances, and especially the dismantling of pensions in the wake of the globalization and digitalization of the U.S. economy (Moen & Altobelli, 2006). In addition to (and in response to) these structural changes, older workers express an interest in managing this phase of life differently. According to the 1996 Health and Retirement Survey, "56 percent of persons age 55 to 65 would prefer to gradually reduce their hours of work as they age." (General Accounting Office, 2001: 27). As people's experiences of and desires for retirement are changing, are organizational policies and the legal environment that guides them changing as well?

Studying phased retirement allows us to examine processes of human resources policy change: how companies and other organizations that want to be more flexible and creative figure out what they can do, and, also, how new employment practices become common, and even expected, over time. In other words, phased retirement provides a strategic research site (Merton, 1968) for investigating organizational change. We investigate four questions. First, what is phased retirement and why might it benefit older workers and the organizations that employ them? Second, how common is phased retirement in the United States today? Third, what are the barriers to phased retirement programs? In particular, we detail how organizational policies and practices are constrained by multiple federal laws and regulations and by the confusion that ensues from these laws and regulations. Fourth, what are the prospects for expanding access to phased retirement?

We draw on the existing literature and our own research into the development and diffusion of new employment policies and practices to assess the current situation for phased retirement and to evaluate what may be on the horizon. Previous research emphasizes the importance of investigating how employers–and the human resources and benefits specialists who act on behalf of their organizations–make sense of their options and interpret the various laws and regulations that shape organizational policies and practices. We recognize that employment law in the U.S. is not simply "out there," with clear rules that practitioners apply in obvious ways. Instead, employment law develops in significant ways *after* legislation is passed, in regulatory agencies, the courts, and professional circles. Government actors and practitioners alike participate in a collective, iterative process of defining what, exactly, counts as compliance with employment laws (Edelman, 1990, 1992, 2005; Kelly & Dobbin, 1999; Kelly, 2003). This means that the laws and regulations surrounding any employment policy or practice are a moving target, and that professional associations and practitioner groups are active agents in shaping what that target looks like.

These dynamics are particularly important to understand when an employment practice is regulated by numerous laws and regulations that intersect in confusing and potentially contradictory ways–as is the case for phased retirement. The title of this article, "Making Sense of a Mess," was inspired by the sense of confusion and frustration that we have heard from human resources managers, benefits specialists, and work-life advocates who are interested in promoting phased retirement but unsure what is possible under current law. We see this confusion as one of the primary barriers to the spread of phased retirement policies and programs, as we describe below, and we hope that this article provides some clarity to scholars, practitioners, and advocates interested in phased retirement.

WHAT IS PHASED RETIREMENT AND WHY IS IT IMPORTANT?

Although phased retirement is sometimes defined quite broadly (e.g., U.S. Department of Labor, 2000), we use the term to refer to the voluntary movement of an older worker from a "full-time" schedule (40 hours per week or more) to a "part-time" schedule (less than 40 hours per week) with the same employer (Hutchens & Grace-Martin, 2004; Pearce et al., 2005). An ideal phased retirement program allows employees to offset the reductions in their salary as a result of their reduced hours by drawing on a portion of their pension benefits.

Of course, there are a variety of work arrangements that allow older people to continue to be engaged in meaningful work and social relationships (Moen & Fields, 2002; Moen et al., 2000). In addition to the phased retirement arrangements defined above, some older workers take part-time "bridge jobs" with a new employer. These jobs are viewed as a "bridge" between a career job and full-time retirement (Ruhm, 1990; Stein, 2000). Others become self-employed in the hopes of gaining more flexibility regarding when, how much, and with whom they work. Some older Americans choose to retire from paid work but pursue volunteer work that involves a serious time commitment and utilizes at least some of the skills from their previous careers (Moen 2003a, b; Freedman, 1999). Finally, some older workers find it useful to retire from their career job and then get rehired–by their same employer–as a contract worker who works 1,000 hours or less per year and supplements his or her wages with pension benefits (Penner et al., 2002; Willett, 2005). These "retire-rehire" arrangements are a common "work around" solution to current regulations and pension plan rules that require workers to retire before they can start drawing any pension benefits. These arrangements may be legally questionable, however. The IRS recently commented that these arrangements constituted a "sham transaction," although the regulatory agency did not immediately call for them to be discontinued (Pearce et al., 2005).

Why should we care about phased retirement? There are several reasons that phased retirement options that are truly voluntary are attractive to employees and employers alike. First, many older workers are interested in continuing to work–but working differently–in their 50s, 60s, and beyond. In addition to the national data cited above, the Retirement and Well-Being Study (a longitudinal survey of older workers and retirees in upstate New York) found that 35% of workers in their 50s and 60s preferred to work less, compared with 19% who wanted full retirement (Moen et al, 2000; Moen & Altobelli, 2006). When interviewed two years later, the researchers found that many of the older workers who were interested in reduced work schedules had fully retired instead largely because they found themselves confronted with two options: continuing working at least full-time and often more, or retiring completely (Moen & Altobelli 2006). Of course, many older workers will want to continue working full time and phased retirement programs should not be used to subtly push these employees out. Many older workers will also need to work full-time to keep their salaries up and/or continue having access to essential benefits such as health insurance. But voluntary phased retirement programs could help those older employees who would prefer to continue working, but work in a new way.

Second, phased retirement programs could benefit workers' health and well-being. Research finds that continued engagement in paid or unpaid work in later years is positively associated with subjective well-being (Kim & Moen, 2001, 2002; Moen & Fields, 2002; Moen et al 2000).[2]

Third, organizations could benefit from phased retirement because these programs may help them manage the loss of institutional memory and expertise that will come with the retirement of members of the large Baby Boom generation who now constitute about 40% of the workforce (U.S. Department of Labor, 1999).

Finally, because phased retirement represents a change in existing organizational policies and practices, this initiative may help to create a more flexible work environment for workers of all ages and life stages. Phased retirement programs may challenge the taken-for-granted and ingrained assumptions, present in many workplaces, that valuable work requires a full-time schedule. Phased retirement programs may help shake the "career mystique" that assumes dedicated workers will work full-time from early adulthood straight through to full-fledged retirement and that part-time workers (of any age) are not truly dedicated or valuable (Moen, 2005; Moen & Roehling, 2005).

HOW COMMON IS PHASED RETIREMENT TODAY?

The prevalence of phased retirement is surprisingly hard to document, and depends on whether one is interested in *formal policies*, in *informal practices* currently in place in organizations, or in employers' stated *willingness to try out* phased retirement under certain conditions. A 1999 survey of almost 600 large employers found that 16% reported having a *formal phased retirement program* in place, and that another 28% of these organizations were interested in phased retirement (Watson Wyatt, 1999). Although these figures are commonly cited in the management press, the Watson Wyatt survey was based on a non-random sample of very large organizations and so the representativeness of the sample (and hence the findings) is questionable.

The most representative study conducted thus far surveyed a national sample of 950 work establishments in 2001 and 2002 (Hutchens, 2003; Hutchens & Grace-Martin, 2004).[3] The Hutchens survey asked respondents (generally human resources managers) to:

> Think of a secure full-time white-collar employee who is age 55 or over. One day that person comes to you and says that at some point in the next few years he/she may want to shift to a part-time work schedule at this establishment. Could this person's request to shift to part-time employment be worked out in a way that would be acceptable to your establishment?

Sixty-seven percent of the respondents answered "yes," an additional 15% answered "in some cases," 14% said "no," and 4% said they did not know.

Note that the survey question used here to assess the prevalence of phased retirement is quite complicated, and measures the *stated willingness to allow a phased retirement in the future* rather than documenting current or recent practices. A follow-up question asked if an older worker had actually shifted from full-time to part-time work in the past three years, and 42% of the sample said that had happened. This finding implies that phased retirement is happening–at least informally and occasionally–in more than a third of workplaces today.

Importantly, most of the managers who said phased retirement was possible in their workplaces reported that it would be handled on a "case by case" basis with "no formal policy" (66%), and an additional 10% reported that a formal policy would be adjusted to meet individual circumstances (Hutchens & Grace-Martin, 2004). Phased retirement is thus "often seen as discretionary. An employer may think long and hard about both business prospects and an employee's talents before permitting an employee to take phased retirement" (Hutchens & Grace-Martin, 2004: 10). These findings confirm previous research on the administration of flexible work arrangements, such as flexible schedules and telecommuting (Kelly & Kalev, 2006). Kelly & Kalev (2006) find that organizations have been careful not to promise that employees can work in these new ways; instead, management leaves these decisions up to supervising managers even if there is a formal policy "allowing" flexible work arrangements. When employers follow this strategy, it is more difficult to know what it means that an employer "offers" phased retirement or other flexible work arrangements. In practice, these attractive work arrangements may only be available to a few, favored employees (Kelly & Kalev, 2006; cf. Eaton, 2003).

Which organizations are more likely to have phased retirement programs? The Hutchens study found that phased retirement was more likely to be seen as a possibility in workplaces that had fewer unionized employees, more women, and more experience with flexible schedules, job-sharing, and extended family leaves (Hutchens & Grace-Martin, 2004). In other words, phased retirement seemed easier in organizations that had already experimented with other flexible work arrangements. Other research demonstrates that phased retirement is more common in higher education and in the public sector, largely because these sectors are regulated by different, and more flexible, pension laws (Perun, 2002; Watson Wyatt, 1999; Willett, 2005).

WHAT ARE THE BARRIERS TO PHASED RETIREMENT?

Widespread Confusion About Intersecting Laws

One of the most important barriers to phased retirement is confusion about what is allowed under current laws and regulations. Employers interested in phased retirement programs, and the professionals and consultants who advise them, have been trying to figure out what phased retirement programs should look like in order to be in compliance with the Employee Retirement Income Security Act (ERISA), the IRS Code, the Age Discrimination in Employment Act (ADEA), and the published pension rules developed by companies and their pension plan administrators (Penner et al., 2002; Fields & Hutchens, 2002). These laws and business policies governing the employment relationship and employee benefits are potentially contradictory and definitely confusing.[4]

The confusion and frustration has arisen primarily from questions about how phased retirement programs can work with traditional defined benefit pension plans, which promise a fixed payment after retirement. It is widely accepted that it is easier to set up phased retirement programs for defined contribution plans, such as 401(k) plans. Defined contribution plans generally allow employees to begin drawing on their accrued benefits at age 59 1/2. Defined benefit plans have more restrictive rules about drawing pension benefits while working for pay. Also, these plans often determine benefits based on average pay over the last three years of work–and this would obviously make it unwise to reduce hours and pay at the end of one's career. See Figure 1 for a brief overview of the laws affecting defined benefit plans.

These complications may become less important over time, because defined benefit plans are becoming less popular. Only half of medium and large organizations had a defined contribution plan by the late 1990s (Galinsky & Bond, 1998) and many corporations (including IBM and other "good employers") are shifting away from their defined benefit retirement programs and expressing a desire to get out of the "business" of retirement altogether.

While the legal barriers to phased retirement reflect the difficulty of integrating these arrangements with defined benefit plans, the confusion about phased retirement is widespread. Some employers with defined contribution plans in place are not even sure what the regulatory issues are–but they know that things are complicated and so they shy away from offering phased retirement options. On the other hand, some organizations with defined benefit plans have maneuvered the complicated legal environment and successfully set up phased retirement programs. In fact, the type of pension program in place (i.e. defined benefit or defined contribution) does not predict whether an organization reports that phased retirement is possible (Hutchens & Grace-Martin, 2004).

It is important to reiterate that the regulatory question is how employees can reduce their hours and make up the loss in income by drawing on their pension benefits. The goal of phased retirement programs, as they are being developed today, is part-time work at the same net income (or nearly the same income, representing prorated salary plus partial pension) as one had when working full-time. Of course, in theory, older workers can shift to part-time work without supplementing their incomes with pension benefits. In practice, though, there are three big

FIGURE 1. Regulatory Environment for Phased Retirement Programs with Defined Benefit Pension Plans

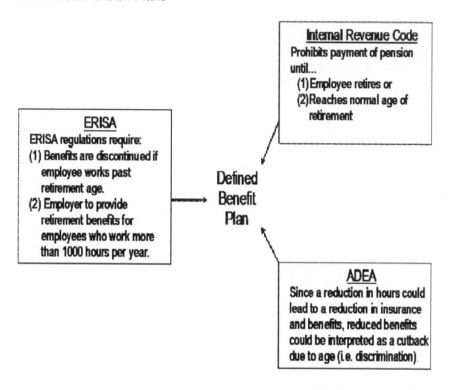

Sources: Employment Policy Foundation 2003, Oakley 2000, Penner et al 2002, NASRA 2002

hurdles to doing so. First, older worker would need to individually negotiate reduced hours with their employer. This is often not an easy thing to do, largely because managers and organizations tend to see jobs–particularly management and professional positions–as indivisible units that require an employee's effort at least 40 hours per week, around 50 weeks a year (Moen & Roehling, 2005; Williams, 2000). Research confirms that employers with more experience with part-time positions are more willing to experiment with phased retirement (Hutchens & Grace-Martin, 2004), but some employers may avoid part-time positions in general and phased retirement in particular. Second, most part-time positions typically do not include benefits. Because employer-based health insurance is generally much less expensive than the health insurance available to an individual or family, losing access to it is a huge disincentive to employees wishing to reduce their working hours. Third, Social Security rules discourage some employees from moving to part-time work. Social Security benefits are based on earnings for the highest 35 years of work. If a worker has already put in 35 years at fairly high wages, cutting back to part-time in the last few years before retirement may not be a problem. But a worker who has not yet worked 35 years–say a woman who took off some years to care for children–might jeopardize later benefits by reducing hours at this point.

Recent Regulatory Action

Although some employers have successfully set up phased retirement programs and others have established informal, "work around" strategies like the "retire-rehire" arrangements, many employers, employment attorneys, human resources professionals, and benefits consultants have felt at a loss about how to roll out phased retirement initiatives in ways that would comply with all the relevant laws and be attractive to the targeted workers. They have been clamoring for some regulatory guidance on what they can and can't do.

In response to these questions, in 2002, the Internal Revenue Service (IRS) began to gather information from employers and their benefits companies, professional associations, and industry groups, about their questions and their vision for phased retirement regulations (U.S. Department of Treasury, 2002). In November 2004, the IRS issued proposed regulations under section 401(a) of the Code for defined benefit plans (U.S. Department of Treasury, 2004). The proposed regulations set requirements for a *"bona fide* phased retirement program" that would allow distributions to be made from a pension plan during a period of reduced-hours employment. The IRS requested comments on the proposed regulations, accepting them through February 2005. At a March 2005 meeting of pension administrators, the Internal Revenue Service assistant chief counsel for employee benefits stated that final regulations would be issued by the end of 2005 (*Human Resources Report*, 2005). The final regulations were listed as a priority action for the IRS in 2005-2006 (Office of Tax Policy & Internal Revenue Service, 2005), but an IRS official told us that the final regulations were "not imminent" when we inquired in June 2006 (personal correspondence). Under the proposed regulations, the key elements of *bona fide* phased retirement programs are:

1. That the reduction in hours is voluntary.
2. That employees are eligible beginning at age 59 1/2.
3. That employees must have worked full-time before the phased retirement begins.
4. That employees must reduce their hours by at least 20%
5. That benefits cannot be paid as a lump sum.
6. That additional pension benefits accrue during the phased retirement period on a pro-rata basis.

(Internal Revenue Bulletin No. 2004-47, November 22, 2004; see also Human Resources Report, March 28, 2005; Watson Wyatt Insider, December 2004; Insight, 2004). One of the most interesting components of the proposed regulations is the creation of a new status of worker. Employees in a phased retirement program will now have an official dual status as "partially retired and partially employed."

Responses and New Questions

The response to the proposed regulations from organizations and benefits experts has been mixed, with both eagerness and concerns about how the proposed regulations would fit with other employment laws (e.g. Carlson, 2005; Caudill, 2005). For example, the January 2005 newsletter for clients of the benefits company Towers Perrin–which is also available to anyone on the web–led off an article about the regulations with the claim that "Companies interested in setting up a phased retirement program–or in building on an informal program that they already have in place–now have some long-awaited guidance from the IRS . . . The IRS proposal is a welcome development for many employers because it puts the government squarely on the side of supporting bona fide phased retirement programs" (Towers Perrin HR Services, 2005). The article concludes by noting that employers who have not considered phased retirement "will likely want to consider them now. Employers who already have informal phased retirement programs will likely want to know what changes might be required to have qualified bona fide programs that meet all the IRS requirements." Other articles in the management press argue that phased retirement will likely take off due to the new regulations, with titles like "Phased Retirement Coming Soon" (Caudill, 2005) and " 'Phased Retirement' Gets a Boost at Hearing" (Brady, 2005).

However, there are some concerns about the proposed regulations, specifically about how the new regulations would intersect with the various existing laws protecting workers and their pensions. A May 2005 article in *Workforce Management* argues (in the headline) that "Proposed Cure Brings New Ills." The article begins with the pronouncement that "Employers may have thought that the proposed regulation on phased retirement would put to rest their concerns about retaining older workers, but they could be in for a new round of headaches" (Workforce Management, 2005). The primary complaint about the proposed regulations presented here is the need to conduct "annual audits of how many hours employees are working" in order to determine what proportion of their pension benefits they are eligible for in that year. Because salaried employees do not generally track their hours, this may introduce "hours of administrative work" (Workforce Management, 2005). The article quotes a Society of Human Resource Management (SHRM) official who says "This is going to be incredibly burdensome, and human resources professionals are the ones who are going to have to deal with it" (Workforce Management, 2005). Although the article does not make this explicit, the issue here is a contradiction between the practices that have arisen around the Fair Labor Standards Act, namely the practice of not monitoring hours for exempt employees, and the requirements of bona fide phased retirement programs under the proposed regulations.

There are also concerns about which workers would be eligible for phased retirement under ERISA's rules regarding benefits discrimination. Pearce and colleagues (2005) note that "The proposed regulations provide that a phased retirement program is an optional form of benefit that must satisfy benefits, rights and features (BRF) testing" required under ERISA. This testing requires employers to show that benefits are not disproportionately available to "highly compensated employees," in order to ensure that employee benefits are not set up for the benefit of executives and senior managers but not lower-level workers. However, as Pearce and colleagues (2005) explain, many employers want to "offer this opportunity on a selective basis" to highly valued employees. Phased retirement–like other flexible work arrangements such as telecommuting–has been sold within management circles as a way to retain and reward valuable employees (Kelly, 1999). Employers are loathe to create new "entitlements" that are promised to all employees; instead they hope to use new work arrangements as part of a less standardized reward system where select employees get access to attractive benefits as a direct result of their superior performance (Kelly & Kalev, 2006). The BRF testing requirement would push employees to broaden access to phased retirement programs, although there is still some question of which employees will be counted in that testing (Pearce et al., 2005).

Another worry is that "the proposed regulations do not address any potential age discrimination issues, other than to require that participation be voluntary on the part of employees" (Pearce et al., 2005). The article notes that there may be claims of coerced phased retirement under the Age Discrimination in Employment Act of 1967 (ADEA), but that employers will have to turn to the Equal Employment Opportunity Commission (EEOC) for guidance on how to address these concerns. In short, the proposed IRS regulations provide guidance to employers on some issues but, because of the complex interplay of laws covering the employment relationship and employee benefits, employers may now worry that they are taking on new risks with regard to older workers who might report being pushed into partial retirement. Employers are wary about age discrimination laws, which they often view as "very broad and very general" (U.S. Department of Labor, 2000). Continued concerns about age discrimination claims may scare some employers away from phased retirement programs, even though age discrimination suits are hard for plaintiffs to win (Clement & Schwab, 2004).

Will Access to Phased Retirement Increase?

What will happen next? It is possible, but not certain, that employers in the United States are on the cusp of widespread adoption of phased retirement programs. Previous research suggests that regulatory guidance can propel the diffusion of an emerging practice (particularly one that is fairly cheap and attractive to a variety of constituents). For example, Kelly's (2003) study of the diffusion of tax-free spending accounts for child care describes a fairly similar regulatory process that resulted in the widespread and quick adoption of these new benefits. In that case, benefits consulting companies requested IRS guidance of the new spending accounts that they wished to market to employers. The IRS provided proposed regulations in 1985 that criticized some of the elements of the expense accounts, but also clarified what types of expense accounts would be allowed as non-taxable benefits. The benefits consulting companies quickly shared this news through the business press and began marketing their administration of expense accounts to current and new clients. Employers responded in large numbers, in part because the tax-free spending accounts were a cheap way to respond to growing pressure from employees for "family-friendly" benefits. Phased retirement programs are developing in a similar fashion. The

IRS guidance is being welcomed by employers and their agents, the programs being discussed are not costly to employers, and the programs allow employers to respond to growing interest among older employees for new ways to work. Phased retirement programs may soon become the norm, at least for medium and large employers, those more apt to have a number of formalized human resources policies.

On the other hand, there are several potential roadblocks to the widespread diffusion of phased retirement, despite the recent regulatory guidance. Phased retirement programs implicate *multiple laws* that are regulated by different federal agencies and monitored by different experts and professions within organizations. The regulatory guidance offered by the IRS has begun to clarify matters but does not solve the problem of how to guard against age discrimination claims. Neither does it establish whether it will be cost effective to monitor the hours of salaried employees who are exempt from the Fair Labor Standards Act. The answer to that question may depend on whether benefits consulting companies and human resource professional associations can facilitate the process of seeking regulatory guidance from other agencies and/or develop inexpensive administrative tools for monitoring hours.

It is also unclear whether, in the opinion of employers, the bona fide programs laid out in the regulations will assist them in retaining valuable older workers. There are two parts of the proposed regulations that seem to conflict with the way employers would like to use phased retirement. First, the age requirement (age 59 1/2 or older) may exclude too many workers in their 50s who are also interested in scaling back their hours. Programs with this age requirement may not help employers retain the employees they are concerned about losing (Workforce Management, 2005). Second, the regulations imply broad access to phased retirement programs–something we are pleased to see for equity reasons–but employers may decide that they are only interested in phased retirement that they can grant selectively to the few employees they are desperate to keep.

CONCLUSION

Phased retirement programs represent one important and attractive way to increase flexibility for older workers while simultaneously benefiting organizations that are worried about the loss of staff and expertise concomitant with the full-speed and full-scale retirements of workers in the large and aging Baby Boom generation (see also Moen, Sweet &

Swisher, 2005). Yet phased retirement advocates have often been baffled by the various intersecting employment laws adopted to protect older workers and their pensions. Recent regulatory developments have clarified when phased retirement with pension supplements is permissible and what would constitute a compliant phased retirement program for the Internal Revenue Service. However, it is hard to predict with any certainty whether phased retirement will be widely adopted. Some regulatory questions and ambiguities remain. It is also unclear whether the *permissible* phased retirement programs will match employers' vision of a *useful* phased retirement program, and whether either fit with the desires of many older workers to retire gradually, over a period of years, rather than "cold turkey."

NOTES

1. This is an open question because previous research has used data from earlier cohorts of employees who retired when the cultural and policy environment fostered a predictable, lock-step exit from full-time work to full-time leisure. But, just as the Baby Boomers are approaching traditional retirement age, that lock-step pattern is unraveling and the policy environment is becoming more uncertain.

2. It is important to note gender differences in the benefits of employment in later life. Retired men who returned to paid work report higher levels of well-being (fewer depressive symptoms, higher mastery, higher self-esteem, higher satisfaction with life) than fully retired men (Kim & Moen, 2000, 2002). Working after retirement did not affect women's psychological well-being, but did seem to improve women's marital satisfaction (Moen, Kim, & Hofmeister, 2001).

3. The sample includes work sites with 20 or more employees and at least two white-collar workers aged 55 or older. The sample was stratified by establishment size, and then weighted to reflect the population of work sites (Hutchens & Grace-Martin, 2004).

4. In the U.S., essential components of a family's financial security, such as health insurance and supplemental retirement income, are provided through employee benefits rather than a public safety net. This means that it is very important for workers to find and maintain employment with an employer that provides these benefits. It also means that the laws regulating the employment relationship per se and the laws regulating employee benefits are both central to understanding the experiences of workers.

REFERENCES

Brady, M. (2005). 'Phased Retirement' Gets A Boost At Hearing. *Life & Health Financial Services, 109* (7), 7, 57.

Carlson, L. (2005). Phased retirement regulations draw mixed reaction from firms. *Employee Benefit News, 19* (3), 1, 52.

Caudill, A. K. (2005). Phased Retirement Coming Soon. *Journal of Financial Service Professionals, 59* (2), 34-36.

Clermont, K. M., & Schwab, S. J. (2004). How employment discrimination plaintiffs fare in Federal Court. *Journal of Empirical Legal Studies 1* (2), 429-458.

Eaton, S.C. (2003). If you can use them: Flexibility policies, organizational commitment, and perceived performance. *Industrial Relations.* 42(2), 145-167.

Edelman, L.B. (1990). Legal environments and organizational governance: The expansion of due process in the American workplace. *American Journal of Sociology, 95(6),* 1401-40.

Edelman, L.B. (1992). Legal ambiguity and symbolic structures: Organizational mediation of civil rights law. *American Journal of Sociology,* 97(6), 1531-76.

Edelman, L. B. (2005). The endogeneity of law: Civil rights at work. In Robert L. Nelson and Laura Beth Nielsen (Eds), *Handbook on employment discrimination research: Rights and realities.* New York: Kluwer Academic Press.

Fields, V., & Hutchens, R. M. (2002). Regulatory obstacles to phased retirement in the for-profit sector. *Benefits Quarterly* (18): 35-41.

Freedman, M. (1999). *Prime time: How baby boomers will revolutionize retirement and transform America.* New York: PublicAffairs.

Galinsky, E., & Bond, J. (1998). *The 1998 business work-life study: A sourcebook.* New York: Families and Work Institute.

General Accounting Office. (2001). Older workers: Demographic trends pose challenges for employers and workers. Report GAO-02-85. Washington, D.C.: Government Printing Office.

Human Resources Report. (2005, March 28). IRS to Issue Phased Retirement Guidance This Year. Official Tells Pension Conference, 23(12), 321.

Hutchens, R. M. (2003). *The cornell study of employer phased retirement policies: A report on key findings.* Ithaca, NY: School of Industrial and Labor Relations, Cornell University.

Hutchens, R. M., & Dentinger, E. (2003). Moving toward retirement. In Moen, P. (Ed.), *It's about time: Couples and careers* (pp. 259-274). Ithaca, NY: Cornell University Press.

Hutchens, R. M., & Grace-Martin, K. (2004). *Who among white-collar workers has an opportunity for phased retirement? Establishment characteristics.* IZA Discussion Paper No. 1155, Institute for the Study of Labor, Bonn. Retrieved on January 15, 2006 from www.iza.org.

Insight. (2004, November 22). Treasury publishes proposed phased retirement regulation. Chicago consulting actuaries. Retrieved from http://insight. chicagoconsultingactuaries.com/Insight/Documents/phasedret.aspx.

Internal Revenue Bulletin. (2004, November 22). Bulletin No. 2004-47. REG-114726-04, 69 Fed. Reg., 2004-47, pp. 857-866. Retrieved from http://www.irs. gov/pub/irs-regs/11472604.pdf.

Kelly, E. L. (1999). Theorizing corporate family policies: How advocates built the 'business case' for 'family-friendly' policies. *Research in the Sociology of Work, 8,* 169-202.

Kelly, E. L. (2003). The strange history of employer-sponsored child care: Interested actors, uncertainty, and the transformation of law in organizational fields. *American Journal of Sociology, 109,* 606-49.

Kelly, E. L., & Dobbin, F. (1999). Civil rights law at work: Sex discrimination and the rise of maternity leave policies. *American Journal of Sociology, 105*(2), 455-92.

Kelly, E.L. & Kalev, A. (2006). Flexible formalization, limited legalization and restructured workplaces: Managing flexible work arrangements in U.S. organizations. *Socio-Economic Review*, forthcoming.

Kim, J. E., & Moen, P. (2001). Is retirement good or bad for subjective well-being? *Current Directions in Psychological Science, 10*(3), 83-86.

Kim, J. E., & Moen, P. (2002). Retirement transitions, gender, and psychological well-being: A life-course, ecological model. *Journal of Gerontology: Psychological Sciences, 57B*(3), 212-22.

Merton, R. K. 1968. *Social theory and social structure.* New York: Free Press.

Moen, P. (2003a). Midcourse: Navigating retirement and a new life stage. In J. T. Mortimer, & M. J. Shanahan (Eds.), *Handbook for the life course* (pp. 267-291). New York: Kluwer Academic/Plenum.

Moen, P. (2003b). Midcourse: Reconfiguring careers and community service for a new life stage. *Contemporary Gerontology, 9*(3), 1-8.

Moen, P. (2005). Beyond the career mystique: "Time in," "time out," and "second acts." *Sociological Forum, 20*(2), 187-208.

Moen, P., & Altobelli, J. (2006). The third age project: Retirement as an incomplete institution requiring strategic selection. In J. Jones, & P. Wink (Eds.), *The crown of life.* New York: Springer.

Moen, P., & Fields, V. (2002). Midcourse in the united states: Does unpaid community participation replace paid work? *Aging International, 27*(3), 21-48.

Moen, P., Fields, V., Quick, H., & Hofmeister, H. (2000). A life course approach to retirement and social integration. In K. Pillemer, P. Moen, E. Wethington & N. Glasgow (Eds.), *Social integration in the second half of life* (pp. 75-107). Baltimore: The Johns Hopkins Press.

Moen, P., Kim, J. E., & Hofmeister, H. (2001). Couples' work/retirement transitions, gender, and marital quality. *Social Psychology Quarterly, 64*(1), 55-71.

Moen, P., & Roehling, P. V. (2005). *The career mystique: Cracks in the American dream.* Boulder, CO: Rowman & Littlefield.

Moen, P., Sweet S., & Swisher, R. (2005). Embedded career clocks: the case of retirement planning. In MacMillan, Ross (Ed.), *The structure of the life course—standardized? Individualized? Differentiated? Advances in life course research.* (Vol 9, 239-257). New York: Elsevier.

Office of Tax Policy & Internal Revenue Service. (2005, August 8). 2005-2006 Priority Guidance Plan. Retrieved January 4, from http://www.irs.gov/pub/irs-utl/2005-2006_guidance_priority_list.pdf.

Pearce, R., Pollack, M. & Hall, R. (2005). Proposed IRS Regulations on Phased Retirement. *Benefits Law Journal, 18*(2), 48-56.

Penner, R. G., Perun, P., & Steuerle, C.E. (2002). *Legal and institutional impediments to partial retirement and part-time work by older workers.* Washington, D.C.: Urban Institute.

Perun, P. (2002). Phased retirement programs for the twenty-first century workplace. *John Marshall Law Review, 35*(4), 633-672.

Ruhm, C. (1990). Bridge jobs and partial retirement. *Journal of Labor Economics, 8,* 482-501.

Stein, D. (2000). The new meaning of retirement. *ERIC Digest, 217,* 1-2.

Towers Perrin HR Services. (2005, January). "Phased retirement programs get a lift from IRS." *Monitor.* Retreived from http://www.towersperrin.com/monitor/webcache/towers/TP_Monitor/jsp/showdoc.jsp?webc=TP_Monitor/2005/01/articles/mon_article_0105b.htm.

U.S. Department of Labor. (1999). *Futurework: Trends and challenges for work in the twenty-first century.* Retrieved January 12, 2006, from http://www.dol.gov/asp/programs/history/herman/reports/futurework/report/chapter1/main.htm.

U.S. Department of Labor. (2000, November 14). *Report of the working group on phased retirement.* Retrieved from http://www.dol.gov/ebsa/publications/phasedr1. htm.

U.S. Department of the Treasury. (2002). Request for Comments on Phased Retirement. *Internal Revenue Bulletin.* Notice 2002-43.

U.S. Department of the Treasury. (2004, Novemeber 10). Distributions from a Pension Plan Under a Phased Retirement Program. *Federal Register* 69, 65108-65117.

Watson Wyatt Worldwide. (1999). Phased retirement: Reshaping the end of work. Bethesda, MD: Watson Wyatt Worldwide.

Watson Wyatt Insider. (2004, December). IRS proposes phased retirement regulations.

Willett, M. (2005). Early retirement and phased retirement programs for the public sector. *Benefits and Compensation Digest, 42*(4), 31-35.

Williams, J. (2000). *Unbending gender: Why work and family conflict and what to do about it.* New York: Oxford University Press.

Workforce Management. (2005). Proposed cure brings new ills to companies. *84*(5), 26-27.

Interests and Concerns of Older Workers: New Challenges for the Workplace

Diana Stork

INTRODUCTION

The trends and predictions are well known. The United States labor force will continue to grow, although at a slower rate than in the recent past, and it will become increasingly more heterogeneous. Government statistics project continuing growth in the representation of women, people of color, and older workers. In order to attract qualified employees and retain experienced talent, especially as a labor shortage looms

(Challenger, 2003), many organizations will devote effort and commit resources to meeting the needs of workers they may not have thought much about in the past. The "graying of the U.S. workforce" (Toossi, 2004) underscores the importance of studying the interests, expectations, and concerns of older workers.

The Bureau of Labor Statistics predicts far-reaching changes in the age composition of the U.S. labor force. The youth labor force is expected to grow from 22.4 million in 2002 to 24.4 million by 2012 (Toossi, 2004). Even so, the median labor force age, which was 36.6 years in 1992 and 40.0 years in 2002, is expected to reach to 41.4 years in 2012 (Toossi, 2004). In 2020, workers age 55 and above will represent 20% of the labor force, up from 13% in 2000. (Toossi, 2002). According to figures from The American Association of Retired Persons (AARP), in "July, 2004, more than 23 million persons aged 55 and older were in the labor force, an increase of nearly one million over the previous 12 months . . ." (Holbrook, 2004). The AARP suggests that older workers are postponing retirement for a variety of reasons including improved health, the lessened physical aspects of many jobs today, higher education levels, and policies and practices implemented by employers to retain older workers. Research conducted by the Boston College Center for Retirement Research suggests, however, that employers would rather hire young workers than older workers, although "more research needs to be done to ferret out exactly why employers prefer younger workers" (Lahey, 2005). As demographics shift, a youth preference would become increasingly costly for hiring organizations. Organizations that have not yet done so are well advised to think differently about their older employees and to invest in attracting and retaining older workers.

This article explores the attitudes, expectations, and concerns of older workers (and, for purposes of comparison, those of younger workers). Questions are addressed about what older workers want from their jobs, how satisfied they are with aspects of their jobs at the moment, and how important work is to their identity. This study finds that older workers are committed, engaged, and satisfied. They want to work, and they want to be valued for their good work.

METHODOLOGY

Subjects

Data for this article were collected from employees of twelve U.S. based work organizations. Organizations of various sizes and from different industry sectors were included. From each organization's Human Resource Information System (HRIS), employees hired in 1997 and 2002 were identified. These two years were chosen to provide a sample of recent hires who began working under similar macroeconomic conditions in the U.S. economy. All 11,064 employees hired in either 1997 or 2002 and still employed by their organizations in 2004 were invited to complete the survey. Similar numbers were hired in the two years, but by 2004, fewer of those hired in 1997 were still employed. Of those invited to participate (those still employed in 2004), approximately a quarter had been hired in 1997; the rest had been hired in 2002. A total of 2,013 employees participated in the survey, for an overall response rate of 18%. Among the 2,013 respondents were 663 younger workers (age 30 and younger) and 415 older workers (over 45 years of age). The younger worker group included 61 people hired in 1997 and 602 people who had been hired in 2002. The older worker group included 161 people hired in 1997 and 254 people who had been hired in 2002.

Instrumentation

The survey instrument (approved by the author's Institutional Review Board) included sections about an ideal job, the current work and organizational experience, work and life satisfaction, identity and work/life issues, and demographic characteristics. Two versions were created–an online version and a paper version.

Procedure

The survey was conducted between January and July of 2004. Most subjects completed an online version. A paper survey was substituted in those organizations where online access for employees was an issue. Subjects were notified by HR about the survey and invited to participate. The research project and the survey instrument were described, and employees were given information about how to contact the researcher or the Institutional Review Board, if they had questions. Employees were assured that no person in their organization would have access to their survey responses, and they learned that the online version was hosted independently, meaning that even the researcher would not see individual survey responses. Written surveys were also sent to an outside data group that appended these data to the online data. Excel spreadsheets were created from submitted surveys and sent electronically to the researcher, who imported them into the Statistical Package for the Social Sciences (SPSS) for analysis (Norusis, 1999). SPSS was used for all data analysis.

Gaps. One researcher-created variable (the *gap*) requires a brief methodological explanation. In the survey instrument, participants were asked to rate the importance of various factors in (a) their ideal job in 2004 and (b) their current job. In the section on the ideal job, respondents were asked to rate factors on a scale of 1 (*definitely not important*) to 4 (*definitely important*) in describing their ideal job. The same list of factors was used in the section for rating the extent to which each factor was present in their current job. In this section, respondents indicated their level of agreement on a scale of 1 (*completely disagree*) to 4 (*completely agree*) to statements such as, "I have control over my work schedule" and "I do work that challenges me."

A variable was created to reflect the difference between respondents' experience of their current job and what they would want in their ideal job. Difference scores were calculated by subtracting respondents' rating of their current job on each factor from the rating of the factor's importance to them in their ideal job.

As noted above, importance in the ideal job section was rated on a 1 to 4 scale for each of the factors; agreement in the current job section was also rated on a 1 to 4 scale. Thus, the difference score (*importance* minus *agreement)* could range from 23 to + 3. A score of + 3 would result from an importance score of 4 and an agreement score of 1. A score of −3 would be calculated from a score of 1 (importance) and a score of 4 (agreement). To learn about those areas in which people feel a significant lack (i.e., they want more of something than they currently have), negative and small positive differences were ignored; a difference of 2 or 3 was required to define a gap. Thus a gap represents a substantial difference between the ideal and the current experience.

RESULTS

With 2,013 respondents and relevant demographic data, it was possible to define sub-samples large enough for legitimate descriptive and comparative analysis. In this article, the focus is on older/mature employees (older than 45) as they compare to younger employees (age 30 and under). This section starts with a description of the sample.

Sample Demographics

Survey data analyzed for this article are from 415 older workers and 663 younger workers. Demographic descriptive data for both groups are presented in Table 1.

Younger and older respondents tended to be female, Caucasian, and college educated. Younger respondents were less likely to be married or partnered. Nearly all of the respondents held full-time jobs, with only a minority having supervisory responsibility. About half were salaried, and a greater percentage of the younger respondents had salaries lower than $45,000 as compared to the older respondents.

For All Results

Comparisons are made between older and younger workers, and all Tables of results include data for both groups. In addition to data for younger workers as a group and older workers as a group, data are also presented for older workers hired in 1997 (n = 161) and for older workers hired in 2002 (n = 254).

Work-Life Identity and Focus

Results on importance and self-definition give a picture of the younger and the older workers which suggest both similarities and differences. Very few older or younger respondents indicated that work was the most important aspect of their life. About 50% of the younger workers and 60% of the older workers rated job and life outside of work as equally important. Defining self in terms of family was less common

TABLE 1. Sample Description

Characteristics	Younger Respondents (N = 663)	Older Respondents (N = 415)
Female	78%	72%
Caucasian	77%	82%
Not Married or Partnered	57%	32%
College Graduate	61%	60%
Income under $45,000	69%	43%
Salaried	50%	58%
Full-time job	92%	92%
Without direct reports	78 %	67%

among older workers than among younger workers. With respect to importance and identity, older workers more often chose a dual focus—work and life outside of work—than did younger workers.

The Ideal Job

In many ways, older workers are not different from younger workers with respect to what they want from a job. For both groups, it was important to do work that makes them proud, have a supervisor whom they respect, have a good relationship with the supervisor, and to be trusted by their supervisor. In addition, rewards, fairness, and time for health, wellness, and family were rated as *definitely important* by almost all older and younger respondents. Table 3 lists the factors that met two criteria: (1) at least 80% of younger and older employees rated the factor as *definitely important* and (2) there was no significant difference in ratings between the older and younger employee respondents.

In addition, both groups reported that they cared about benefits. The vast majority of both groups of respondents rated most benefits (paid time off, health care, family care) as *definitely important*. Education benefits (and opportunities to learn new skills) were rated as *definitely important* by a smaller proportion of older employees.

Focusing on aspects of the work situation and the job itself, several differences emerge between younger and older respondents (Table 4). Compared to young workers, friends and the social or relational aspects of work were not as important to older respondents. By contrast, the nature of the work itself was more important to older workers, with task variety and challenge in the job being rated as *definitely important* by a larger proportion of older workers. In addition, issues of control (when, how, and where they work) were also more important to older respondents, Looking outside the organization, time for friends and time for fun were more important to younger workers; time to volunteer in the community was more important to older workers.

Current Job

The ideal job is just that, an ideal. The feelings of fulfillment, satisfaction, and loyalty that employees may hold relate to the actual job and current work situation. Table 5 gives the percentages of older and younger employees who indicated *completely agree* in response to a set of statements about their current job and work experience. Younger and older employees report that they feel similarly comfortable at work (as

TABLE 2. Identity and Focus

Importance of Job and Life Outside of Work

	Younger Workers	Older Workers (1997, 2002)
Job More Important	4 %	6 % (5%, 6%)
Job and Life Outside Equally Important	52 %	62 % (70%, 59%)
Life Outside of Work More Important	44 %	33 % (24%, 36%)

Chi-Square (Younger and Older) =12.3; p=.002

How I Define Myself

	Younger Workers	Older Workers (1997, 2002)
Work or Leaning Toward Work	16 %	16 % (17%, 15%)
Both Work and Family	40 %	50 % (51%, 50%)
Family or Leaning Toward Family	44 %	34 % (32 %, 35%)

Chi-Square (Younger and Older) =12.1; p=.002

TABLE 3. Similarities in Ideal Job: Percentage Rating Factors as Definitely Important

Job Factors	Younger Workers	Older Workers (1997, 2002)
Doing work that makes me proud	90 %	90 % (92%, 86%)
Having a good relationship with my supervisor	87 %	84 % (81%, 85%)
Having a supervisor I respect	89 %	90 % (91%, 89%)
Having a supervisor who trusts me	94 %	96 % (97%, 95%)
Being in an organization where good performance is rewarded	87 %	88 % (91%, 86%)
Being in an organization where everyone is treated fairly	90 %	92 % (93%, 89%)
Being in an organization that respects personal/family time	86 %	83 % (81%, 84%)
Having time for family	89 %	85 % (87%, 83%)
Having time for health and wellness	85 %	80 % (83%, 79%)
Having time for vacations and travel	81 %	83 % (87%, 81%)

indicated by being themselves and having people know the "real" them), but for both groups, the percentage of workers who feel completely comfortable at work is less than 40%. Older and younger workers responded differently to statements about their current work situation. A higher proportion of older employees reported being happy with the kind of work they do, their current employer, and their supervisor. Older workers also reportedly felt more loyalty to their current employer, would more often recommend the employer to their friends, and were more likely to be happy working for their current employer for the

TABLE 4. Differences in Ideal Job: Percentage Rating Factors as Definitely Important

Job Factors	Younger Workers	Older Workers (df = 1) (1997, 2002)		Chi-Square* Sig. Level
Being able to spend time with co-workers at work	43 %	26 %	(25%, 27%)	24.2 p = .000
Having co-workers who are also friends	30 %	13 %	(18%, 11%)	36.5 p = .000
Task variety	62 %	76 %	(68%, 76%)	11.5 p = .001
Challenging work	69 %	79 %	(78%, 79%)	13.3 p = .001
Learning new skills	85 %	78 %	(76%, 80%)	6.6 p = .010
Opportunities for advancement	89 %	75 %	(76%, 74%)	38.8 p = .000
Having control over work schedule	64%	73 %	(78%, 71%)	9.1 p =. 002
Having control over how tasks accomplished	66 %	72 %	(76%, 70%)	4.7 p = .031
Being able to do regular work from home	36 %	47 %	(46%, 43%)	6.7 p = .010
Having time for friends outside of work	73 %	60 %	(58%, 64%)	18.4 p = .000
Having time for fun	83 %	74 %	(73%, 74%)	9.5 p = .002
Having time to volunteer in community	37 %	45 %	(45%, 44%)	4.2 p = .04
Being proud of the organization I work for	76 %	83 %	(79%, 88%)	7.6 p = .006

*Chi-Square (for Younger and Older), with Continuity Correction

TABLE 5. Describing the Current Job: Percentage Who "Completely Agree"

	Younger Workers	Older Workers		Chi-Square* (df = 1) Sig. Level
I can easily be me at work	37 %	37 %	(36%, 37%)	.01 p = .9 (ns)
People at work know the real me	33 %	34 %	(37%, 31%)	.43 p = .5 (ns)
I am happy doing the kind of work I do	37 %	47 %	(49%, 45%)	9.6 p = .002
I am happy working for this employer	47 %	56%	(57%, 55%)	8.3 p = .004
I am happy with my supervisor	50 %	57 %	(61%, 54%)	4.5 p = .033
I feel a lot of loyalty to this employer	34 %	52 %	(62%, 46%)	30.5 p = .000
I would recommend this employer to friends	46 %	58 %	(59%, 57%)	13.9 p = .000
I am happy to work for current employer for rest of career	28 %	52 %	(55%, 49%)	57.0 p = .000
I feel fulfilled at work	18 %	28 %	(33%, 24%)	10.7 p = .001
I am very satisfied with my job	28 %	40 %	(46%, 36%)	16.3 p = .000

* Chi-Square (for Younger and Older), with Continuity Correction

TABLE 6. Percentage of Younger and Older Respondents Experiencing a Gap Between Ideal Job and Current Job

Job Factors	Younger Workers	Older Workers (1997, 2002)		Chi-Square* (df = 1) Sig. Level	
Having control over work schedule	26 %	18 %	(12%, 22%)	7.7	p = .005
Being able to do regular work from home	39 %	32 %	(29%, 33%)	4.9	p = .027
Being in an organization where good performance is rewarded	22 %	15 %	(11%, 18%)	7.6	p = .006
Having opportunities for advancement	23 %	17 %	(15%, 19%)	4.6	p = .03
Being in an organization where everyone is treated fairly	28 %	21 %	(23%, 19%)	5.6	p = .018
Having flexible work policies and programs	18 %	16 %	(11%, 18%)	.64	p = .4(ns)

* Chi-Square (Younger and Older), with Continuity Correction

rest of their career. A larger proportion of older workers reported being both fulfilled at work and satisfied with their job.

In addition, twenty-two percent of younger respondents and 43% of older respondents indicated that they were "always" focused on work when they were at work ($p = .000$). In other words, almost twice as large a proportion of older employees, compared to younger ones, reported that they were not distracted by non-work matters when they were at work.

Overall Satisfaction

In addition to asking about particular aspects of work, respondents provided information about how satisfied they were with their work life, their life in general, their personal/family life, and their work/life balance. On a 1 (*very dissatisfied*) to 5 (*very satisfied*) scale, the two groups reported similar levels of satisfaction, except with respect to their work life. Younger workers had a mean work life satisfaction score of 2.61; older workers' mean score was 2.94. This difference is significant ($t = 3.6$; $p = .000$), indicating that older employees reported greater satisfaction. In terms of proportions, 54% of younger employees and 65% of older employees reported being *satisfied* or *very satisfied* with their work life (*Chi Square*, with continuity correction = 12.4; $p = .000$).

Analysis of Gaps Between Current and Ideal Experience

Another way to look at satisfaction and dissatisfaction is to focus on individual aspects of the job experience and ask whether there are differences between what people would like to experience and what they actually experience. The gap variable (described in the Methods section) is an indicator of substantial difference between what is ideally desired in a job and the current experience.

Table 6 presents results for job factors about which at least 15% of older respondents experienced a substantial difference or gap. Notable gaps are experienced around issues of control–control over work schedule and being able to work from home. Gaps are also experienced with respect to how performance is rewarded, opportunities for advancement, flexibility, and the fair treatment of employees. It is important to note that, with but one exception, a significantly higher proportion of younger workers experienced gaps in these same areas.

DISCUSSION

Results from this study suggest that older workers are engaged with work, but not in a way that overwhelms their life outside of work. Few older workers defined themselves only in terms of work or saw their job as more important than their life outside of work. The majority of older workers in this study can be classified as *dual-centric*; they value both domains–work and life outside of work equally. The concept of dual-centricity was introduced to describe a work-life identity uncovered in the Families and Work Institute's (FWI) study of successful global leaders (Galinsky, 2000). In contrast to work-life balance, dual-centricity does not imply a zero-sum game; more engagement at work does not have to mean less with family. Among the interesting FWI findings were that dual-centric executives felt more successful at work than either work-centric executives or family-centric executives. Dual-centricity seemed also to affect stress, with a significantly lower proportion of dual-centric adults reporting moderate or high levels of stress than executives who are not dual-centric. In the current study, older workers were classified as dual-centric more often than younger workers. Younger workers, compared to older workers, placed more emphasis on life outside of work than on work.

What do older workers want from work? What would define the ideal job for them? Results of this study show that in many areas, younger and older workers are looking for similar things. Both groups want a healthy relationship with the supervisor, want to be trusted at work, and want to work in an organization that treats people fairly, rewards good performance, and respects personal and family time. They also want time for life outside of work, notably family, health, and wellness. Such results are consistent with what others, like Babcock (2005), report that people want from their jobs. In addition to pay and benefits, he reports that employees value a good relationship with the supervisor, management recognition of good performance, and the ability to balance work and life. Some of the other factors that Babcock identified are ones that older workers and younger workers in this current study valued differently.

Domains of difference between what older and younger workers want in a job are important to highlight. In essence, older workers seemed to care more about the job itself and how they accomplished the job, and less about the social context or organizational opportunities. For older workers, what they do and how and where they do it mattered more. In contrast, social relationships with co-workers are less important to older workers than to younger workers.

How well are current work situations meeting the needs of older workers? Results of this study suggest that older workers are more satisfied than younger workers with many aspects of their work lives. For older workers, the current work experience seems to be closer to their ideal than is the case for younger workers. Even so, less than 60% of the older workers are happy with their supervisor, are happy working for their current employer, or would recommend the employer to their friends. Such figures are troubling. With the coming labor shortage, it will be even more important for organizations to meet the needs of all workers. And a higher proportion of those workers will be older than we are accustomed to seeing in the workplace.

From the employer perspective, data on retention of older workers may create a false sense of security. Spherion (2003) reports that retention is higher among older workers than among younger workers, with 55% of older workers (and 43% of younger workers) planning to stay with their employer for the next five years. In the current study, over half of the older workers said they would be happy working for their current employer for the rest of their career. Less than 30% of younger workers felt that way. But, with changing workforce demographics and the coming labor shortage or "job boom" (Kaihla, 2003), employers who do not address the needs and concerns of older workers will find themselves disadvantaged in the labor marketplace.

The AARP (2005) presents a compelling business case for hiring and retaining older workers. In addition to examining the economics of older workers as employees, the AARP also challenges some myths regarding older worker creativity and productivity. In another report, the

AARP (2004) examined employer practices that would make an organization an attractive place for older workers. They suggested that organizations need to put in place programs and policies that address issues like pay, benefits, and health care, as well as programs that deal with the design of jobs and careers. In the present study, results suggest that older and younger workers care about policies and practices that support their well being (health care benefits, for instance), but that older workers care even more than younger workers about the actual job and how they work. Older workers want jobs that use a variety of skills and are challenging. Among the suggestions made to employers by Janrog (2004) is that older workers need more challenging work and greater task variety. Older workers also want greater control over their work schedule and how they accomplish their tasks. Many would like to do more of their regularly scheduled work from home.

Older workers are becoming a dominant demographic group in the workplace. But, we have evidence (Lahey, 2005) that employers prefer younger workers to older workers. Even if this finding was incorrect, the perception of age discrimination among older people (AARP, 2002) may limit their view of options and opportunities. Managers hold negative stereotypes about older workers, seeing them as "high-cost, inflexible, out-of-date liabilities" (McEvoy & Blahna, 2001).

Some companies that have begun to institute innovative programs and policies designed to attract and retain older workers are seeing some success. The CVS drugstore chain has doubled its 55 and older workforce in the past ten years, and Baptist Health South Florida now employs about 2,500 older workers, in their total workforce of about 10,000 (Mullich, 2003). Home Depot and Deloitte Consulting are other well-known companies making a concerted effort to attract and retain older workers (Coy & Brady, 2005).

Research by the Families and Work Institute (Bond et al., 2005) and Spherion (2005) discuss what organizations can do to attract and retain older workers. Among them are programs and policies that support work-life concerns, address fundamental pay and benefits needs, and promote job and career enrichment and flexibility. One of the most interesting findings of the Spherion study was that the employer view and the employee view of what would keep workers in their current positions was different enough that the report is actually titled, "The Great Divide: The Employer-Worker Disconnect." This underscores the importance of additional research to understand what older workers want and need. In addition, individual organizations should invest in learning about the needs and preferences of their own employees. It is undoubtedly the case that, with further research, there will be some generalizable findings about what older workers want, but there will always be organizational differences that reflect the diversity of organizations–their industries, their histories, and their cultures.

NOTE

With sponsorship and funding from Simmons College School of Management and Bright Horizons Family Solutions, original data collection and analyses for the New Workforce Realities project were carried out in 2003 and 2004. Diana Stork served as Principal Investigator and was an Associate Professor at Simmons School of Management. Fiona Wilson was a researcher on the project team and is an Assistant Professor at Simmons College. A project report, The New Workforce Reality: Insights for Today, Implications for Tomorrow was published in January 2005 by Simmons School of Management and Bright Horizons Family Solutions.

REFERENCES

American Association of Retired Persons (2002). *Staying ahead of the curve: The AARP work and career study.* Washington, DC: AARP Knowledge Management.
American Association of Retired Persons (2004). *Staying ahead of the curve 2004: Employer best practices for mature workers, executive summary.* Washington, DC: AARP Knowledge Management.
American Association of Retired Persons (2005). *The business case for workers age 50+: Planning for tomorrow's talent needs in today's competitive environment.* Washington, DC: AARP Knowledge Management.
Babcock, P. (2005). Find what workers want. *HR Magazine*, April, 51-56.
Bond, J. T, Galinsky, E., Kim, S. S., & E. Brownfield. (2005) *National study of employers: Highlights of findings.* Families and Work Institute.
Challenger, J. A. (2003). The coming labor shortage. *The Futurist*, September-October.
Coy, P. & D. Brady. (2005). Old, smart, productive. *Business Week*, June 27, 78-86.
Galinsky, E. (2000). *Dual-centric: A new concept of work-life.* Families and Work Institute.
Holbrook, D. (2004). *Breaking the silver ceiling: A new generation of older workers redefining the new rules of the workplace.* Congressional Testimony, September 20.
Jamrog, J. (2004). The perfect storm: The future of retention and engagement. *Human Resource Planning*, 27(3), 26-33.
Kaihla, P. (2003). The coming job boom. *Business 2.0*, September, 97-105.
Lahey, J. N. (2005). *Do Older Workers Face Discrimination?* Boston College, Center for Retirement Research.
McEvoy, G. M. & M. J. Blahna. (2001). Engagement or disengagement? Older workers and the looming labor shortage. *Business Horizons, 44*(5), 46-52.

Mullich, J. (2003). They don't retire them. They rehire them. *Workforce Management*, *82*(13), 49-54.
Norusis, M.J. (1999). SPSS 9.0 Guide to Data Analysis. Upper Saddle River, NJ: Prentice-Hall.
Spherion. (2003). *Emerging Workforce Study.*
Spherion. (2005). *The Great Divide: The Employer-Worker Disconnect.* Spherion Emerging Workforce Study Report.
Toossi, M. (2002) A Century of change: The U.S. labor force, 1950-2050. *Monthly Labor Review*, May.
Toossi, M. (2004). Labor force projections to 2012: The graying of the U.S. workforce. *Monthly Labor Review*, February.

An Ergonomic Approach to the Aging Workforce Utilizing This Valuable Resource to Best Advantage by Integrating Ergonomics, Health Promotion and Employee Assistance Programs

Robert W. Boyce

INTRODUCTION

January 1, 2006 marked the sixtieth birthday of the first members of the Baby Boomer Generation. This generation of 79 million Americans born between 1946 and 1964 is half again the size of the previous generation. (Welch & Bazar, 2006). The median age of Americans is increasing. Estimates of the US Bureau of Labor Statistics predict that by the year 2015 there will be 55 million workers 45 years of age or older. In addition, older Americans are choosing to continue to work even after retirement seeking extra income to supplement pensions and retirement plans. Fortunately the business sector has needs for this resource as these individuals bring a wealth of expertise and skill to the worksite.

While Americans are living longer as a result of improved medical services and technology they are often suffering from the ill effects of sedentary life styles, such as poor nutrition, obesity and lack of regular exercise. The affects of aging and poor lifestyle behaviors present a challenge for the employer to maintain high productivity and low insurance cost. To meet this challenge, employers must develop and support ongoing occupational assistance and health programs to address the needs of the aging American worker. In fact, a physically conditioned, disease-free older individual can not only be a productive worker but can outperform their poorly conditioned younger counterpart.

Individuals age at different rates due to factors such as lifestyle, genetic make-up, the environment, economic and social support. (Kowalski-Trakofler et al., 2005) Add to this the variables of an individual's skills and experience along with each job's specific requirements and it becomes difficult to predict performance of a job based on an individual's age alone. A company experiences a maturing process as well because their employees continue to grow older and accrue age related issues that affect their abilities. It is important to have programs in place that integrate employee assistance, ergonomics and health promotion to respond to these factors.

The purposed of this paper is to alert health professionals to integrated approaches that would be of assistance to older workers. In this paper the author seeks to:

- discuss the physiological effects of aging and de-conditioning.
- address these issues with an integrated program involving ergonomics and health promotion.
- discuss workplace issued related to aging workers and to recommend actions to address these issues.
- illustrate suggested programs through case studies performed by the author.

UNDERSTANDING THE PHYSIOLOGICAL EFFECTS OF AGING AND DE-CONDITIONING

It is difficult to assess the physiological effects of aging because of de-conditioning, nutritional, disease, psychological and genetic factors. Individuals do not age at the same rates. The following is a brief synopsis of the physiological effects of aging (ages 45 to 74 years) on the cardiovascular, pulmonary, musculoskeletal and nervous systems, and temperature regulation in relation to job performance.

Cardiovascular System

The pairing of the worker with a job is highly dependent on the aerobic capacity of the worker and the physical demands of the job (Astrand, 1967). Aerobic capacity is greatly influences by an individual's cardiac output, the amount of blood pumped per minute. Cardiac output is the amount of blood the heart can pump per beat (stroke volume) and the number of beats per minute (heart rate). Any change of stroke volume or heart rate has a major impact on an individual's cardiac output. It would be ill advised to evaluate aerobic capacity of an older individual based only on their resting heart rate. Resting heart rate does not appear to change with age. Resting stroke volume has been shown to decrease 30% from age 25 to 85 (Schulman et al., 1992). Interestingly enough, no age related decline in resting stroke volume was reported for those free of coronary artery disease (Rodeheffer et al., 1984). As a result, disease-free individuals appear to have no change with age in resting heart rate and resting cardiac output (Graves et al., 2006). Maximal cardiac output is the principal measure of aerobic capacity. It has major implications in the selection of employees for physically demanding occupations. Maximal cardiac output decreases with age and it is related to decreases in maximal stroke volume and maximal heart rate. Maximal heart rate declines proportionally with age, about one beat per year, and this decline may be the single greatest factor for the reduction of cardiac output as one ages. However, because of the variations in maximal heart rate among individuals, it is possible that a younger person could have less heart rate capacity than an older counterpart simply because of these variations in individual maximum heart rate. Using aerobic fitness tests that depend on a predicted maximal heart rate formula to estimate aerobic capacity to test job applicants is fraught with error because of this heart rate variance and can be discriminatory to older individuals.

Older individuals have higher systolic and diastolic blood pressures with the same work loads (Astrand et al., 2003). Thus when a job entails high physical exertion it may be necessary to screen blood pressure at the actual level of physical work required by the job.

Work performed by the arms causes a significantly higher blood pressure in rhythmic work (low loads repeated) or isometric work (sustained contraction). Therefore, in older groups it may be hazardous to exercise with the arms, especially for those with cardiovascular disease or individuals who are unconditioned.

An individual's ability to sustain aerobic work is strongly related to their oxygen consumption capacity. Ergonomists believe that an allowable work intensity for a given work time is to be based on a given percentage of one's maximum aerobic capacity (Garg, 1991). It is interesting to note that at 50% of the maximum aerobic power older individuals have the same heart rates as their younger counterparts. Because of the decline in maximal heart rate with age the relative work rate and feeling of strain experienced by a 65 year old at a heart rate of 110 beats per minute is not experienced by a 25 year old until a heart rate of 130 beats per minute. Thus, the younger person is working at a higher rate for the same amount of strain as the older one. Older individuals with lower maximal oxygen capacities worked at lower rates than their younger counterparts, but the relative workload (percentage of maximal oxygen consumption per minute) was the same (Astrand et al., 2003; Astrand, 1967).

Despite the decreases in maximal aerobic capacity that occur with age some believe that occupational work capacity remains undiminished. (Muller, 1962; Snook, 1971) Snook and Irvine (1968) found no relationship between age and estimates of continuous working capacity (Snook & Irvine, 1968). This author has noted that in the work setting the complexity of factors involving work capacity makes it difficult to predict workplace outcome by using a single measure of body function such as aerobic fitness. Therefore, a primary goal of a work performance test is to make it highly similar to the actual job.

Even though aerobic capacity declines with age, research consistently demonstrates that physically active older people maintain a higher aerobic capacity than their sedentary counterparts (Astrand et al., 2003). It has been reported that the decline experienced by physically active persons throughout their life is half that of their sedentary counterparts (McArdle et al., 2001). Some subjects who were physically active maintained the same maximum as they did 33 years earlier (Astrand et al., 1997). The remarkable endurance capacity of older individuals who continue to train can be seen in marathon runners up to the 9th decade of life. The best time for an 86 year old male is 12.9 minutes per mile and for an 80 year old female is 12.5 minutes per mile for 26 miles. (McArdle et al., 2001). Therefore, staying physically trained and keeping a healthy body weight over a lifetime has a profoundly positive effect on one's aerobic capacity as one ages.

In summary, it is apparent that in terms of cardiovascular fitness and job performance, there is a great variation between individuals no matter what their age. Meaning that an older individual, because of their skill and efficiency of movement, can perform the same tasks as well as if not better than an inexperienced younger individual, despite the higher aerobic capacities of that younger individual. Therefore, it is the duty of EAP and other health professionals to identify the proper evaluation procedures to match an individual with a job. For jobs with high physical demands, the cardiovascular, or aerobic capacity test, are highly valuable in the selection and retention of employees. Employee retention is directly related to placing the individual in jobs in which they can comfortably perform. For example, those that are placed in jobs that are too physically demanding are more exposed to injury, experience greater job stress and are more likely to resign.

Pulmonary System

The ability to expand the chest, (Babb, 1999) maximal expiratory flow, and lung volume reserves (Smith & Serfass, 1981) decrease as a result of adult aging. Vital capacity decreases 40% to 50% by age 70 (Smith & Serfass). Overall there is approximately a 20% increase in the work of the respiratory muscles (DeVries & Adams, 1972). In well-trained subjects followed for 33 years the average reduction in maximal pulmonary ventilation was only 5% (Astrand et al., 2003). However, even though there are reductions in pulmonary function it is rarely the limiting factor in work or exercise as there is usually more than enough ventilator capacity to fully oxygenate the blood. The exception would be with those with disease or limited lung volumes.

The pulmonary system is an integral part of the cardiovascular system and therefore affects aerobic capacity tests. After an initial pulmonary screening, the aerobic capacity test is, once again, the primary determinate as to an individual's suitability for physically demanding jobs such as police and fire fighters.

Musculoskeletal System

The health of the musculoskeletal system is of primary concern in the workplace. Musculoskeletal disorders as a result of repetitive trauma and sustained postures have led to problems, such as carpal tunnel syndrome and back injuries and are a major concern of employers in regards job performance, productivity and reduced costs. Many of these disorders can be reduced or avoided with an integrated approach involving occupational health and safety, health promotion and EAP.

Bone loss is a major concern in the aging years especially in women as it is a precursor for fractures and disability. Women start losing bone mass about age 35 at approximately 1.0% a year. Approximately 50% of women and 12% of men over 50 suffer from osteoporosis. Males begin bone loss approximately 50 years of age at a rate of 0.4%. By the age of 80 the trend has reversed itself (McArdle et al., 2001). Nutritional status such as calcium intake along with physical activity and genetics factors play an important role in bone retention making it difficult to determine the actual bone aging process (O'Flaherty, 2000).

The average strength of a person 65 years old is 75% to 80% of a 20 to 30 year old. Strength decline is greater in the legs and trunk than in the arms (Gremby & Saltin, 1983); the decline in strength is primarily due to the loss of muscle mass (Akima et al., 2001).

Isometric strength and muscular endurance was compared in persons 17 to 70 years old. It is interesting to note that there were decreases in strength but no significant differences found in muscular endurance (Backman et al., 1995). This muscular endurance characteristic can more than make up for the decrease in strength in certain jobs.

Anaerobic capacity, the ability to generate high levels of peak blood lactate, declines with age. Older individuals had a higher blood lactate with sub-maximal workloads but lower levels at peak exertion (Astrand, 1960). Blood lactate is often associated with muscular fatigue and increased recovery time following intense exertion such as needed for physically demanding occupations. Intramuscular blood flow is slower in older individuals and that reduces the removal of lactate and increases recovery time (Tzankoff, 1979).

Older individuals respond to vigorous training with marked and rapid improvements into the ninth decade of life (McArdle et al., 2001). A 12-week muscular training study of 60 to 72 year old men demonstrated an improvement rate of 5% per training which is similar to younger men. A significant fast and slow twitch muscle fiber hypertrophy, size increase, accompanied the strength improvement (McArdle et al., 2001). The reduction of physical strength with age is generally believed to be potentially hazardous in jobs requiring high muscular forces such as lifting, lowering, and carrying moderate to heavy loads, and pushing and pulling of heavy carts on broken or inclined floors (Kowalski-Trakofler, 2005). For the health professional, this means that proper physical fitness training and work-hardening programs can yield significant improvements in the strength and endurance of the older worker.

The loss of flexibility is associated with the increased incidences of falls and other injuries. (Graves et al., 2006). Flexibility decreases as a result of such factors as disease, deterioration of joints and degeneration of collagen fibers (Graves et al., 2006). The incidence of arthritis and joint inflammation increases drastically beyond the age of 45 (Kowalski-Trakofler et al., 2005). It appears that the rate of deterioration of flexibility accelerates beyond the age of 65. The loss of spine flexibility and degeneration associated with the aging process is a major concern. Spinal degeneration is associated with injuries that may result from activities such as the lifting of heavy objects or work related automobile accidents. Shoulder muscle fatigue is identified as a major concern for older workers experiencing decreased joint mobility and it is associated with jobs requiring elevated arm activities (Herberts et al.,1980). Once again, the need for coordinated efforts between safety, health promotion and occupational assistance programs is clear.

Nervous System

A review of literature by Kowalski-Trakofler et al. (2005) discussed changes in the cognitive processes resulting from aging in relation to ergonomics. They report aging can cause decreases in information processing time or speed, working memory, attention abilities, and perceptual abilities. These have work place implications; for instance working memory can affect the ability to learn new tasks such as computer skills, or recall of complex or uncommon procedures. Attention capacity may make it more difficult to perform multiple tasks. More time may be needed to perform these tasks or to select targeted information on complex displays. Although these changes have been reported, research has also indicated that such changes demonstrated in the laboratory do not parallel changes in actual work performance particularly in jobs that rely on accumulated knowledge and skill (Kowalski-Trakofler et al., 2005).

Sensory and motor performance can be thought of in three parts, perception of the incoming data, choice of responses to the data and the detailed timing and phrasing to carry out a chosen response. Of these, timing and phrasing are little affected by age. For example, the time to raise a finger to a light stimulus is similar in those from 20 to 60 years of age (Welford, 1958; 1981). Reaction time has been reported to decrease 15% by the age of 70 years (Elia, 1991). Increased sensory deficits, such as hearing and/or vision, and requirements for higher thresholds of perception may be related to an increase in falls (up to 35% to 40% in persons older than age 60 years) (Ogawa et al., 1992; Schut, 1998). The ability to locate and identify textures and surfaces becomes impaired. This makes it increasingly difficult to grasp, hold and manipulate small smooth objects. The sensory decline may inhibit one's ability to detect pressure cues such as pressing a button. Sensitivity to pain caused by thermal stimuli may be reduced increasing the risk of injury in cases where thermal shielding is required (Pirkl, 1995).

However, Giniger, Dispezier and Eisenburg (1984) found that age was not significantly related to performance, absenteeism, accidents, or turnover on jobs requiring speed (example sewing machine operators, M = 57 years) or on skilled jobs (example quality control examiners, M = 49 years). The complex nature of a particular job and the adaptability of the individual to specific tasks make it difficult to take physiological characteristics, especially measured out of the work environment, and relate it to job performance.

Temperature and Fluid Regulation

The ability to regulate core temperature is affected by the aging process. (Falk et al., 1994; Young, 1997). Aerobically demanding tasks may be more difficult for older workers to perform as a result of their reduced ability to regulate temperature in the heat or the cold. (Goldberg & Ellis, 1996; Kemper, 1994). This could be explained in part by the reduction of skin blood flow with aging (Graves et al., 2006). This exposes the older worker to greater risks of dehydration in hot working environments. However, another study found that older women tended to maintain core temperatures as well as or better than younger women in cold work environments. Note that the rate of musculoskeletal disorders increases in cold work environments. This is a result of such factors as the increase in friction within and around the tendons and joints; and the use of protective gear such as gloves which can require increased force and coordination to complete the task.

Elements of an Ergonomic Workplace Program

The goal of ergonomics is to increase the efficiency, productivity, comfort and safety of the employee and to decrease errors, accidents, injuries and illnesses. The use of ergonomic principles determines the capabilities and limitations of people and then attempts to build or redesign a work environment around these capabilities. They are also used in prescribing worker selection methods and the developing of worker training programs (Garg, 1991). The effectiveness of ergonomic principles can be increased by coordinating them with other initiatives such as health promotion and occupational assistance programs.

Identification of risk factors in the work place is a primary objective of ergonomics. The risks vary considerably depending on the industry and the type of job that is to be performed. A biomechanical risk factor analysis, as it applies to musculoskeletal disorders (MSDs) includes force, awkward postures, static postures, repetition, dynamic factors, compression and vibration. Other modifying factors are intensity, duration, temporal profiles and temperatures (Ergonomics program, Federal Register, 1999).

The core set of elements for an effective program for workers of all ages has been studied by the United Stated Accounting Office in a Report to Congressional Requesters (1997). The core includes management commitment, employee involvement, identification of problem jobs, development of controls for problem jobs, training and education for employees and appropriate medical management.

Management commitment is a key element. This involves the assigning of staff, establishing goals and evaluating the results. It entails communicating with the staff the importance of the program, making resources available and assuring employees are protected especially if they report hazard conditions.

Employee involvement promotes health by enhancing motivation and job satisfaction, improving problem solving and increases the likelihood that the employees will accept the changes. Involvement includes creating committees and encouraging prompt reporting of musculoskeletal disorders and potential job problems.

Identification of the problem jobs is a component for the gathering of information to identify the conditions that contribute to musculoskeletal disorders (MSDs). The identification process would include reports of MSDs, symptoms, and discomfort, fatigue and stress profiles. This process would also review OSHA 200 logs and other reports and conduct interviews of employees and management. A more complex review would identify problem jobs before they are a problem. This may require performing walk-through observational surveys, interviews and the use of checklists to score hazards such as awkward postures, forceful exertions, repetitive motions and vibration. Employers may have to make priority lists as to which areas need primary attention.

Analyzing and developing controls for problem jobs involves a number of activities. These include worker observations, interviews and questionnaires, as well as measurements of surface heights and reach distances at the work area. Videos, photos and biomechanical calculations may be used. Further steps may include brainstorming with the ergonomic team, consulting with organizations such as insurance companies, OSHA, trade organizations and vendors.

Controls have a suggested hierarchical order: engineering and then administrative. Engineering controls, eliminates or reduces the exposure to the hazard. This is of primary importance to ergonomics. These include workstation layout, tool design or changing the way materials, parts and products are transported. Administrative controls deal with workplace practices and policies such as, exercise, rest breaks, rotating workers to different jobs and providing training to ease the task demands.

Training and education includes overall ergonomics awareness to learn to recognize hazards, reporting procedures and to identify and control problem jobs. Targeting of special groups because of the jobs they hold, and risks they face and their roles in the program are important.

Medical management should be familiar with the jobs. Areas of involvement include giving prompt evaluation, encouraging early reporting of symptoms and ensuring employees do not fear reprisal. They are to give employees with diagnosed MSDs or other conditions restricted or transitional duty assignments as necessary until effective controls have been installed and conduct follow-up monitoring.

Suggested Actions for a Proactive Ergonomic Approach to the Older Worker

A progressive program that is sensitive to the needs of an older population and unconditioned worker takes into consideration the aging process and an attitude of trans-generational ergonomic design. This process of designing for all generations is all-inclusive and based on the premise that good design benefits everyone regardless of age (Pirkl, 1995; Kowalski-Trakofler et al., 2005). The following are suggested targets incorporated within the core elements of an ergonomics program that this author has found to be effective in addressing the needs of the older worker.

- Develop procedures to evaluate the new hires in order to place them in jobs that make use of their experience and physical capacities while meeting the needs of the employer. Assigning an older employee to an unfamiliar task may increase their risk of injury. An employee's prior experience with a task greatly reduces the risk of injury.
- Develop techniques to monitor how long it takes a new hire to become accustomed to the job, or when there are significant changes in the task duties of an existing employee. In the case of the older worker, consider allowing for a longer probationary period to become accustomed to the new task.
- Develop procedures to accommodate those with special needs such as those with injuries or physical impairments. This may require modification of workstation and tool design for the older individual as well as task rotations and shift breaks to allow sufficient time for recovery.
- Develop systems to monitor the employees targeting the ergonomic risk factors (force, awkward postures, static postures, repetition, dynamic factors, compression and vibration). Consider the use of body part discomfort profiles and fatigue curves as primary tools for monitoring the work stress of employees, particularly older or special needs individuals.
- Use a continuous improvement process for all workers and special accommodations for the aging workers (Kowalski-Trakofler et al., 2005). In this process you gain commitment of leadership, collect and analyze baseline data, set goals, implement intervention, collect and analyze results, report to management and start over.

- Acknowledge the older employees' contributions to the workplace and ensure that they are accepted (Kowalski-Trakofler et al., 2005).
- Involve the older employees in the ergonomic and safety processes to instill ownership and gain the input of their unique capabilities and experiences (Kowalski-Trakofler et al., 2005).
- Provide skills training packaged in an acceptable program that is unique to the needs of the older individual (Kowalski-Trakofler et al., 2005).
- Train employees and management in the early warning signs of musculoskeletal disorders. Early detection is the key to avoiding musculoskeletal disorders (MSDs) in the older employee. Small musculoskeletal irritations that are incurred early on can, over time become major musculoskeletal disorders months later.
- Types of training should be task specific and include general ergonomics, postural awareness, age-awareness and employee wellness (Kowalski-Trakofler et al., 2005).
- Involve the older employee in physical conditioning and nutritional programming and its promotion among the employees. Using comfort and fatigue profiles identify those body parts that need specialized strength, flexibility and endurance conditioning. Provide programs such that the older employee can perform these exercises during lunch and shift breaks.

WORK PLACE ISSUES FOR THE OLDER WORKER AND RECOMMENDED ACTIONS

Reviews by Garg (1991), Kowalski-Trakofler et al. (2005), and Astrand et al. (2003) reported the following findings regarding work place issues for the older worker and recommended actions:

Musculoskeletal

- Design workstations and tasks to avoid working conditions that require prolonged unusual postures (Garg, 1991).
- Static postures seem to lead to higher strain in older individuals (Garg, 1991). Allow for regular stretching breaks and add more tasks to a given workstation that would require the employee to change positions more frequently.

- Shoulder muscle fatigue has been identified as a major concern for older workers who have reduced joint mobility. Shoulder muscle fatigue has been associated with and jobs requiring elevated arm activities (Garg, 1991). It is recommended that the workstation be designed so that the arms are kept below shoulder level and avoid repetitive motions requiring reaching above the head.
- Reduce cumulative trauma disorder exposure of the upper extremities as the risk increases with age (Garg, 1991). Most studies show that repetitive motion injuries are more prevalent in workers aged 40 to 60 years. These tend to develop over time. Monitor body part discomfort to identify developing problems so they can be addressed promptly.
- Design controls and switches so they don't require tight pinching or grasping, or large wrist deviations and/or forces (Garg, 1991).
- Reduce the time spent on the on jobs that require a lot of grip strength or provide mechanical assists. Develop fixtures for the holding of products to relieve hand stress. Choose tools and hand-held devices that are appropriately sized for the hand.
- Design jobs so that older workers do not have to exert as much physical force in material handling operations. Restrict the maximum loads of workers 45 years of age and older to 20% of the maximum loads recommended for their younger cohorts (Garg, 1991).
- Consider the physical training level of the older employee. In a literature review by Kowalski-Trakofler et al. (2005), they reported that a sample taken by Kovar and La Croix (1987) found a large portion of subjects 55 to 74 years of age had difficulty stooping or crouching (28%) lifting of carrying 25 pounds (23%) or standing on their feet for two hours (22%) and walking up 10 steps without a rest (15%).

Sensory and Cognitive

Operative controls should be kept to a minimum and the relationship between controls and the movements they affect should be compatible for the older workers (Garg, 1991).

- Illumination required for satisfactory visual functioning increases with age. Older workers require more light, 50% more for those age 40 to 45 and 100% more for workers over 55 than for those workers under 40. Glare is also major problem for older workers (Garg, 1991). Review the lighting in workstations to ensure it is

adequate and properly designed to be bright enough and without unnecessary glare. Improper lighting and excessive glare can contribute to fatigue, headaches, eyestrain, etc.
- The visual contrast should be maximized between the task and the background. Information on control panels for example. Also, increase visual display size to counter the effects of presbyopia. Fine work may be unsuitable for some older workers (Garg, 1991).
- The older worker may have less tolerance for heat (Garg, 1991) and require more time to adjust to hot environments.
- In the older worker, some hearing loss may require a higher signal to noise ratio (Garg, 1991).
- Older workers appear to be more susceptible to problems arising for time and production standards (Garg, 1991). Self-paced activities would be more suitable for some older workers.
- Older workers need a well-cushioned shoe. This heel pad, which is the primary shock absorber for the foot, declines with age and attention should be given to appropriate shoes and floor surfaces (Astrand et al., 2003).

Training and Scheduling

- It is recommended that the older employee will be aided by longer training sessions; practice with written instructions, and videos demonstrating the desired job. Active training and pre-training can reduce both discrimination and decision errors. Memory training may greatly reduce or eliminate age differences in performance (Garg, 1991).
- Reduce the amount of rotating shifts or night work for the older worker (Garg, 1991). Increase number of rest breaks during the shift.
- The older worker may need more time to rest between shifts and additional breaks during the shift to adequately recover. A fatigue survey will help identify those workers.
- Older workers need to drink water more frequently and not wait until they are thirsty. The older worker tends to be less hydrated due to lower cellular water as well as the possible side effect of many medications.

CASE STUDIES

The following case studies illustrate an approach that promotes optimal work design regardless of age.

Case 1

This large international manufacturing plant had over 8 to 9 musculoskeletal disorders per month. The average cost to the plant was in excess of $6,000 per injury. The plant experienced high employee turnover. Employees were assembling small parts and the job required static postures, primarily sitting, and the use of the fingers and hands to assemble the parts. The goal was to identify the cause of the injuries and to design programs and solutions to prevent them. A committee, consisting of a nurse, a safety representative, an outside consultant (the author), engineers, and human resource personnel was formed. The committee received direction from management to address the issue.

Questionnaires were developed for the regular workers and for the injured employees. Several key components of the general questionnaire were: their specific job, length of employment and extent of discomfort for each body part.

Utilizing the results of the questionnaires the team was able to target the workstations that caused the most physical discomfort and those body parts that were experiencing the greatest discomfort. The injured employees' questionnaire allowed us to identify tools that needed redesign. It also targeted new work processes discovered by the previously injured employees and these solutions were applied to their workstations. Participating employees were interviewed and were instrumental in this discovery process. The basic findings from the injured employees showed that 90 percent of the injuries occurred within the first three months of employment.

Based upon the information gained from the questionnaires the following interventions were implemented. Managers and employees were trained to recognize musculoskeletal disorders and to address them promptly. Those stations where force was applied were given to employees that were younger and had greater upper body strength. Some workstations were redesigned. Jobs were rotated regularly and several operations were applied at each station to reduce the repetitive stress on a single body part. Employees were encouraged to use both the right and left hands to balance the workload between the two hands. A regular stretching program was introduced and pre and post data was collected over a six-month period. Feedback was provided to managers and employees concerning program results. The program involved shutting down the production line five times a day for stretching exercises. Exercises were tailored for each workstation according to the body part discomfort profile and employees were trained to conduct the exercises.

Results

Within six months of implementation, a cost avoidance saving was reported as a result of eliminating repetitive trauma illnesses. Productivity savings were realized from reduction of work motion and the quality of product was increased. In feedback surveys, employees reported an increase in the quality of work, productivity, and morale, as well as improved comfort, a greater sense of safety, and a desire to continue exercises.

Case 2

A manufacturing plant conducted an ergonomic review to improve the safety of its workers and processes. The plant had an excellent safety record even though certain jobs involved heavy labor in heated and cold conditions. In certain jobs there were chances of caustic chemical exposure. The hazardous conditions of the job required a self-pacing component for the workstations. The age of the employees ranged from the twenties into the mid sixties with an average age of 42 years. There was little employee turnover in the plant. The program was necessary due to the fact their workforce was aging. A safety committee was formed that consisted of the safety director, an ergonomic consultant (the author), plant management and employees from various areas of the plant. The employees completed a questionnaire that identified the type of job, work processes and a body part discomfort profile. The employees with injuries or musculoskeletal conditions were interviewed and their workstations were evaluated. An ergonomic review of the plant was conducted. A report proposed a prioritized list of work condition improvements to reduce hazards.

The discomfort profile identified the body parts that were having the most discomfort. This revealed that the low back experienced the most discomfort. The office staff had the most back discomfort even though other jobs required considerable physical labor. The older employees were dispersed in all the job operations. One intervention involved instituting a back strengthening program that included warm-up exercises similar to the material handling needs of the jobs. Muscles in the abdominal areas, as well as the arms and legs were targeted for the warm-up session. The back muscles (erector spinae) were targeted for the heavy muscular resistance conditioning. A back extension machine was used to train the back muscles. Once workers were accustomed to the exercise, they performed 10 repetitions to muscle fatigue once per week. The condition and fitness level of the employee was the delineating factor for the loads used in the conditioning program. All participants were medically screened before the program. Age was not a delineating factor in this study.

A pilot group of twenty employees was run through pre and post testing using a MEDX back extension machine.

Results

Back strength increased by an average of 50 lbs. per employee. Participants reported an increase in ability to lift safely, safety awareness, back comfort, work quality, production, morale, and home/recreation quality.

It is interesting to note that even though this job had high environmental and physical demands the older employees were successfully performing their duties. The older employees were seasoned and well conditioned to the tasks. They were aided to this end by the exercise program, which targeted a specific body part to improve the comfort and work process.

Case 3

A large call center had been operational for approximately eight months. The job required sitting for nearly 8 hours per day while addressing customer's concerns. This type of job was not physically demanding other than long periods of sitting. The human resource department reported an unacceptably high employee turnover rate. The workstations had up-to-date ergonomically designed seating and workspaces.

An exercise and ergonomic questionnaire was administered to 393 employees (71% female). The questionnaire included body part discomfort, fatigue and injury assessments. The discomfort scale ranged from 0 to 5 with 5 being very uncomfortable. Fatigue was measured in two-hour time intervals starting at 5 minutes and continuing to the end of the 8 hour shift on a similar ranking scale of 0 to 5.

Results

Over 40% of the workers reported high levels of discomfort (3 to 5) for their low backs. Back discomfort was not found to be related to age.

It also revealed that those who were physically active had less low back discomfort. For example, 53% of the "inactive" category was experiencing low back discomfort of 3 to 5 versus only 33% of the "HEPA" category (health enhancing physical activity). A similar positive relationship was found with the in-house fitness club membership.

The areas of most concern were spine and shoulder related. Of those employees with discomfort, 71.0% reported the discomfort occurred over time (176 + 40.6 days). This is a primary risk factor for musculoskeletal disorders and showed that measures were needed to stop the cumulative effects causing the discomfort.

The fatigue curves over the shift revealed a significant upswing in fatigue between hours 6 to 8 (1.18 + 1.39 to 2.46 + 1.50, $p < .05$). An intervention involving exercise and nutrition was recommended to decrease fatigue experienced late in the shift.

Case Study Discussion

Primary tools for monitoring the health of the employees, especially the aging workers, are discomfort and fatigue profiles. These tools quickly alert supervisors to individuals requiring help, identifying work stations needing improvement, and providing a way to tailor exercise and health programs to their workers. The data collected is also a valuable asset for training employees to recognize ergonomic risk factors in their specific job. The information prepares management to rapidly address issues experienced by new hires while they become accustomed to the job and prevent potential injuries and expense. It reveals increasing body part discomfort over time and fluctuations in fatigue levels in a timely manner allowing for intervention.

In Case 3 the fatigue curve proved to be an excellent way to address the concerns of the aging and deconditioned employee by monitoring fatigue levels and targeting increases in fatigue during the shift. For instance, an individual that is experiencing high levels of fatigue at the beginning of the shift may not be recovering sufficiently from the day before. Persons coming into the work environment continually fatigued, especially on a particular body part may require more rest breaks and/or more recovery time between shifts until they become accustomed to the job. This is especially important to those newly hired and the older employee. For instance, in Case 3, the call center, employees that became injured on the job took more time to finally become accustomed to the job. The injured employees required 33 to 54 days to become accustomed to job whereas non-injured needed only 15 to 31 days. This also occurred in Case Study 1.

CONCLUSIONS

The workforce is aging and the business sector has a need for older employees as they bring unique experience and skills to the worksite. In light of this, organizations need to have a grasp of the physiological changes that occur over time in order to develop the methods to address the evolving capabilities of their employees while meeting the demands of the workplace. An integrated approach involving ergonomics, health promotion and employee assistance programs can produce positive results. It is important to have a monitoring system in place, such as found in the OSHA 200 logs. A comfort and fatigue profile will help to identify potential MSDs before they become severe. In addition, through the health promotion programs, specific exercise directives, supported by the efforts of the EAP, can be especially beneficial to the older worker and can be designed to address the specific issues raised by the comfort and fatigue profile. Employee participation in these exercise and nutrition programs can dramatically ameliorate the affects of aging and de-conditioning as well as their psychosocial effects. Finally, approaching ergonomics from the basis of trans-generational design addresses the needs of all workers regardless of age. The case studies cited demonstrate the potential economic benefits of such programs as evidenced by increased productivity and reduced costs. Other benefits include improved employee morale and comfort.

REFERENCES

Akima, H., Kano, Y., & Enomoto, Y. (2001) Muscle function in 164 men and women aged 20-84yr. *Med. Sci. Sports Exerc.*, 33, 220-226.

Astrand, I. (1960). Aerobic work capacity in men and women with special reference to age. *Acta. Physiol. Scand.*, 49 (suppl. 169), 67.

Astrand, I. (1967). Degree of strain during building work as related to individual aerobic capacity. *Ergonomics*, 10, 293-303.

Astrand, P. O., Bergh, U., Kilbom, A. (1997). A 33-year follow-up of peak oxygen uptake and related variables of former physical education students. *J. Appl. Physiol.*, 82(6),1844-1852.

Astrand, P.O., Rodahl, K., Dahl, H.A., & Stromme, S.B. (2003). *Textbook of work physiology, physiological bases of exercise* (4th ed.). Champaign, IL: Human Kinetics.

Babb, T.G. (1999). Mechanical ventilatory constraints in aging, lung disease, and obesity: Perspectives and a brief review. *Med. Sci. Sprts. Exerc.*, 31, S12-S22.

Backman, E., Johansson, V., Hager, B., Sjoblom, P., & Henriksson (1995). Isometric muscle strength and muscular endurance in normal persons aged between 17 and 70 years. *Scand. J. Rehabil. Med,.* 27(2),109-117.

DeVries, H. A., & Adams, G. M. (1972). Comparison of exercise responses in old and young men. *J. Gerontol.*, 27, 344-348.

Elia, E. A. (1991). Exercise and the elderly. Clin. Sports Med. 10, 141-155. *Ergonomics program*, 64 Fed. Reg. 225 (Nov. 23, 1999) (29 CFR Part 1910).

Falk, B., Barr-Or, O., Smolander, J. et al. (1994). Response to rest and exercise in the cold: effects of age and aerobic fitness. *J. Appl. Physol.*, 76, 72-78.

Garg, A (1991). Ergonomics and the aging worker, an overview. *Experimental Aging Research*, 17(3), 143-155.

Giniger, S., Dispenzieri, A., & Eisenberg, J. (1984). Older workers in speed and skill jobs. *Aging and Work*, 7(1), 7-12.

Goldberg, J. H., & Ellis, R. D. (1996). Human factors/ergonomics. *Encyclopedia of Gerontology: Age, aging, and the aged*, (pp. 715-725). San Diego, CA: Academic Press.

Graves, S. B., Whitehurst, M., & Findley, B. W. (2006). *ACSM resource manual for guidelines for exercise testing and prescription* (5th Ed.). Baltimore, MD: Lippincott Williams & Wilkins.

Gremby, G., & Saltin, B. (1983). The aging muscle. *Clin. Physiology,* 3, 209-218.

Herberts, R. Kadefors & Roman, H. (1980). Arm positioning in manual tasks. *Ergonomics.* 23(7), 655-665.

Kemper, H.C.G. (1994). Physical work and the consequences of the aging worker. *Work and Aging.* London: Taylor & Francis.

Kovar, & Lacroix (1987). Aging in the eighties, ability to perform work activities. *NCHS Advance Data.* 136, 1-12.

Kowalski-Trakofler, K. M., Steiner, L. J., & Schwerha, D. J. (2005). Safety considerations for the aging workforce. *Safety Science,* in press. Retrieved November 16, 2005, from Science Direct database.

McArdle, W. D., Katch, F. I., & Katch, V. L. (2001). *Exercise physiology—energy, nutrition and human performance* (5th ed.). Baltimore, MD: Lippincott Williams & Wilkins.

Muller, E. A. (1962). Occupational work capacity. *Ergonomics*, 5(3), 445-452.

O'Flaherty, E. J. (2000). Modeling normal aging bone loss, with consideration of bone loss in osteoporosis. *Toxicological Science*, 55, 171-188.

Ogawa, T., Spina, J. R., Martin, W. H., et al. (1992). Effects of aging, sex, and physical training on cardiovascular response to exercise. *Circulation*, 86, 494-503.

Pirkl, J. J. (1995). Trangenerational design: Prolonging the American dream generations. *The Journal of the American Society of Aging*, (Spring) XIX, 1-14.

Rodeheffer R.J., Gerstenblith G., Becker L.C. et al. (1984). Exercise cardiac output is maintained with advancing age in healthy human subjects: Cardiac dialation and increased stroke volume compensate for a diminished heart rate. *Circulation* 69, 203-213.

Schulman S. P., Lakatta E. G., & Fleg J. L., et al. (1992). Age related decline in left ventricular filling at rest and exercise. *Am J Physiol*, 263, H1932-H1938.

Schut, L. (1998). Motor system changes in the aging brain: What is normal and what is not. *Geriatrics*, 53, S16-S19.

Smith, E. L., Serfass R. G. (1981). Exercise and aging: The scientific basis. Hillside, NJ: Enslow.

Snook, S. H. & Irvine, C. H. (1968). Maximum frequency of lift acceptable to male industrial workers. *American Industrial Hygiene Association Journal*, 29, 531-536.

Snook, S. H. (1971). The effects of age and physique on continuous-work capacity. *Human Factors*, 13(5), 467-479.

Tzankoff, S.P. (1979). Age-realted differences in lactate distribution kinetics following maximal exercise. *European Journal of Applied Physiology*, 42, 35-40.

Welch, W. M. & Bazar, E. (2006, December 30). N.J. woman enjoys celebrity of being 1st baby boomer. *USA Today*, pp. 4A.

Welford, A. T. (1958). *Aging and human skill*, London: Oxford.

Welford, A. T. (1981). Signal, noise, performance and age. *Human Factors*, 23(1), 97-109.

Worker protection, private sector ergonomics programs yield positive results. (1997, August 27) *United States general accounting office: report to congressional requestors,*. Rep.No. B-277451.

Young, A. J., Lee, D. T. (1997). Aging and human cold tolerance. *Exp. Aging Res.*, 23, 45-67.

Index

Milton Keynes UK
Ingram Content Group UK Ltd
UKHW031149141024
449569UK00024B/956